S0-EVF-100

Rayne

SOON THE NEWS WILL BE SHOES

Rayne

RAYNE:
Shoes for Stars

Michael Pick

ACC Editions

To Eiji Takahatake
In grateful friendship

© 2015 Michael Pick
World copyright reserved

ISBN 978 1 85149 793 5

The right of Michael Pick to be identified as author of this work has been asserted by him in accordance with the Copyright, Designs and Patents Act 1988

All rights reserved. No part of this publication may be reproduced, stored in a retrieval system, or transmitted in any form or by any means electronic, mechanical, photocopying, recording or otherwise, without the prior permission of the publisher

Every effort has been made to secure permission to reproduce the images contained within this book, and we are grateful to the individuals and institutions who have assisted in this task. Any errors or omissions are entirely unintentional, and the details should be addressed to the publisher.

British Library Cataloguing-in-Publication Data
A catalogue record for this book is available from the British Library

Frontispiece: Rayne advertisement in *Vogue*, 1945. In 1945, at the end of a gruelling war, the British nation was physically tired and longing for peace-time pleasures denied to them by rationing and Utility clothing. Sadly, Austerity measures were to prove even more draconian in many ways and the last vestiges of rationing only ended in 1953. Rayne was but one of thousands of manufacturers giving hope and colour to drab lives through their advertising and products. CONDÉ NAST

Title page: The famous yellow shoe box emblazoned with Royal Warrants and the world-famous Rayne logo formed part of the pleasure of unpacking the new shoes nestling in the tissue paper within. The sleek lines of the black satin diamanté-embellished stiletto–heeled design epitomise the 'floating feet' concept of shoe design from the mid 1950s-60s. RAYNE ARCHIVE

Printed in Italy
Published in England by ACC Editions, an imprint of ACC Art Books Ltd., Woodbridge, Suffolk

Contents

Foreword – 6

Introduction – 11

Chapter One – 16
Theatrical Steps: Henry & Mary Rayne 1898-1920

Boots – 38-41

Chapter Two – 42
From Stage to Society Shoes: Joseph Edward Rayne 1920-1950

Cleopatra – 68-69

Chapter Three – 76
New London Look: Edward Rayne 1951-1992

Oliver Messel and the Bond Street Shop – 108-111

Designers – 132-135

Chapter Four – 144
Shoemakers to the Royal Family

Handbags – 174-179

Rayne Today 180

Endnotes – 182

The Rayne Factory – 184-185

Bibliography – 186
Acknowledgements – 188
Author's Biography – 189
Index – 190

Foreword

Above: Peggy Cummins, one of a number of beautiful international stars adorned by the consummate elegance and comfort of Rayne shoes both on and off the screen and stage. PEGGY CUMMINS

Below: Julie Harris, the Oscar-winning British film costume designer, dressed a galaxy of stars, including Joan Crawford and Kay Kendall, as well as The Beatles. She usually utilised Rayne shoes for the artists in her charge. Interestingly, as a girl in the 1920s, she even wore an H. & M. Rayne costume herself as a 'pearl' in Madame Vacani's annual dancing academy pageant. JULIE HARRIS

Peggy Cummins

I had just finished making a film with Rex Harrison called *Escape* and was crossing the Atlantic on the *Queen Elizabeth* when we hit a terrible storm. Most of the passengers were unable to leave their cabins, but two intrepid voyagers made their way to the Dining Room. I was one and Edward Rayne was the other. He was not much older than me, but was already popular in fashionable circles – not least because of the elegant and original shoes made by his family company.

This was the beginning of a very long friendship and long after my wedding in 1950, my husband often played golf with Edward, and we were entertained by him and his wife Morna at their flat in Mayfair and their house on the Sussex coast.

I was married wearing Rayne shoes and still have them along with the beautiful dress made for me by Worth in Grosvenor Street. I had the train removed and wore it to many dances, with the shoes, which now sadly show how much I loved them !

I am delighted to contribute to the Foreword to this book and to know that Edward's younger son Nick and his wife Lulu have revived the family company and are creating beautiful shoes again.

Julie Harris

My career as a film costume designer for some 85 films or so began at the end of the Second World War and *Holiday Camp* (1947) was my first great success.

When it came to sourcing and supplying the shoes for stars and actresses, I would very often accompany them to Rayne, as they had the finest shoes with the most interesting designs. Before rationing ended, we had to account to the Board of trade for all coupons issued for clothing including shoes or they were disallowed.

For the lovely Kay Kendall in the comedy *Simon and Laura* (1955) or Joan Crawford in *Esther Costello* some dramatic clothes were partnered with elegant Rayne shoes. *Darling* (1965) with Julie Christie won me an Oscar and Rayne shoes were worn in the film, also in the Bond films for which I designed: *Casino Royale* (1967) with Ursula Andress and Deborah Kerr, and *Live and Let Die* (1973) with Jane Seymour. There were also the famous Beatles films, *A Hard Day's Night* (1964) with Anna Quayle and *Help!* (1965) with Eleanor Bron.

Rayne shoes were always fashionable in the most interesting ways, I even used them in *Rollerball* (1975), and over the decades Rayne quite regularly dyed white satin pumps to the colour of the many clothes I had designed.

So many British companies contributed to the success of our films and Rayne was a wonderful part of this.

Anna Harvey

I first met Sir Edward Rayne (or Eddie, as he was affectionately called) many years ago when he was MD of Harvey Nichols and also Chairman of the British Fashion Council. His love of fashion and of shoes in particular was infectious and I loved visiting the Bond Street shop just to look in wonder at the shoes. The shop itself was a work of art – designed by Oliver Messel it was beautiful to behold. You can still see rooms decorated by Messel at the Dorchester, but sadly his lovely interior for Rayne has not survived, however the famous brand does, which is wonderful.

Bruce Oldfield

All dress designers seek to maximise their talents and commercial skills and I am no exception. The name of Rayne with its world-famous clientele of stage and film stars, not to mention three Royal Warrants, was a perfect match for me in the mid-eighties, when I expanded my business. Rayne was known for its collaboration with Delman shoes and with Christian Dior. Shoe designer Roger Vivier had worked with Edward Rayne, who had already called on the talented home-grown designing skills of Mary Quant and Jean Muir, amongst others – and myself.

Rayne had their own shoe factory at King's Cross and it proved a fascinating and sometimes steep learning curve with young Nick and Lulu Rayne to find out how my original designs could be translated into fabulous shoes, whilst retaining the essence of my own personality in the eventual designs we made. I described the process in my book *Bruce Oldfield's Season*.

One other thing I remember well is the 1950s Oliver Messel-designed Rayne shop in Bond Street, an almost other-worldly setting of great glamour. It reflected a fading era, but was a great theatrical backdrop for selling beautiful shoes, including mine, and the Oldfield-Rayne collaboration is now part of British fashion history.

Bruce Oldfield famously designs dresses for international stars and notable clients, including the late Diana, Princess of Wales. As part of his continually evolving relationship with the UK fashion industry, Edward Rayne invited Oldfield to be one of his 'Young Designers' in 1985, resulting in several shoe collections. BRUCE OLDFIELD/ALAN WICKES

Facing page: A typical example of Rayne's eye-catching advertising campaigns that began in the 1970s. Having emerged from the testing era of change in the 1960s, the Rayne image was again updated with a new advertising formula. By personalising advertisements in the early 1970s with an eye-catching image of the benign head of the company in the background and witty by-lines, a large image of the featured Rayne product was cleverly incorporated into the dynamic editorial of influential monthly fashion and society-conscious magazines. *Harpers & Queen* with 'Jennifers Diary' was an ideal vehicle of the times for these successful advertisements, here featuring a range of luxurious embroidered slippers. RAYNE ARCHIVE

Below: A shoe box designed by Oliver Messel (1904-1978), a leading British stage, film and interior designer of the time, noted for his mid-18th century Austro-German baroque pastiches, he was commissioned by Edward Rayne to design the Old Bond Street shop in 1959. The acclaimed result had spin-offs including his Rayne window displays and this enticing shoe box. RAYNE ARCHIVE

Nicholas Rayne

I consider that I was born with a lady's shoe in my mouth as part of the fourth generation of Rayne shoe-manufacturing and grew up as part of the family firm with the knowledge of the extraordinary history behind it. As these other contributions to the Foreword make clear, Rayne was internationally famous for most of the 20th century.

I worked at Rayne in its many departments for eight years after university and like all the family felt great sadness on the night that it was sold in 1987, but was always hopeful that the company could begin again. Seven years ago the exciting possibility of its re-launch occurred.

It is with great pride and affection that I am lucky enough to have re-launched Rayne shoes as a 21st-century brand with the Rayne family once more leading the concept and design, after an interlude of almost 25 years.

As this book shows, Rayne was one of the greatest ladies' shoes companies in the world, known for excellence in design and manufacture and worn by the most chic and beautiful women in the world and our intention is to become this again.

Lulu Rayne

I started at Rayne when I was 19 years old as the assistant handbag buyer. Little did I know that I would first marry a Rayne and then leave the ladies' shoe business completely for almost a generation only to return to Rayne again after all these years away.

Whilst the world has certainly changed in the intervening years, I think that fashion has moved back in Rayne's favour as style, glamour, luxury, and heritage – all part of Rayne's DNA – are now more in vogue than they have been for many years.

"Edward Rayne, your new collection of brocade slippers is clear evidence of the designs you have on innocent womanhood. Where will this course of action lead you?"

"Down the slippery path, my lord."

RAYNE
15-16 Old Bond St, W1.

Choisy: available in five delectable brocades Red, Brown, Light Green, Turquoise and Navy. £12.95.

Rayne tells a velvet shoe story
for glamorous autumn evenings. Two of his fashionable heroines: *Serena*, velvet all over, highlighted by shimmering diamanté. In black, brown, green or wine. And *Terese*, prettily velvet trimmed over nylon mesh. Black, brown, navy, or green. Both at £11.19.6.

RAYNE

Introduction

H. & M. Rayne Ltd was not only a leading British manufacturing company for almost a century, but also internationally famous throughout most of the twentieth century. Although it began as a theatrical costumier, Rayne became one of the world's pre-eminent manufacturers of fashionable women's luxury shoes. They even gained three Royal Warrants and supplied galaxies of shoes for stars.

The history of shoe-making in Britain is both long and complex, reflecting changing needs as much as new fashions linked to increasing purchasing power. In the first decades of the 20th century, utility outweighed appearance amongst all but the very rich, as most of the population would have to walk at some time upon unpaved or dirty roads, streets and pavements in all but the most sophisticated surroundings. Until well into the 20th century, horse-drawn transport was universal: the resulting dirt and dust were the enemy of elegant shoes for both sexes, crossing sweepers were not universal.

Late 18th-century and early 19th-century fashion plates often show women's footwear to be slight and delicate. Yet from the 1840s, women's feet were only ever glimpsed and rarely seen until skirt lengths began to rise in the 1910s. The most elegant and decorative of shoes were worn in houses for dinners, dances and special occasions, such as weddings, when carriages took guests almost to their host's door, where awnings and a red carpet over the city pavement protected the feet and footwear.

It follows that in spite of increasing mechanisation of boot and shoe manufacture during the latter half of the 19th century, for which Northampton became particularly famous, there was a particular metropolitan market for the more delicate of women's shoes and boots, often hand-made.

The late Sir Edward Rayne (1922-1992), the third generation to run the family company of H. & M. Rayne, was quoted as saying that until after the end of the First World War, the only women to wear truly original if not fashionable shoes were either actresses or prostitutes. By which he meant that the fetishistic element inherent in much of the laced or be-ribboned footwear seen on stage was meant to heighten the allure of the actress at a time when a glimpse of ankle or stocking was truly shocking.

Facing page and page 15: The two seductive advertisements commissioned from Martin Battersby (1914-1982) – British artist, set and fabric designer, collector and decorative art historian – reflect Edward Rayne's keen interest in the most fashionable designers of his day. The irascible Battersby gained an impressive clientele, including dress designer Hardy Amies, Lady Diana Cooper, Lady Kenmare and the Pierre Hotel in New York. The shoes are taken from both the Miss Rayne and Rayne collections, c.1962. MARTIN BATTERSBY ARCHIVE

Below: Sir Edward Rayne (1922-1992) was the third generation to head the family business. An acclaimed bridge player, he was afflicted by poor sight from his teenage years, but became immersed in every detail of his business, always seeking positive innovations. RAYNE ARCHIVE

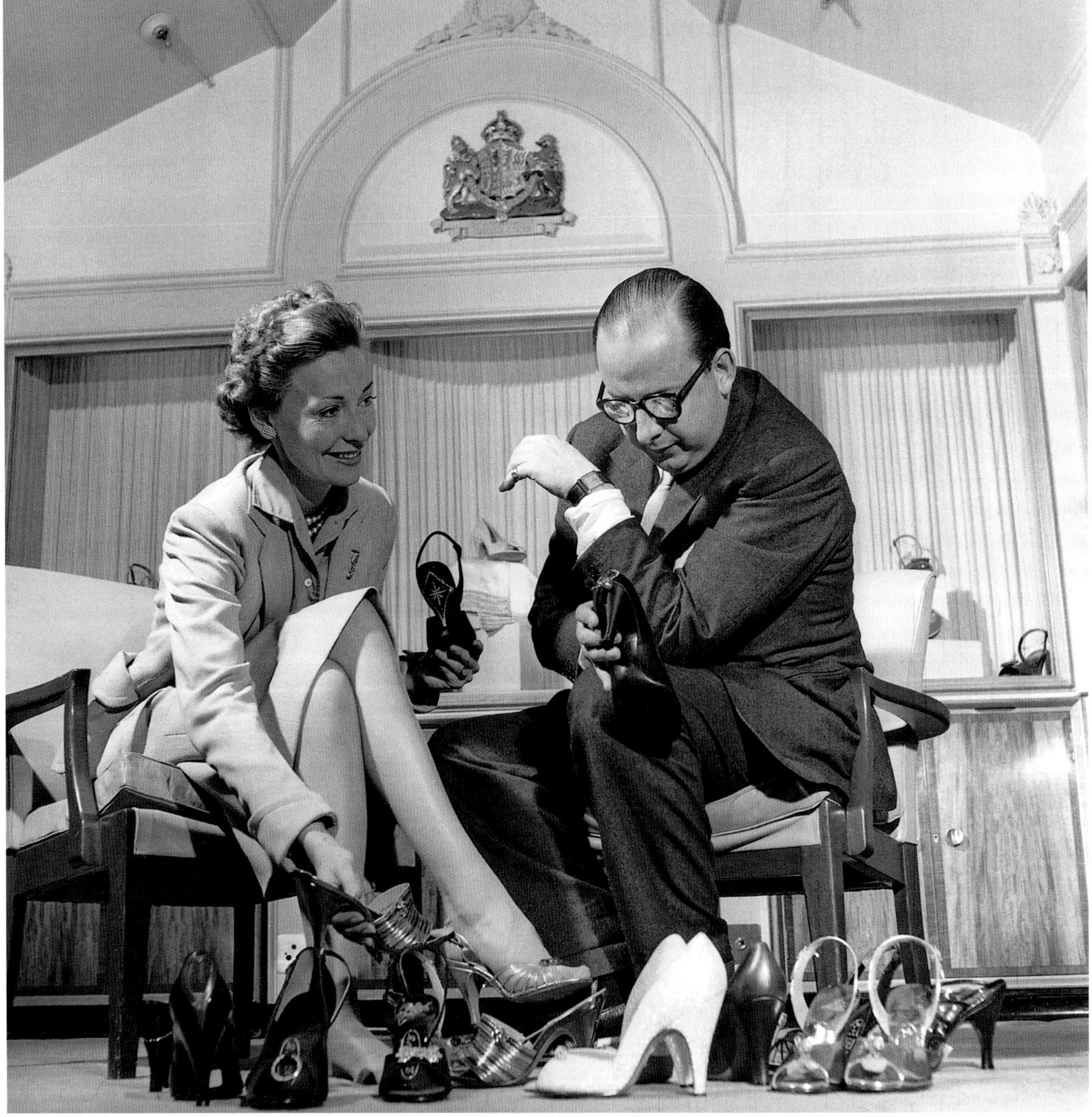

Sir Edward was well-placed to make his comment, as H. & M. Rayne were essentially theatrical suppliers and shoes were an important part of this business. Late Victorian and Edwardian Britain enjoyed a nationwide vogue for theatrical performances, often on a gigantic scale with London productions touring the country. Costumes and shoes were needed in abundance but, by 1920, the theatre had peaked and cinema was seen as a threat. In that year, H. & M. Rayne began retailing their shoes through a Bond Street shop, as well as premises on Regent Street, stocked with elegant shoes suitable for ladies. They were scarcely alone on Bond Street, but Rayne shoes had a reserved distinction to their styling and immaculate manufacture, quickly written up in the press, including *Vogue*.

One of the effects of the First World War was most visible in the radical change in women's clothing, notably shorter skirts and less bulky lines. The modern young woman, as she was universally referred to in the press, danced to jazz rhythms, increasingly rode in cars – rather then carriages – and had a taste for cigarettes, cocktails and make-up. She also wore patterned or coloured silk stockings and her shoes became as sophisticated as her dress. Inevitably, many of the older generation found this all rather shocking, as these changes in fashion seemed to go far beyond the behaviour of recent 'fast women', such as Lillie Langtry or even most actresses.

Even in the 1930s, London's West End street-walking prostitutes, such as Martha Watts, wore particular designs of shoes to advertise their services to men in the know. In the 1940s many of these distinctions evaporated as fashion and shoe design rapidly evolved and it was after this period that H. & M. Rayne shoes came to epitomise the most sophisticated manufactured women's footwear, the name spoken of in the same terms as Delman in the USA, Ferragamo in Italy or Perugia in France.

Rayne also came to have three supreme accolades unknown to any foreign shoemakers, namely Royal Warrants from HM Queen Mary, HM Queen Elizabeth The Queen Mother and HM Queen Elizabeth II. Famously above fashion, but fashionably dressed, these royal clients and others of the Royal Family, were able to confide in H. & M. Rayne, who in turn were able to create shoes for many varied occasions, often in collaboration with the royal dressmakers Norman Hartnell and Hardy Amies.

Facing page: Known as a convivial man, Sir Edward Rayne is seen here in a Bond Street showroom explaining the latest shoe designs to an admirer, c.1955.   RAYNE ARCHIVE

Below: In keeping with his constant search for further business opportunities, Edward Rayne launched the company brand of nylon stockings in the late 1950s. Rayne shoe collections followed and necessarily complemented the new dress collections in London, Paris and New York; the sought after nylon stockings also reflected seasonal changes and were presented in beautiful packaging, c.1960.   RAYNE ARCHIVE

In common with other well-known and distinctive shoemakers world-wide, Rayne had many of the world's most elegant and famous women as clients, such as Vivien Leigh, Marlene Dietrich and Elizabeth Taylor. The shoes were consistently chosen for wear on stage and screen, although often scarcely visible on film, but famously replicated in Egyptian styles for two Cleopatras: Vivien Leigh and Elizabeth Taylor. London couturiers, such as Sir Norman Hartnell and Sir Hardy Amies, designed shoes specially for their collections, and Stanley Kubrick's commissioned designs from Amies for *2001: A Space Odyssey* included shoes, which were made by Rayne in their factory.

The younger fashion designers of the 'mini' era, such as Jean Muir, also designed for Rayne; and, latterly, Bruce Oldfield – particularly known for his designs for Diana, Princess of Wales – designed a collection of shoes for Rayne. The Princess had been the youngest member of the Royal Family to wear shoes from Rayne, at a time when virtually all the royal ladies found beautiful shoes and bags in the enticing Oliver Messel-designed Bond Street store.

Over the course of a century, H. & M. Rayne had evolved from a stall on London's Waterloo Road into one of the most prestigious and glamorous businesses in the world. Now run by Nicholas Rayne, the great-grandson of the founders, the Rayne history is one that reflects the many storms surrounding British business in the 21st century and the battle to adapt to changing tastes and times.

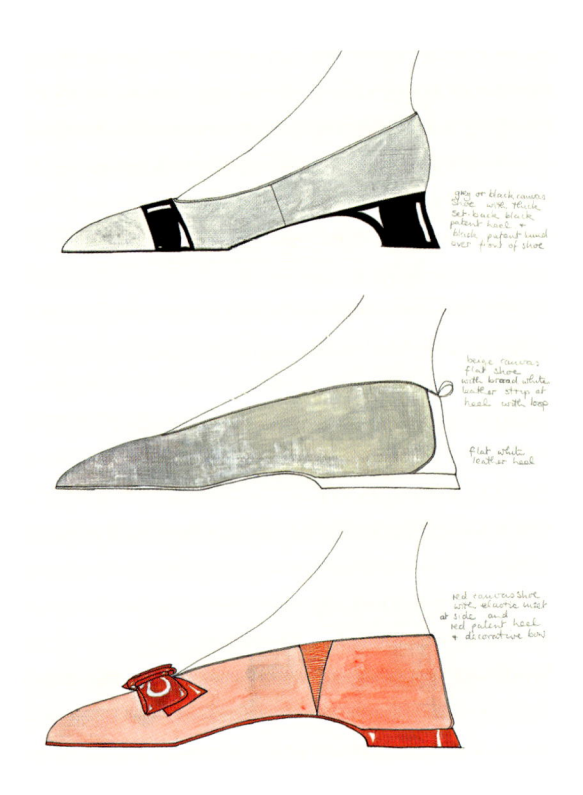

Above: Sir Hardy Amies (1909-2003) collaborated on shoe design with Edward Rayne. He not only designed Rayne shoes for his dress collections, but also consulted Rayne over his designs for clothes made for HM Queen Elizabeth II. This led Stanley Kubrick to commission dress and shoe designs from Hardy Amies for his iconic film *2001: A Space Odyssey* (1968). Some of the futuristic Amies designs by in-house designer Ken Fleetwood (1930-1996) are seen here. HARDY AMIES ARCHIVE

Right: Sir Norman Hartnell (1901-1979) was Britain's leading dress designer of the 20th century and put London fashion onto the world map. Like Rayne, he had three Royal Warrants and his shoe designs for the royal ladies were executed by Rayne. He used Rayne shoes for his collections from the 1920s and befriended young Edward during the war. These sandals were designed for Rayne c.1958. JEAN MATTHEW ESTATE

Facing page: Martin Battersby advertisement showing Edward Rayne peering through from behind the latest 'Miss Rayne' collection, c.1962. (See p.10 for the other Battersby advertisement). MARTIN BATTERSBY ARCHIVE

Mr. Edward Rayne was so pleased with this bright young beauty from the 'Miss Rayne' Autumn Collection that he asked Mr. Martin Battersby to paint it. The artist thoughtfully added a picture of Mr. Rayne, and some charming baubles of his own. The original shoe is available in the peachiest of suedes, lightly edged with calf, in six joyful colours. The price is eight guineas.

Miss Rayne

Martin Battersby.

H. & M. RAYNE LTD. 152 REGENT STREET · 15–16 OLD BOND STREET.
29 BRUTON STREET, MAYFAIR · 57 BROMPTON ROAD, KNIGHTSBRIDGE · HIGH STREET, GUILDFORD, AND LEADING STORES.

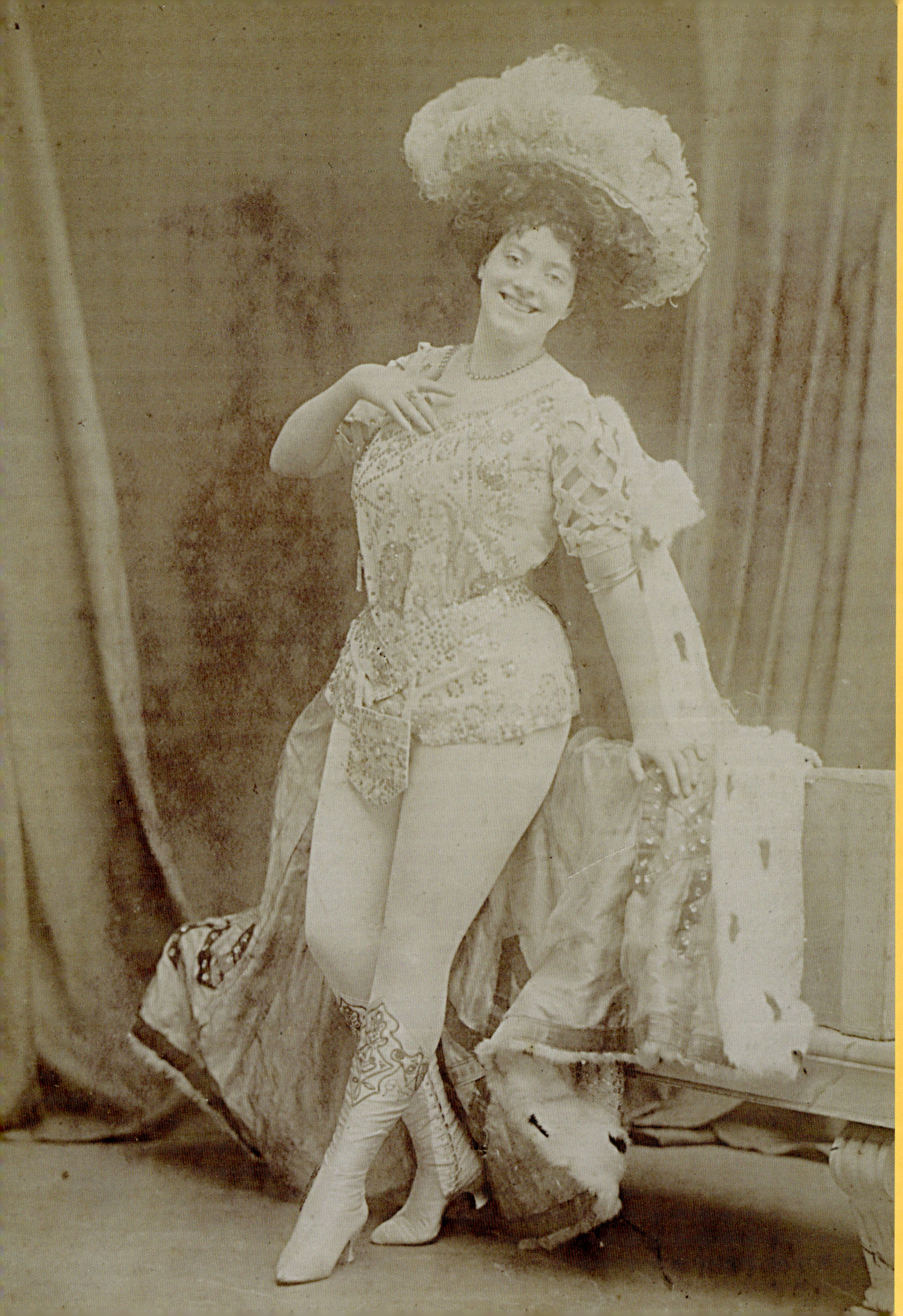

1

Theatrical Steps:
HENRY & MARY RAYNE
1898-1920

Keturah Daveney lived locally in Walworth and in 1909, at the age of 14, went to work in the Boots and Shoes Department in the Rayne factory: "I was given a piece of linen with the button-holes already cut out, then I had to hold a piece of fine cord (called 'gimp') round the edge of the hole and work the buttonhole stitch over the top. No 'gimp' must show when the stitching is finished." Her friend and colleague explained, "when you can sew perfect button-holes you will work button-holes for satin boots or shoes and the piece of satin you work on is called a 'fly'. For High Boots you might have eight button-holes to stitch. When you are done you hand over the 'fly' to Bessie and she will sew it on to the uppers which will be then stitched on to the boot. Do you understand?" I answered "Not yet, but I will eventually." This led to three more months of practise, when the forelady 'Lottie' pronounced them perfect and gave her green satin boot 'flies' for buttonholes to be made, the boots for the pantomime 'Puss in Boots'. "Mind you don't prick your finger, because if a spot of blood gets on the 'fly' it is spoilt" (Kids Over The Water by Angela Cousins. Mereo, Cirencester, 2014, pp85-89)

As with so many successful 20th-century businesses, the later glamour of H. & M. Rayne shoes had its feet rooted firmly in the most fertile ground of Victorian London, then the richest and most successful expanding capital city in the world. The capital of the vast British Empire encouraged the hard work and initiative that gained enormous rewards for large numbers of entrepreneurs. The Rayne family history is one of commercial success with advances and reverses and it began in the interesting area of Lambeth around the Waterloo Road, a fast-developing area of varied shops and businesses encouraged by the transformation effected by the huge expanding railway station with its bustling traffic.[1]

The young Mary Clark (1863-1911) was born in Walthamstow, where her father was a decorator. At the time of her marriage on 21 September 1884 to Henry Rayne in St Anne's Church, Soho, both were aged 21 and both gave their address as being at nearby 9 Little Newport Street; no occupation is given for her. Henry was then a waiter, as was his father James Rayne. Soho was an extension of theatreland, its bustling life filled the local restaurants with actors and theatregoers, and the inspiration for Henry and Mary to begin a business as theatrical costumiers.

Previous page: Kitty Lord exemplifies the full talents of the H. & M. Rayne Ltd, Waterloo Road, Lambeth work-rooms. Miss Lord, the 'Chanteuse Excentrique Anglaise' not only had costumes made for her by H. & M. Rayne, but they probably also sold her the figure-shaping 'symmetricals', which were worn under the 'fleshings'. Kitty Lord's career peaked between 1894-1915. Born Kate Anna Emma Burbidge, she performed aged eleven at The Grand Musical Hall in Islington and subsequently in the major London Halls, appearing with Fred Carno, Maurice Chevalier and Gladys Cooper. She toured the British Isles and also appeared in Paris and Naples. In 1915 she married bank clerk Cyril Parker. They later ran into legal difficulties in Buenos Aires during a Latin-American tour. © MUSEUM OF LONDON

Facing page: These H. & M. Rayne silver braid, silver and red sequin embroidered pink satin boots, seen worn by Kitty Lord, an 'Eccentric Singer' (p.16) around 1905 have cotton linings, leather soles and covered Louis heels. They fastened with pink silk laces through eighteen pairs of pink-painted metal eyelets. Miss Lord's bravado matched her outrageous boots in private life. In November 1904 she was stopped for passing a policeman 'like a flash of lightning', having taken the wheel of a car *en route* from Blackpool to London, whilst the driver enjoyed his cigar. She said, "Don't make any mistake. I shall be awfully disappointed if I don't get a summons." (*Lancashire Evening Post*, 17 November, 1904). © MUSEUM OF LONDON

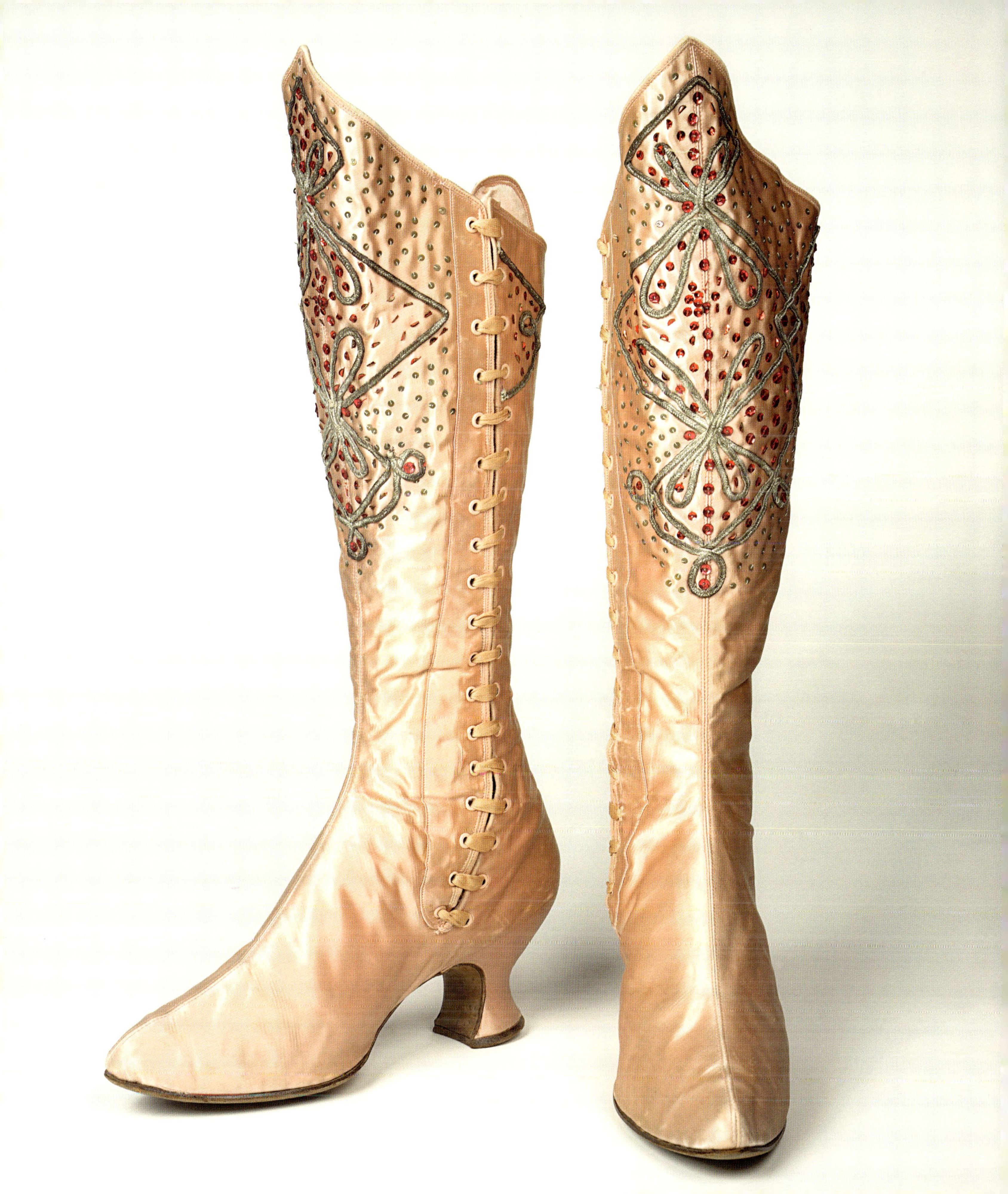

Family legend has it that they began at the bottom with a street-market stall in Lambeth – away from the established West End businesses – almost certainly in the thriving market along The Cut, south-east of Waterloo Station. Surviving photographs of the area from before the First World War display streets of terraced housing alternating with commercial streets such as the Waterloo Road or The Cut, full of every variety of shop and restaurant on a scale unimaginable today. At the Waterloo Road end was social reformer Emma Conns' Royal Victoria Hall and Coffee Tavern in the New Victoria Palace Theatre (built in 1818 and today known as the 'Old Vic' theatre). Theatre goers and actors also thronged the area. The subsequent extensive nature of the Rayne business is a testament to Henry and Mary's hardiness, coping with all weathers and tough customers with determination, helped by the plentiful and cheap labour force available.

Edward Henry Ryan's father, James, was born around 1840 in the garrison town of Cahir, Ireland (just before the Potato Famine of 1845-1852) when it was a garrison town. He enlisted in the Duke of Cornwall's Regiment and was a Private in the 32nd regiment at Devonport, where his eldest son was born, 21 January 1863; Edward later served in India.

As young man, Henry travelled to America and held a variety of jobs. Next he worked as a waiter in Paris, where he learned fluent French. The French pronunciation of 'Ryan' no doubt gave him and his father the idea of changing his surname to 'Rayne'. It proved advantageous on the establishment of H. & M. Rayne as theatrical costumiers. Not only did their competitors have quite exotic names, but also Irish names were not then chic in the wake of the political problems, known as 'The Irish Question', an especially contentious issue after the Fenian Rising in 1867. There was also a popular and very beautiful actress treading the Dublin boards at this time, Eveleen Rayne (born Daisy Evelyn Lyster) famous for playing 'Moya' in *The Shaugraun*, the Irish melodrama by Dion Boucicault. She was much photographed and illustrated in the burgeoning press of the day; like several other actresses at the time, she married into the peerage. Although her first son was illegitimate, the second became Earl Fitzwilliam, so the name of Rayne was well known.

Apart from the usual Victorian plethora of public houses, the Waterloo Road area was most notable for its theatres. The Canterbury Music Hall at 143 Westminster Bridge Road, could boast performances by the celebrated Arthur Lloyd performed, as well as a host of minor artistes, such as Charlie Chaplin's father and Charlie himself. Opposite was Gatti's Palace of Varieties – known as Gatti's-in-the-Road. Dan Leno appeared here as did George Leybourne, Little Tich, Harry Vance, Marie Kendal, and Marie Lloyd; it was also the venue for scottish comic Harry Lauder's first London appearance and he became

Facing page: A pair of Rayne theatrical shoes, c.1913-16, worn by Sir Johnston Forbes-Robertson (1853-1937) as Hamlet. Black lace-up shoe made of bands of suede and velvet. He was generally considered the finest Hamlet of the 19th century. He first played the role at the age of 44 and last played it in 1916, probably the date of these unusually modern shoes. He also filmed the role in 1913. © MUSEUM OF LONDON

21

a sensation. Gatti's also had a second premises in Villiers Street, Charing Cross, where the same artistes appeared, often on the same night. In fact, such was the ideal nature of the location that they would quite often cross the road to appear at The Canterbury and could also perform in other music halls on the same night, including the Camberwell Palace, the Paragon on the Mile End Road and the Granville at Walham Green, before returning to Gatti's for their final performance. Today, the area is so re-developed that this is hard to imagine.

Such intense activity gives a good indication of the audience numbers available for an evening's entertainment. There was usually also food and drink available on the premises. The extensive 1900 menu for The Royal Cambridge Theatre of Varieties on Commercial Street in London's East End, for example, included no fewer than seven different champagnes. The variety of entertainment on offer can scarcely be appreciated in the London of today. Rayne profited from this – the need for costumes, make-up and shoes was increasing; it meant greater investment, more manufacturing and supervisory staff and more business for H. & M. Rayne.

The 1901 Census lists the Rayne family as living at 68, Amity Street, Raynes Park – a modest Victorian house. On Census day, Mrs Rayne was in fact absent. At home were daughter Mary Elizabeth (aged 14 and already a shop assistant) and sons James Henry (8), Joseph (8) and Charles (7); all were to be highly active in H. & M. Rayne's business. Also at home were Jessie (4) and Susie (3) as well as a housekeeper and 13-year-old servant girl, Beatrice Buck. Also present were three visitors: a theatrical floquier, a silk seamstress and a bookbinding worker. The house was close to bursting and with growing children, the family moved to a larger house 'Hazelmere', 71, Lambton Road, the parallel street.

By 1895, *Kelly's Directory* listed Rayne as 'theatrical costumiers, shoemakers, hosiers wigmakers and theatrical perfumers' at 115 Waterloo Road. The listing states Henry and Mary 'Mrs' – underlining her position in the company.[2] As *Kelly's* 1895 entries show, there were many women in London operating as independent traders in all manner of commercial undertakings, not least in the clothing industry and the theatrical costume trade at that time. Near Rayne's premises there were also outfitters, shirt and shoemakers' shops, but Rayne was the only local theatrical costumier of note.[2] The city guides reveal that they had become a major business; others equally prominent such as Auguste, Alia, or Nathan were all located in the Drury Lane area, whilst Simmons was nearby in King Street St James's, indicating their proximity to the main seats of dramatic art.

Facing page: H. & M. Rayne Ltd. faced enormous competition in their field and were careful to advertise their services and wares in all manner of publications. The latter decades of the 19th century were ones of great expansion of printed matter and processes. The advertisement makes interesting reading and was undoubtedly closely scrutinised on the train journeys undertaken all over the British Isles by theatricals. The content of the preparations on offer was not so closely scrutinised and one wonders what health dangers lurked within. RAYNE ARCHIVE

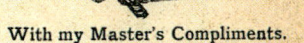

Another facet of the Waterloo Road establishment was the proximity in neighbouring York Road of a considerable number of theatrical agents' offices and inexpensive actors' lodgings, apart from better hotels, so that actors of all talents were increasingly familiar with Rayne. The further redevelopment of Waterloo Station, especially from 1900 to 1910, involved the demolition of the west or facing side of Waterloo Road across from Rayne's premises, then including the neighbouring buildings at 117 and 119. Deterioration of the surroundings contributed to the Raynes opening premises at 49 Charing Cross Road. In the music-hall star Dan Leno's memoirs, *Hys Booke* (published in 1901), an advertisement underlines the importance of the location at that date, stressing the superb transport links: 'Opposite Waterloo Tram Terminus' and 'Buses and trams pass the door every minute'. In addition, the advertisement contains the Manx logo, marked 'Trade Mark', rendered as whirling legs in striped or plain pantaloons, the business employing the usual messengers, known as ' boy runners', who would deliver items to theatres with great speed.

The connection with the Isle-of-Man and the use of the Manx symbol is said to refer to Mary Rayne's family background pre-dating her birthplace in Walthamstow. Her daughter Jessica was also nicknamed 'Manx', but there may be another reason, as with the adoption of the Rayne name by her father-in-law and husband.

The 1907 advertisement offers 'Historical and Fancy Costumes, Wigs, &c. Suitable for Bazaars, Tableaux, Mrs. Jarleys' Waxworks, Attendants at Stalls, School Entertainments, &c., can all be hired at most reasonable terms'

('Mrs Jarley's Waxworks' refers to the establishment in Dicken's novel *The Old Curiosity Shop*, based upon Ferguson's Waxworks at the Drury Lane end of Museum Street, known to Dickens, a keen amateur actor.)

The advertisement then states: 'The largest and most modern stock of Theatrical Costumes and requisites in London' and significantly announces:

> MONA POWDER : If you want to look your best, use MONA POWDER for producing a beautiful complexion. Largest sale of toilet powder in the Kingdom, prepared in 4 shades ; Naturelle, Blance, Crème and Rose : sample box sent on receipt of 9 stamps.

In the history of British women using cosmetics or 'enamelling' their faces beyond the foot-lights, this is significant, as is the diversification indicated further with:

> ELIXERINE : a remarkable discovery, a certain preventative and immediate cure for the falling out of the hair, dandruff, &c., An absolute producer of hair sold in large bottles 3s 6d sufficient to show a marvellous growth.

> Testimonials proving the excellence of our preparations from
>
> Madame Adelina Patti   Sir Henry Irving
> Miss Ellen Terry   Miss Ada Blanche
> Miss Marie Lloyd   Mr Dan Leno. &c.

Another striking full-page Rayne advertisement of the period depicts a bouquet of roses, each rose the face of a period stage star

> A BOUQUET OF ROSES : TRY MONA POWDER : PRODUCES A LOVELY COMPLEXION : as used by the Elite of the Profession and MOST BEAUTIFUL WOMEN OF THE DAY........

The least familiar amongst the legendary names in the testimonials is that of Ada Blanche, who featured as 'Robinson Crusoe' in pantomime at Drury Lane wearing a suitably furred short garment above the fleshings covering her shapely legs as shown in a photograph in the influential magazine *The Sketch* on 31 January 1894. Miss Blanche held the record for appearing as Principal Boy in Drury Lane for seven consecutive seasons – 1892-98. Miss Blanche also displayed a fine pair of court shoes with small heels, an indication of Rayne's growing fame in this sphere.

Musical productions were more valuable for Rayne than dramatic ones, as they utilised very many pairs and replacement shoes, often for enormous casts.[3] Rayne catered for all contingencies, advertisements of the late 1890s in *The Era* not only offered the metal

Above: Mona Powder was a staple of the H. & M. Rayne range of theatrical make-up powders. Family legend asserts that the Rayne family came from the Isle of Man (Mona), hence the early Rayne logo of the three legs. Certainly one of Henry and Mary Rayne's children was nick-named 'Manx' and by 1919 their son Joseph had re-named the Waterloo premises Manx House. It is just as likely that the legs symbolised the famously swift delivery service of the Rayne messengers delivering from Waterloo to the stage doors of theatres all over London. MICHAEL PICK COLLECTION

make-up box 'RAYNE'S PATENT ENAMEL MAKE-UP BOX. CLOSED. OPENED. With Removable Plate Glass, 7s. 6d. If fitted complete, every requisite, Gents., 15s.' but also costumes of roaring lions, and 'the Boxing Kangaroo, a great success as introduced by Yorick the Fool at Wulff's Circus. A sure Pantomime Draw...'. One December 1892 sale included 'Cat, Dogs, and Monkeys' Dresses, also several Harlequin and Clowns' Dresses Second-hand, Cheap and Good Condition' . They also advertised mechanical properties, hence the roaring lions. Though the make-up received rave reviews: "... grease paints and rouges which will not become oily in warm weather as other preparations do...", shoes were undoubtedly Rayne's speciality.[4]

A rare survival of an H. & M. Rayne theatrical travelling make-up box for a time when actors almost all travelled by train between engagements with trunk and case. This ingenious box contains the remains of a full make-up kit for some actor of the early decades of the last century. Made of black enamelled tin, it is both robust and light. The mirror folds out and all manner of interesting tins and colourings remain within – there is even a surviving rabbit's foot for the application of rouge and powder. RAYNE ARCHIVE

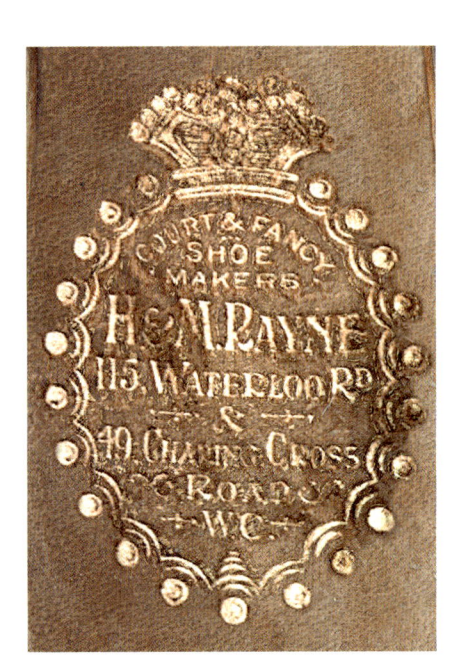

A pair of H. & M. Rayne Ltd white satin shoes with small Louis heels and rectangular buckles decorated with glass brilliants, the a bar/strap closure fastening with a button. These shoes were suitable for dyeing to match the colour of any dress or could have been worn to any formal occasion such as a ball or wedding. They may have been intended for stage use, but are possibly amongst the earliest non-dancing shoes to have survived. The insole bears both the Waterloo Road address and that of the first Rayne retail shop at 49 Charing Cross Road. c.1910. RAYNE ARCHIVE

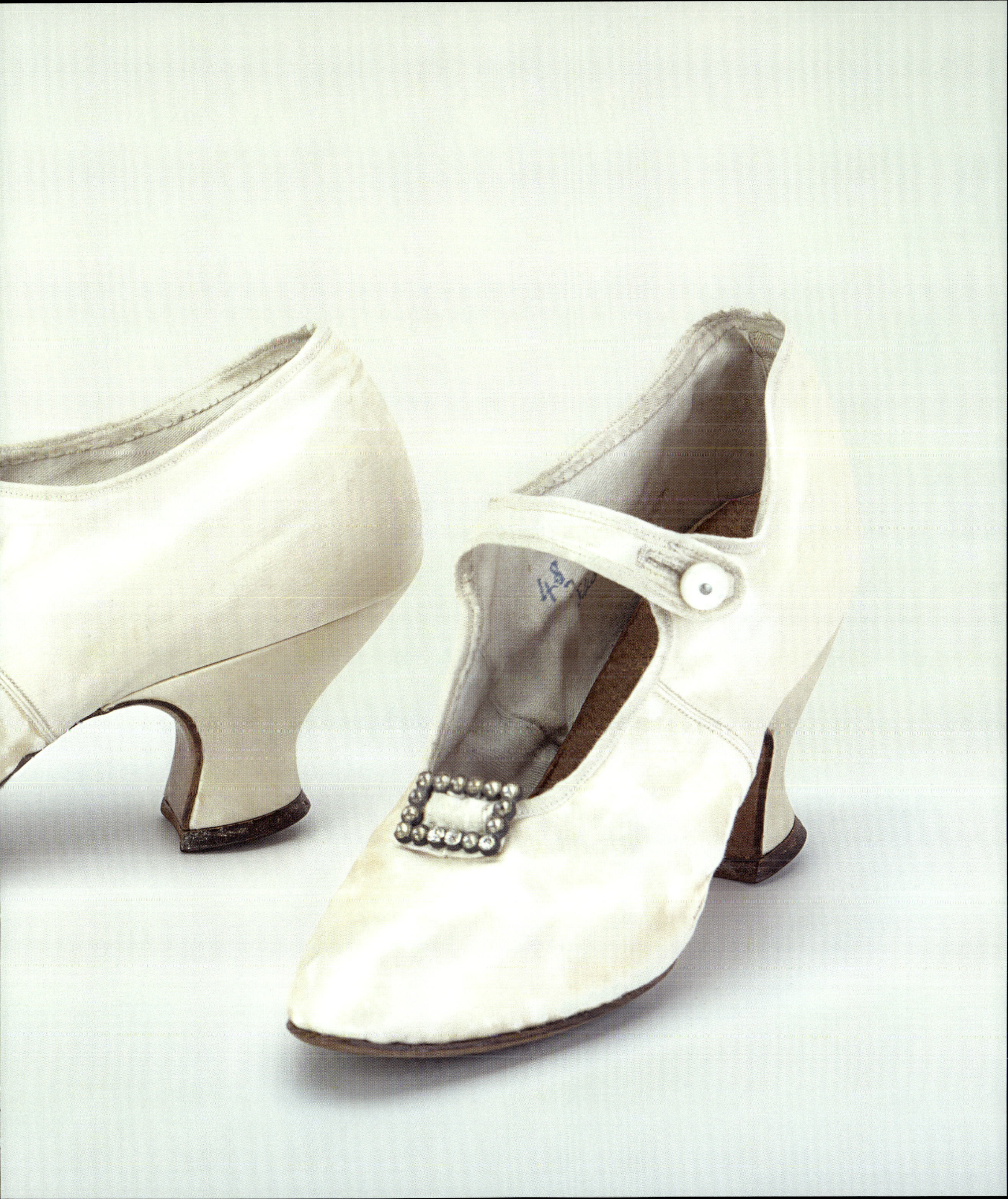

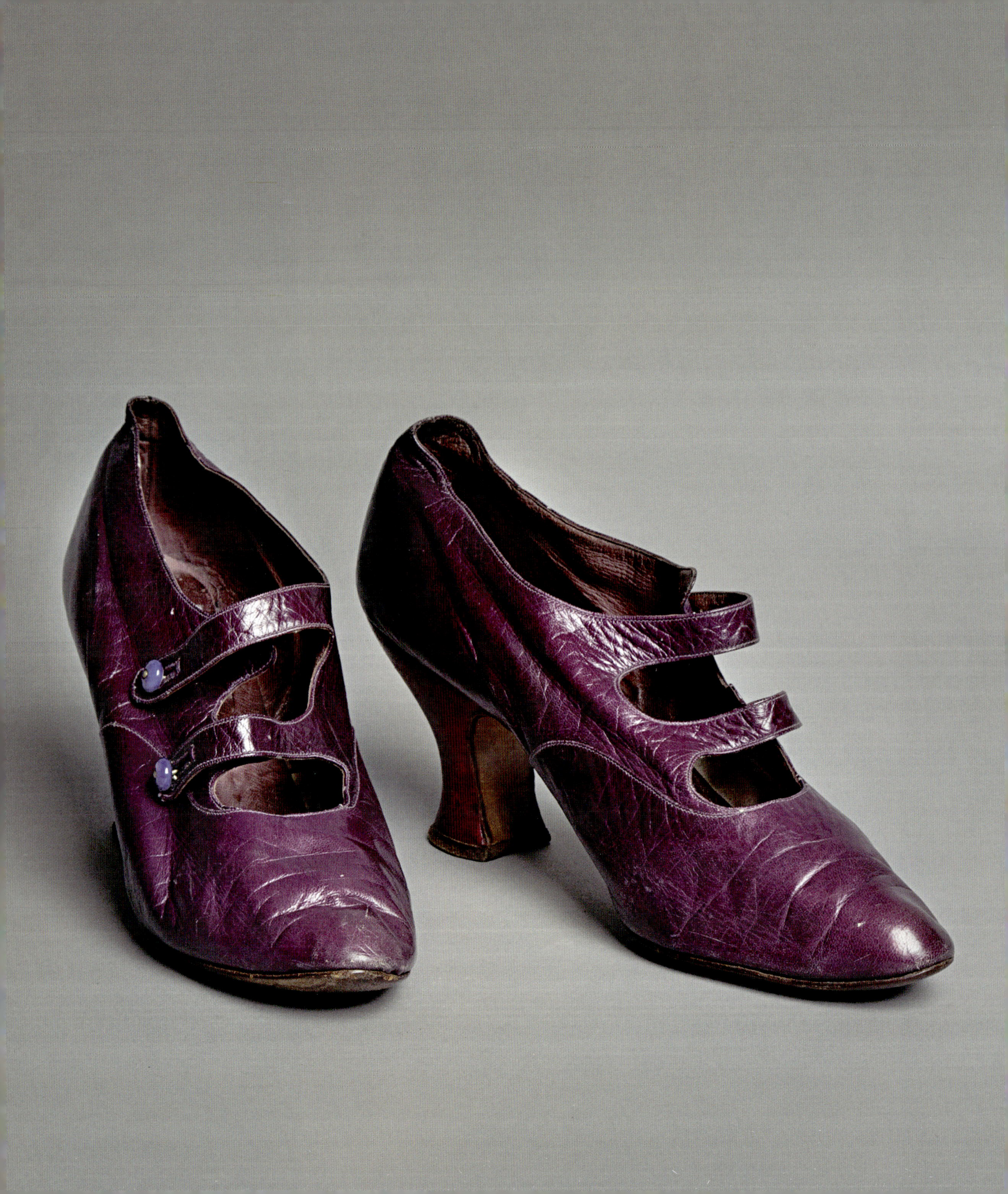

London in the decades around Queen Victoria's Golden Jubilee in 1887 until the outbreak of war in 1914 was not merely the 'hub of the Empire', often said to be Piccadilly Circus, it was the largest and richest city in the civilised world. The building of Shaftesbury Avenue included many of the new theatres built at this time, all vying with one another to draw in the public with lavish productions, many of them light-hearted to the point of inanity.

The proximity of Bermondsey, for centuries at the heart of the British leather industry with its tanning processes so well described some thirty years earlier by Henry Mayhew in his books, probably contributed to the materials and labour source for the shoe-making part of H. & M. Rayne, although by the latter quarter of the 19th century there was a great number of boot and shoe retailers in London, as well as manufacturers. In the late 1870s, The Leather, Hide and Wool Exchange was built on the corner of Leathermarket Street, and St Crispin's Church was dedicated to the patron saint of leather and shoes. In spite of the new factories such as those for Hartley's Jam or Peak Freans biscuits introducing cleaner and more pleasant variety to Bermondsey manufacturing, the old leather-based trades were still strong in Henry and Mary Rayne's day.

Not just steam power, but the use of gas for lighting and heating, were utilised in addition to the handworkers and finishers available and the rapidly widespread adoption of electricity for lighting extended winter working hours in a less unhealthy manner. These same power sources made streets, shops and places of entertainment all more seductive.

Many illustrated journals of the period devoted much space to London theatrical productions, photographs of the stars appearing in the same issues as royalty, aristocratic women or politicians and other famous men and women, especially concentrating on the events of 'The Season'. Women's clothes visible in such periodicals and on the stage had a clear influence on women's fashion in general, augmented by newspapers and items found in the many department stores or shops. The 'Gaiety Girls' or stars such as Lillie Langtry – Rayne clients – were national figures and their houses and clothes were 'news'. Theatre programmes included the names of production designers or suppliers, increasingly with the line 'Shoes by H. & M. Rayne' or just ' Shoes by Rayne', regularly to be seen over the next seven decades attached to many legendary productions. This was the best advertisement of all. As women's dress began to be less elaborate and skirt hems began to rise after 1910, women's feet and shoes became visible and the design of boots and shoes worn during the day ceased to be purely utilitarian for all but the poorest. *A Pocket Atlas and guide to London* (1900) indicates the trend in dress and fashion, explicitly stating that in theatres, 'full dress is no longer required, except in the opera houses'.

Facing page: A pair of H. & M. Rayne double-bar day shoes in a daring magenta kid leather with Louis heels and blue glass buttons. It is rare to find surviving day shoes of this period. c.1910. NORTHAMPTON MUSEUMS

A pair of H. & M. Rayne red leather four-bar shoes with unusual central button fastenings lined with white leather and with high black leather Louis heels, insole or sock gilt-stamped: 'Court & Fancy Shoe Makers H & M Rayne 115 Waterloo Road and 49 Charing Cross Road WC'. c.1910.   © MUSEUM OF LONDON

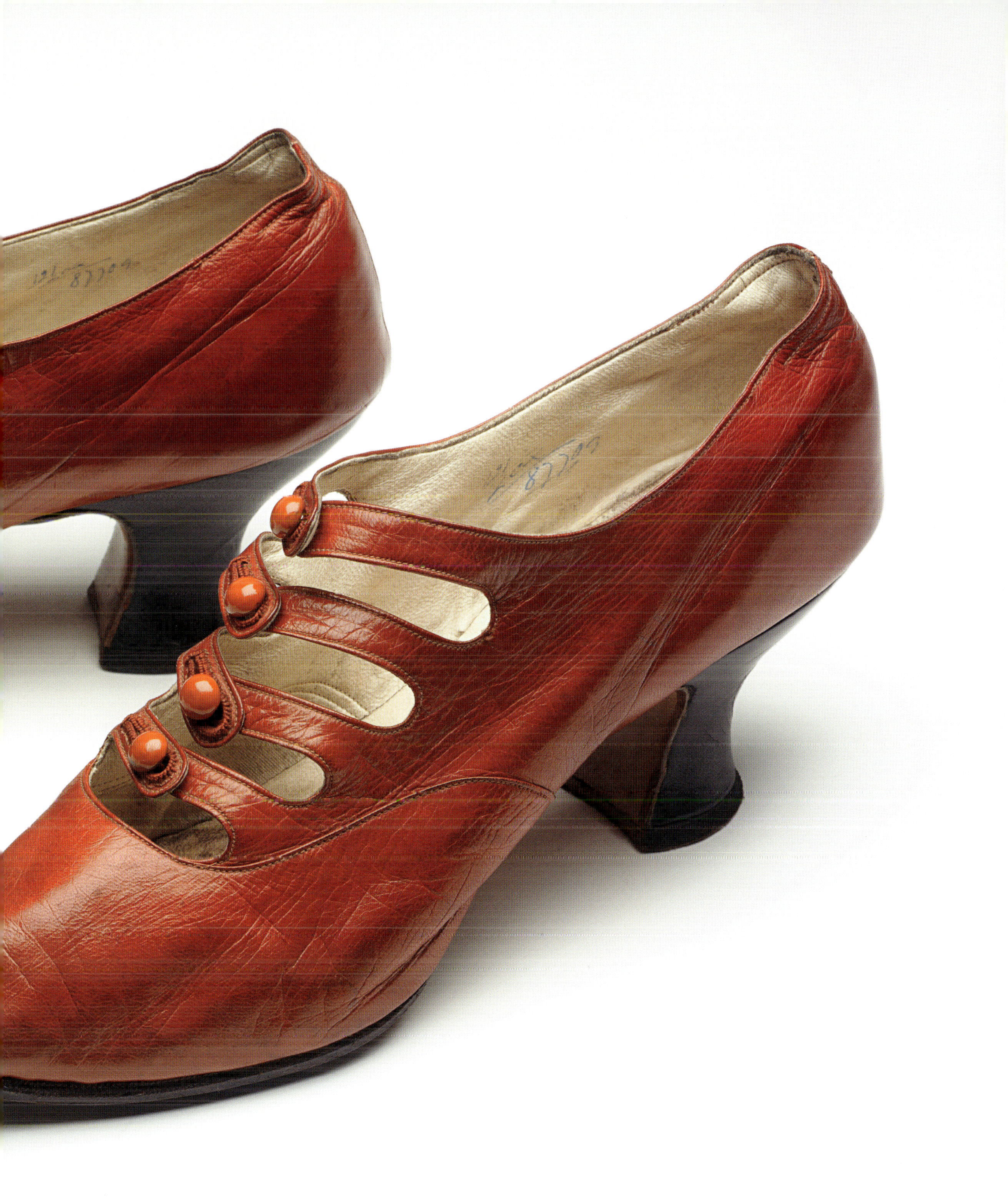

By this time, Henry's brother Himalaya (1871-1942) had also joined the company. Known as 'Himmy', he was supposedly given his eccentric name because his parents were travelling to India on the SS *Himalaya* when he was born. Himmy had left a job in Glasgow – where he knew the music hall artist Harry Lauder – to join H. & M. Rayne. Mary had become less involved in the business as she was busy with their six children. In later years, she suffered from depression. Mary, who had been the mainstay of the theatrical costume business, had to leave the company when she suffered a mental breakdown after the birth of her eighth child and was latterly looked after in an institution. By the time of her death in 1911, they were living at 71 Lambton Road and also had a house on the cliffs at Kingsdown, Ringwould between Deal and Dover. The significance of the extended family became apparent with the opening of the West End commercial shoe shops in 1920, after the death of Henry in 1915.

In 1900, in the London of Henry and Mary Rayne's day, there existed some 48 theatres, not only requiring a multitude of costumes for a constantly changing repertoire, but also catering to the many productions touring Britain, where cities and towns all had theatres and music halls until the growth of cinemas began to take away their audiences.[5] By 1910 there were 30 music halls and 44 advertised theatres in London alone; Rayne occupied four buildings with the upper storeys connected by lifts, shoes were made in various workshops on differing floors, which was impractical but possible in the days of low overheads and wages.

Lavish stage productions, such as those by George Edwardes (regarded as the inventor of British musical comedy) at Dalys, the Prince of Wales, Adelphi and, most notably, The Gaiety with its 'Gaiety Girls', all added to the demand for stage shoes. Not only were shoes required for show-girls to dance in, but the growth of ballet productions, even as part of a 'variety' bill, brought increasing fame and fortune. For example, the 1905 production of *The Spring Chicken* ran for 401 performances and featured famous 'Gaiety Girl' Gertie Millar; the costumes designed by Mr Wilhelm: 'dresses executed by Jays Ltd, Paquin and Morris Angel Ltd. Shoes H. & M. Rayne'. 'Mr Wilhelm' was actually William Charles Pitcher (1858-1925), an Englishman who worked on almost 200 productions at a time when things German and artistic were considered notable, reflecting the influence of Prince Albert, husband of Queen Victoria.

This endorsement by a leading star of the Victorian and Edwardian stage marks the beginning of advertising by emulation. Presumably many women idolised Miss Fanny Brough and could have afforded 'Dandy Shoes' or others sold in Rayne's Charing Cross Road shop set amidst theatreland. Frances "Fanny" Whiteside Brough (1852–1914) was admired in Shakespearean roles, 'refined' comedy, and also in Oscar Wilde's 1895 *An Ideal Husband*. In 1902 she created 'Mrs Warren' in George Bernard Shaw's *Mrs Warren's Profession*. The endorsement of such a leading performer must have added to Rayne's commercial success. RAYNE ARCHIVE

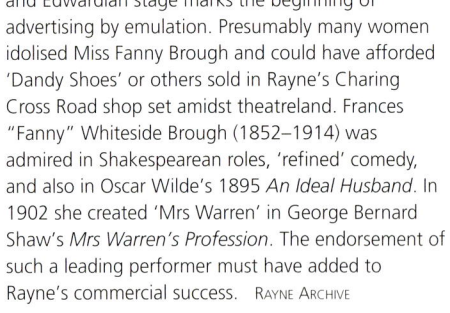

In an advertisement in the programme for *Humpty Dumpty* at the Theatre Royal, Drury Lane, the 1903-1904 pantomime featuring Dan Leno, H. & M. Rayne were already showing their future path. Rayne's advertisement states, 'The whole of the shoes in this presentation are made by Messrs H. & M. Rayne, the Largest Manufacturers of Theatrical Shoes in the World'. A bold claim indeed; though, given the cut-throat jealousies of stage or commercial activities, it is unlikely to have been unsubstantiated.

Sadly, little is known about the daily life of the Rayne family or about the workforce or the premises at that time, nor do any photographs seem to have survived, but they were promoting their new shoe outlet at 49 Charing Cross Road as 'Theatrical & Modern Boot & Shoe Makers' illustrating a buttoned shoe with a bow trimming and a Louis heel:

'The DANDY shoe as worn by the PRINCIPAL ACTRESSES. Miss Haidee Wright says "Delighted with Shoes".'

Haidee Wright was a very famous character actress in her day and starred in the long-running play *Milestones* by Arnold Bennett and Edward Knoblauch. Bennett considered her 'a strong, "vibrant" (as they say) personality, always interesting.' (*Journal*, Friday October 29 1915). She came from a large family of actors and her work extended to Broadway and into films from 1915, as therefore did the appearance of Rayne shoes. The smallest type above the address indicates the future direction of the Rayne business: 'Every grade of Boots and Shoes for Ladies Outdoor Wear at Moderate Prices.'

A rare glimpse of Henry Rayne and the Waterloo Road premises has been left by Keturah Daveney, who lived locally in Walworth and at the age of 14 in 1909 went to work in the Boots and Shoes Department of the factory above the retail and hire premises. 'The window displays showed off dresses and suits made of satin or other stylish materials, like silks and georgette, or other shimmering materials. Top hats were often made of the same materials with boots

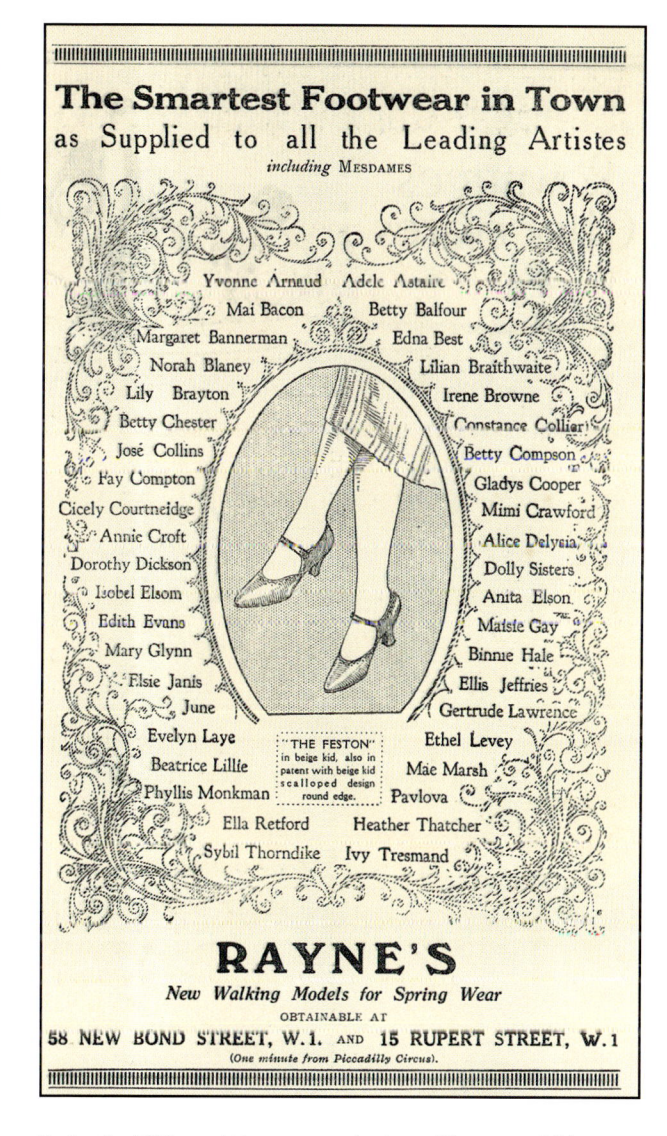

During the 1920s, as skirts grew ever shorter and feet more visible, H. & M. Rayne were providing elegant shoes for almost all the beautiful women seen on the London stage. After 1920, they also had a Bond Street shop catering for affluent Mayfair shoppers. This roll-call of some of the greatest actresses of the period indicates the quality and diversity of Rayne shoe designs. The kid shoes reflect the 1920s taste for the lady-like colour beige; it vied with eau-de-nil. Rayne were consistent advertisers in theatre programmes for over seven decades. RAYNE ARCHIVE

ROYAL OPERA HOUSE
COVENT GARDEN
By arrangement with THE GRAND OPERA SYNDICATE, Ltd.

EDMUND RUSSON has the honour to present

FOR FOUR WEEKS ONLY, SEPT. 8th to OCT. 4th,
Evenings at 8.15.   Matinees, Wednesdays and Saturdays at 2.30

ANNA PAVLOVA

SUPPORTED BY

LAURENT NOVIKOFF   ALEXANDRE VOLININE

IVAN CLUSTINE
BALLETMASTER

HILDA BUTSOVA   SOPHIE FEDOROVA

M. PIANOWSKI   FR. VAGINSKI
(Assistant Balletmaster)

J. ZALEWSKI   AND   O. OLIVEROFF

CORPS DE BALLET

ORCHESTRA OF 60 PERFORMERS

Leader and Solo Violin   -   -   Mr. H. WYNN REEVES

Conductor   THEODORE STIER

PIANOS SUPPLIED EXCLUSIVELY BY CHAPPELL
FOOTWEAR SUPPLIED TO Madame PAVLOVA & HER TROUPE BY H. & M. RAYNE

General Manager, for Madame Anna Pavlova, EDMUND RUSSON to whom all communications must be addressed

---

Above, facing page and overleaf: Internationally famous for her depiction of 'The Dying Swan', Anna Pavlova (1881-1931) enjoyed world-wide popularity. She was the first ballet dancer to tour the whole world. Her public endorsement of H. & M. Rayne shoes followed the provision of various items to Diaghilev's 'Ballet Russes', then including Nijinsky. Pavlova made London her base in 1912 and Rayne advertisements in programmes and magazines came to include her valuable endorsement of their outdoor footwear in the early 1920s when they had moved from their Charing Cross Road shop to nearby Rupert Street and opened their Bond Street shop.

p.34 Rayne Archive; p.35 © Heritage Image Partnership Ltd./Alamy; p.37 Condé Nast

---

and shoes to match. It was really delightful to see all these beautiful clothes adorned with pearls and diamontes (*sic*), shining in the coloured lights when the windows were lit up at night.' The effect on passersby in this hectic commercial corner of London can be imagined, patrons of the Old Vic, music halls and train station included. (*Kids Over The Water*, Angela Cousins, Mereo, Cirencester, 2014, pp.85-89)

Even with the advent of 'moving pictures', theatre was predominantly the entertainment of choice amongst the population during the last quarter of the 19th-century. The controversial creation of Shaftesbury Avenue in 1885 included many splendid new theatres, including the London Pavilion in 1885, the Lyric in 1888, the Apollo in 1900, the Hicks Theatre (soon to be the Globe) in 1906, and the Queen's Theatre in 1907. This prompted Rayne to augment the Charing Cross Road business with another location in Rupert Street, just off Shaftesbury Avenue.[6]

Rayne's reputation for excellence attracted Danish born dancer Adeline Genée. Classically trained and famed in Europe, she began her London career in 1897 at the Empire Theatre of Varieties in Leicester Square, where she stayed for ten years. Although principally known as a classical ballerina, in 1905 she also appeared at Daly's Theatre for 400 performances of *The Little Michus*, for which the various styles of dancing – often not *en pointes* – necessitated a large variety of shoes in beautiful leathers or fabrics, many based on 18th-century designs. Those by Rayne with Louis heels worn by Genée, or members of her company, in various productions and preserved in the V&A reveal the superb craftsmanship.

Genée was soon added to the significant number of stars wearing Rayne footwear. Credited with re-inforcing ballet in the USA, she was engaged by Florence Ziegfeld in 1907 and billed as 'The World's Greatest Dancer'. She married an American in 1910 and divided her time between London and America, refusing an offer from Diaghilev to join his company. Her influence on Rayne seems to have extended beyond endorsing their advertisements – Mdlle Genée says 'The Boots and Shoes are perfect' – to awakening interest in the American market for their products during her visits there. It was probably her influence that brought the orders from Diaghilev in 1911 for various products for his Ballet Russes, as surviving invoices show, star, Nijinsky.

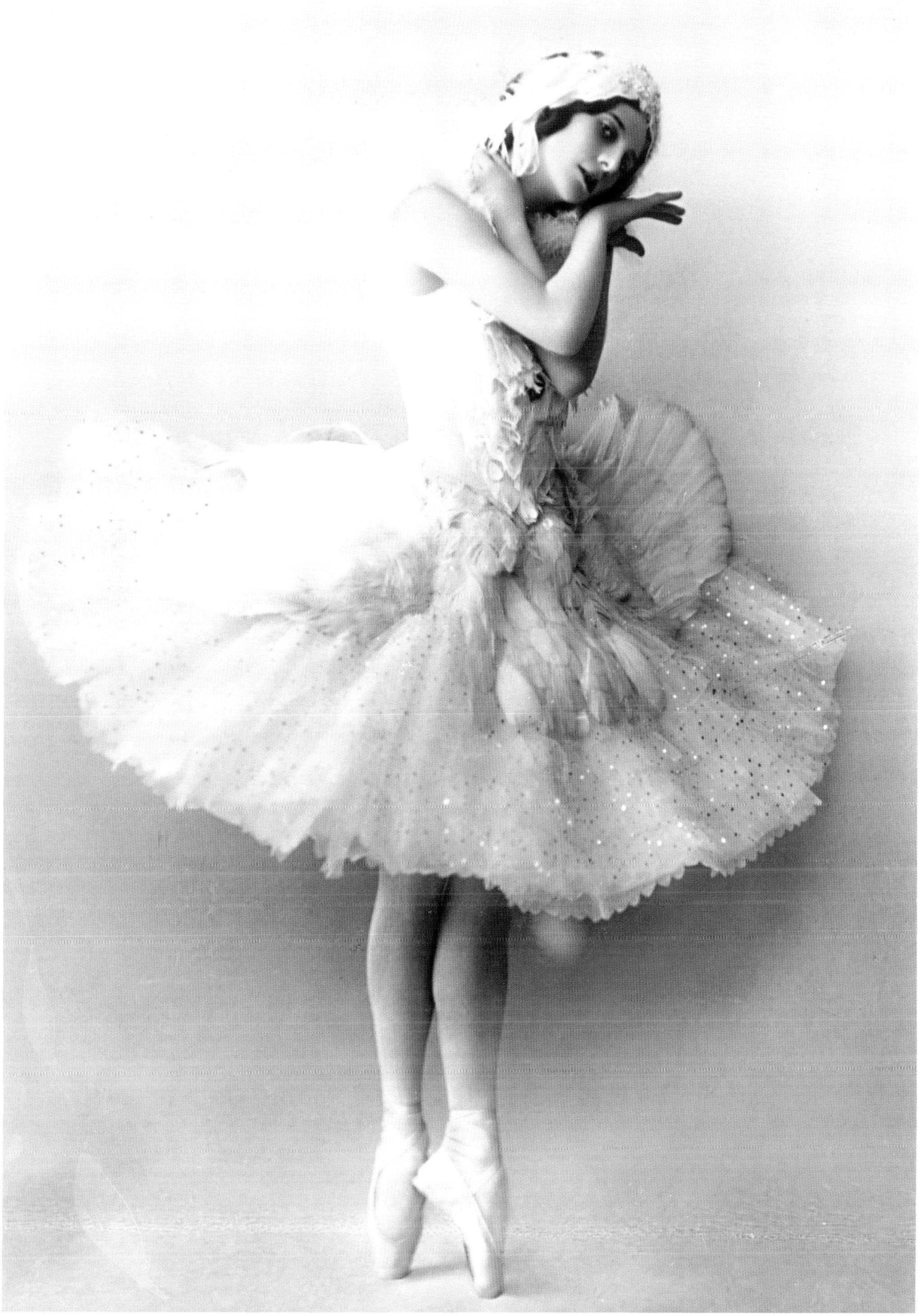

Other advertisements proclaimed Rayne's leading position in the industry:

'Sole Agents for the leading Milan Toe Shoes'.

'Suppliers to all the leading Theatres and Opera Houses. Makers to Mdlle. Pavlova & the Imperial Russian Dancers and the Royal Russian Opera Ballet – Mdlle Lydia Kyashi says 'Shoes fit perfectly'.

Rayne had added Anna Pavlova to their list of stars by 1910. Most famous today for her portrayal of 'The Dying Swan', choreographed for her by Fokine in 1905, she had briefly been part of Diaghilev's company in 1909. Though she continued to tour the world, in 1912 she made her home in England buying a house off Hampstead Heath in North London. She often wore stage shoes from Rayne and these reflect the capacity of their craftsmen to produce individually fashioned pointe shoes.[7] As Pavlova's feet were remarkably rigid, she had a piece of strengthening hard wood added to the soles and the box of the shoes was curved to give power to her small toes. Ballet purists of the day considered this to be deceitful, but Pavlova found her balance significantly improved, although she often removed the device or had photographs doctored, so that her feet appeared to be in the traditional pointe shoes. In fact, her modifications greatly influenced subsequent developments in the construction of pointe shoes, which today include a 'shank' to stiffen the sole. Pavlova's performances and her own ballet troupe accounted for some substantial orders from Rayne.

Pavlova's patronage helped the business to move forward – in the 1920s she became one of the first celebrities to be photographed promoting a product, namely Rayne off-stage shoes. By the First World War, cinema had really begun to take hold and had become a major force in reducing the number of music halls and the form of 'variety' on offer; Gatti's Music Hall at Charing Cross had already been turned into a cinema by 1910. Always with an eye to the future, Mary Rayne was already supplying shoes for film productions by this date. Theatre audiences declined significantly after 1918 as a torrent of British, European and American silent movies swept the cinemas. All they needed were subtitles and music accompanists and occasionally a variety act or two. The success of *The Jazz Singer* in 1927 ushered in the Odeon era of The Talkies during the 1930s and sounded the final death kneel of the Variety Act.

The history of H. & M. Rayne's success always lay in the directors' ability to build on their strengths and diversify. Edward Senior realised that Rayne's own hand-made shoes were not just glamorous adornments for the feet of stars on stage, but could be marketed as luxurious and desirable footwear for the most fashionable of women.

Madame Pavlova wears Rayne's Shoes both on and off the stage

All the Footwear for this Ballet supplied by

H. & M. RAYNE

Footwear-de-Luxe

58 New Bond Street

and at 15 Rupert Street

Shaftesbury Avenue (One Minute from Piccadilly Circus)

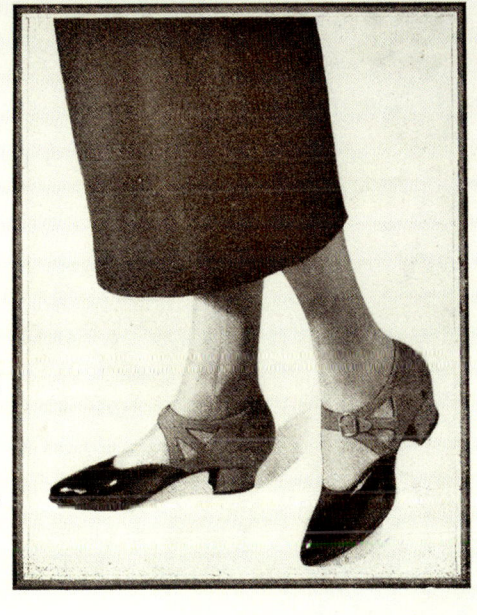

The Inimitable Quality

IT has ever been the privilege of the House of Rayne to create footwear for those women of taste who must be exclusive. It is this experience and discrimination which give to a Rayne Shoe that natural, unstudied distinction which has yet to be successfully imitated.

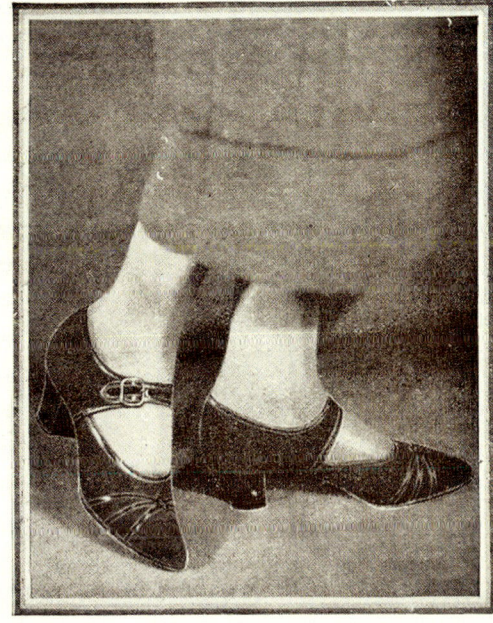

'*Madison*'
In Patent and Coloured Deerskins, or in Patent and Black Suède. Or with vamps of Tan Calf and backs of coloured Deerskins

'*Florida*'
In Black and Coloured Deerskins, with fancy strappings of Glacé Kid. Also in White Kid, strapped Patent, and in Patent strapped with dull Kid

'*Berkeley*'
A new Rayne model. In Nut Brown Doeskin, with fancy strappings in Glacé Kid of the same shade. Also in Black Antelope; strappings in Patent Kid Or Patent Kid; strappings in Black Antelope. This model can also be had in *White Deerskin, with Black Kid strappings*

Write for Price List of Rayne's Blocked Toe Ballet Shoes as supplied to the Russian Ballet.

Boots

From the preceding pages it is evident that H. & M. Rayne Ltd. were well versed in the design and manufacture of all types of footwear and were adept at the making of what were often the Cinderella of fashion: boots.

Check! The new high Button Boot for the low hem-line by Rayne

AGENCIES FOR RAYNE SHOES IN PRINCIPAL CITIES

Left: A late 1940s advertisement links the glamour of the past with what appears to be a folded jewelled fan or lorgnette and a vignette of a carriage with what was the latest post-New Look revival utilised by Christian Dior: high buttoned boots with checked gaiters. They were not only a fashion statement, but practical whilst Europe shivered through post-war fuel shortages. Rayne Archive

Facing page: The Rayne archive held an extraordinary quantity of historic footwear, which inspired their designers, not least Jean Matthew, seen here. Various boots and other footwear contrast nicely with the contemporary platform-soled sandal she is wearing. c.1952. Rayne Archive

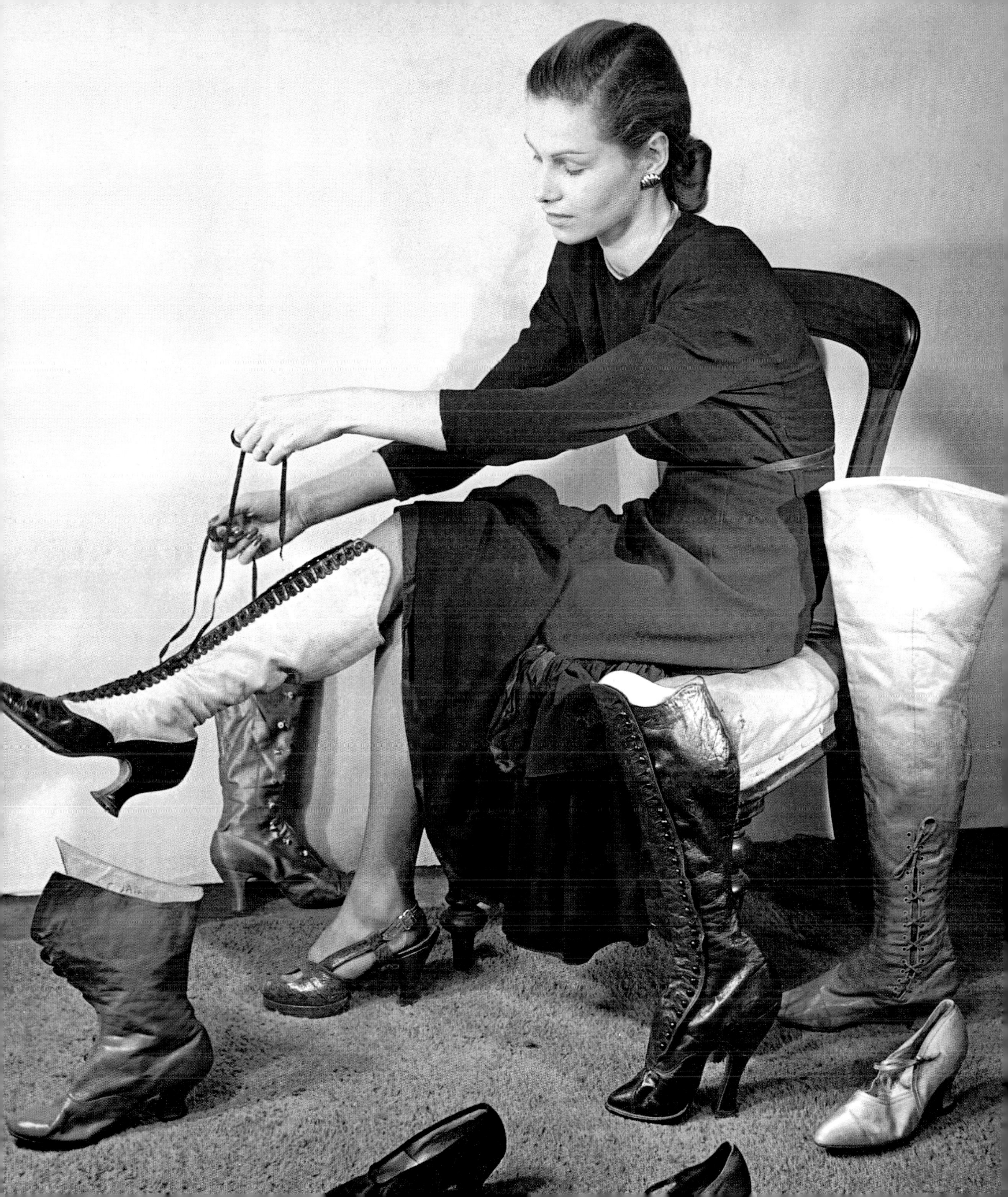

Three-quarter length boots were also popular amongst all ages and a note preserved in the archives of Historic Royal Palaces contains the information that HM Queen Elizabeth The Queen Mother particularly liked the 1970s grey suede versions, which were re-ordered at least three times.

'Town And Country'.
Above left: A pair of Rayne fur-edged chic black town ankle boots c.1985.
Bottom left: The tan country equivalent with leather stacked heels and horsey connotations visible in the strap and buckle around the heel. c.1975.
TRACY DOLPHIN COLLECTION

Below and facing page: Edward Rayne ("The Cobbler") and Norman Hartnell ("The Little Woman Round The Corner") may have had a self-deprecating sense of humour, but when it came to fashion innovation they blazed with inspiration. These vinyl boots were made for a Norman Hartnell show – probably to his design – and fashion shoot in 1960, as Jean Matthew's stock book design (below) shows. The lurex trim was enhanced with diamanté bobbles to the zips, but that version clearly defeated photographer and model. MICHAEL PICK COLLECTION

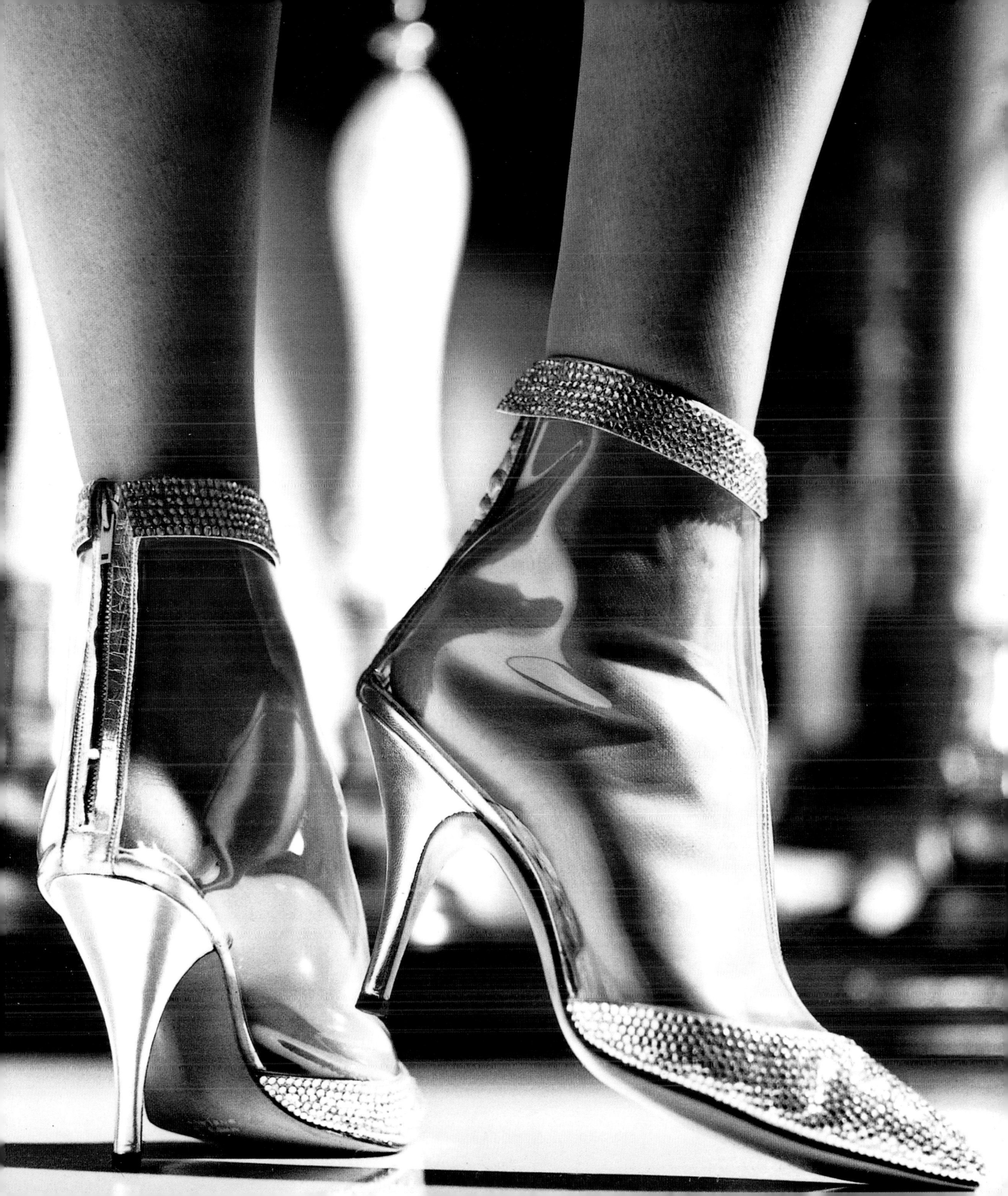

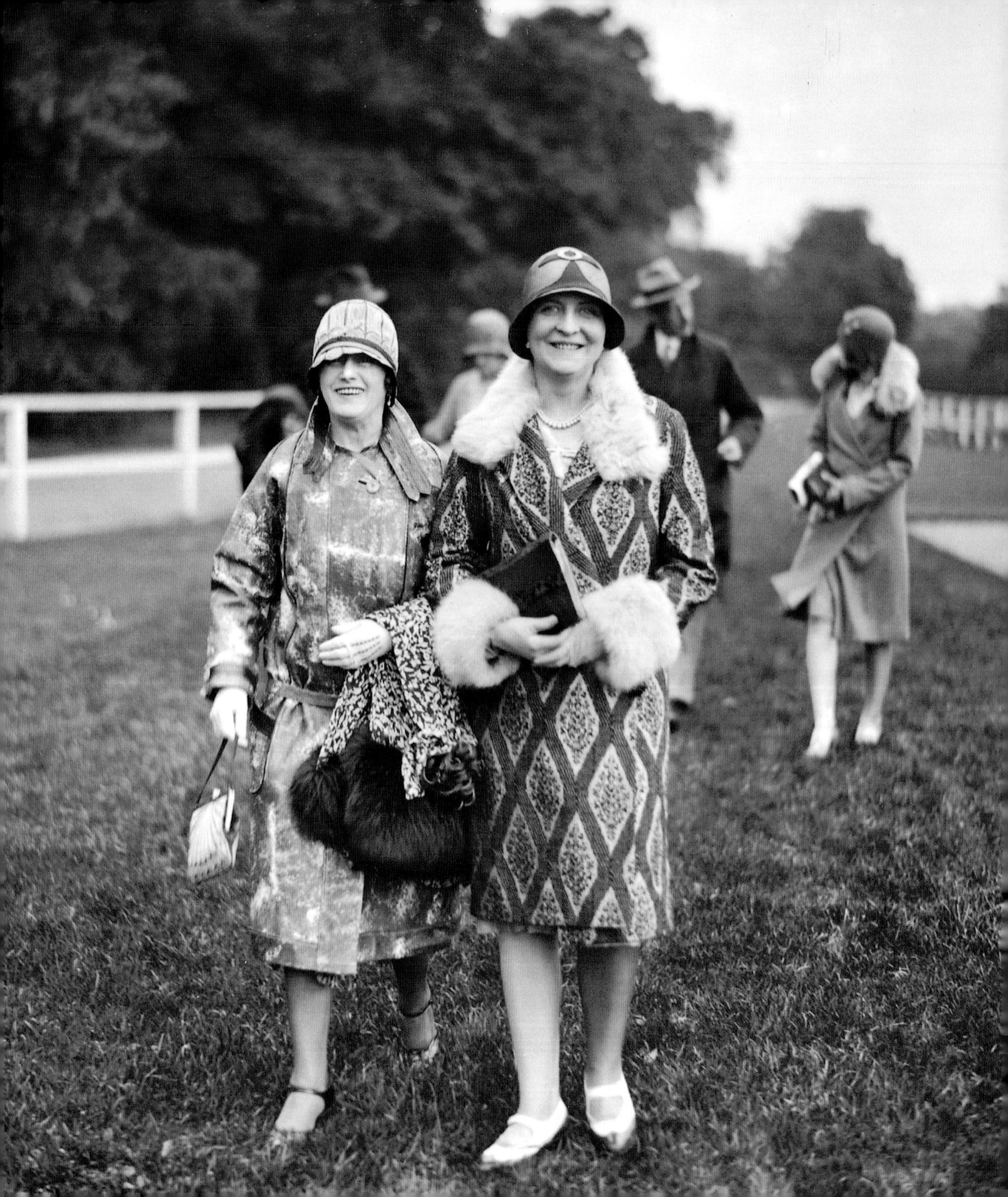

2

From Stage to Society Shoes:
JOSEPH EDWARD RAYNE
1920-1950

Previous page: A rare example of Rayne shoes photographed outside at the Queen's Bays v 10th Hussars Polo match held at Hurlingham, London on 16th June 1928. Worn by Mrs Joseph Edward Rayne, here with her close friend Mrs Arthur Franke, who sponsored her Presentation at Court in July 1932. Mrs Rayne (right) is wearing light summer shoes with a striking Jazz Age ensemble. The first polo match played in Britain was between the 10th Hussars and 9th Lancers in 1869, followed in 1874 by the first to be played at Hurlingham. The UK polo governing body evolved into The Hurlingham Polo Association (HPA) in 1925. The grounds were used as farm-land during the Second World War. RAYNE ARCHIVE

Below: After his war-time service as a decorated officer, Joseph Rayne began to turn H. & M. Rayne Ltd. into a shoe-retail business. After 1920 it attracted a discerning, fashionable clientele to the new Bond Street shop. At the beginning of the Jazz Age, new dance crazes changed as rapidly as fashions in clothes from season to season and feet were the focus of much attention. In 1957, Cecil Beaton typically deprecated past London fashions, the shoes of the 1920s reminding him of 'plumbing'. These silver mesh bar shoes prove how false memory can be, their chic zig-zag lines and glittering surfaces thrust upwards by small Louis heels fasten with a strap and exude sophistication, as Rayne shoes would do for decades to come. RAYNE ARCHIVE

In 1920, the first Rayne fashionable shop was opened in new Bond Street to cater for the most discerning Mayfair clientele. This was none too soon, for in January 1920 *Vogue* editorial indicated that British women were not only attracted to French shoes, but also catered to by French shoemakers, 'The Last Entente of France and England' over round toes and boat-shaped lasts 'were made especially for the British market. Joseph Edward Rayne went into battle.

Of the children of Henry and Mary Rayne, the second son Joseph Edward was the most charismatic. For some now unknown reason, he preferred to be called by his second name Edward, perhaps because it was the same as the then Prince of Wales, but was also bafflingly known in the business as Joe or Joseph and after the First World War, Major Joseph (from now on referred to as J.E.R.). Nevertheless, he was the one most imbued with his parents' entrepreneurial flair and, as so often in family businesses, his own son Henry Edward felt the force of his autocratic manner and all the family rivalries.[1]

After his successful wartime career and marriage, J.E.R. nurtured a growing distaste for the original and lucrative theatrical costumier business. His son, Henry Edward (known as Edward), much later observed that the physical side of handling and renting of what often amounted to little more than used clothes was distasteful to his father, as was the financial irritation of constant losses from unpaid bills due to many failing productions. This also applied to the copious rental business and provision of stage shoes. However, the company specialised in their traditional business until the end of the Second World War, but with the business directly administered by other family members under the overall direction of J.E.R. He successfully evolved the H. & M. Rayne luxury shoe retail business utilising the Waterloo Road factory as the main manufacturing base until 1938. It is significant that on leaving for war in August 1914, Edward designated his occupation as 'Theatrical Costumier'. On returning he gave it as 'Shoe Manufacturer' and the business writing paper he used is headed with the Waterloo Road address, by then known as 'Manx House', in keeping with the old logo, but reflecting the perceived changing status and taste of Joseph Edward Rayne in the new post-war world.

As a young man, J.E.R. was a member of The Honourable Artillery Company and joined the Territorials in February 1911. He was singled out by his father for an extended educational tour of the continent to learn German, French and Italian. No doubt he also observed shoes and shoe manufacturing, but no detailed record survives of his time abroad. The most enduring result of his 'Grand Tour' was his infatuation with the talented American opera singer Meta Reddish (1890-1967), whom he met in Italy. Chaperoned by her brother Claude,[2] Meta Reddish made a successful European debut in 1911 at the San Carlo Opera House in Naples, where her voice and beauty attracted the attention of an anonymous admirer, who sent her a diamond and ruby watch.[3]

Meta and J.E.R. met in 1913 when staying at the same *pensione* in Naples. In June 1914 she visited London, and J.E.R. took her with friends from Florence, Guy Bridgewater and Baron de Peverelli, on an excursion to Box Hill in Surrey. Meta had been due to sing at La Scala when war broke out and she returned home to America via engagements in Lyons and Spain.

With Meta in America and J.E.R. then serving his country in Europe, their relationship relied on letters crossing the Atlantic. 'We heard from Edward Rayne [J.E.R.], who has gone to the Continent with the 1st contingent of British officers and is a member of Lord Roberts staff and a Captain of the Royal Engineers' wrote Claude of him in August 1914. Subsequently, Edward fell from his horse and broke a collar bone, re-joining with the Intelligence Corps in January 1915. As a 2nd Lieutenant, J.E.R. was decorated by both the French and British governments and promoted to Major on demob in 1919.[4] Meta and J.E.R. eventually married on 4 November 1919 at All Saints Church in Roehampton.

Meta's career extended to performances in the flourishing opera houses of South America, but after her marriage in 1919 she performed only rarely: in 1923 with the Liverpool Symphony Orchestra at the London Aeolian Hall, and in the July that year she gave what amounted to her farewell performance at the Albert Hall in front of a stellar audience, including Dame Nellie Melba. According to *The Times*, she had 'one of the finest voices of her day... clear golden tones from low B flat to G in alto.' J.E.R.'s marriage to such a distinguished artist enhanced his social standing and ultimately the fame of Rayne shoes. This is in marked contrast to the carefree pre-war world of the Rayne brothers, when Henry was firmly in charge of house and business.[5]

The Rayne siblings built on their parents' success, resolving that in business one cannot stand still in a fast-changing world. The theatrical costume business had been a financial success, augmented by Mona theatrical make-up and their own shoes. New forms of entertainment and dwindling public support for the theatre in its full-blown Edwardian form, dictated the transformation of the shoe manufacturing side of their business into a larger retail venture.

In 1920, the new shop at 58 New Bond Street built upon the success of the Charing Cross Road shop and established the family leadership of J.E.R. The new shop was elegantly decorated with much solid wood forming the various cabinets and shelving – in the manner of grand shops of the period – it had scarcely changed by the time Brigitte Bardot was photographed trying on shoes in 1955 (see p.112). At the time this simplified and solid style typified stable values during visibly changing times, as Britain emerged from the cataclysm of the First World War and the Jazz Age began.

Above: This 1920 advertisement in *Vogue* reflects the laudatory editorial given to Rayne shoes for the next seventy years. Rayne relied on artists' renderings of their models for their advertisements until the 1960s, the Pavlova photographic page (see p.37) being a rare exception. The emphasis upon artistic inspiration for their designs was clearly considered more suitable for the ultra-fashionable nature of their products. The wealth of detail and expensive components advertised, belies the shoes' humble origins in the Rayne factory at Waterloo and their anonymous designers. 1920. CONDÉ NAST

Change was particularly visible in women's dress and in the newer forms of entertainment, such as the expanding network of cinemas and the gradual movement away from music halls and vaudeville to 'revue'. And, of course, fashions in dress often copied novelties seen on stage or screen, including radically new shoe designs. Women's changing role in society was markedly visible in the fashion for less restrictive and more youthful clothing; younger women were more assertive in life, often as a result of their own participation in many aspects of the war and the marked dearth of young men.

Women's fashionable dress had already discarded the elaborate, layered styles of the preceding decades and skirts were above ankle length by 1914. By 1920, not only were legs and shoes on display as dresses, especially for the evening, became ever shorter and skimpier, but a variety of shoes was now an essential part of the fashionable young lady's wardrobe. The mood of the time is encapsulated by Martin Armstrong in this extract from his 1921 poem 'Miss Thompson goes Shopping': *Serenely down the busy stream/Miss Thompson floated in a dream./Now, hovering bee-like, she would stop/Entranced before some tempting shop,/Getting in people's way and prying/At things she never thought of buying:/Now wafted on without an aim,/Until in course of time she came/To Watson's bootshop. Long she pries/At boots and shoes of every size —/Brown football-boots with bar and stud/For boys that scuffle in the mud,/And dancing-pumps with pointed toes/Glossy as jet, and dull black bows;/Slim ladies' shoes with two-inch heel/And sprinkled beads of gold and steel —/*

Above: A well-loved pair of pale violet satin-covered Rayne afternoon shoes with elegant trailing embroidery and pierced decoration around the toes. The embroidery suggests *art-nouveau* or Arts & Crafts influence, but the design of the shoe is clearly of the early 1920s before the Paris Exhibition of 1925 made *art deco* motifs fashionable (as seen on p.42).
NORTHAMPTON MUSEUMS

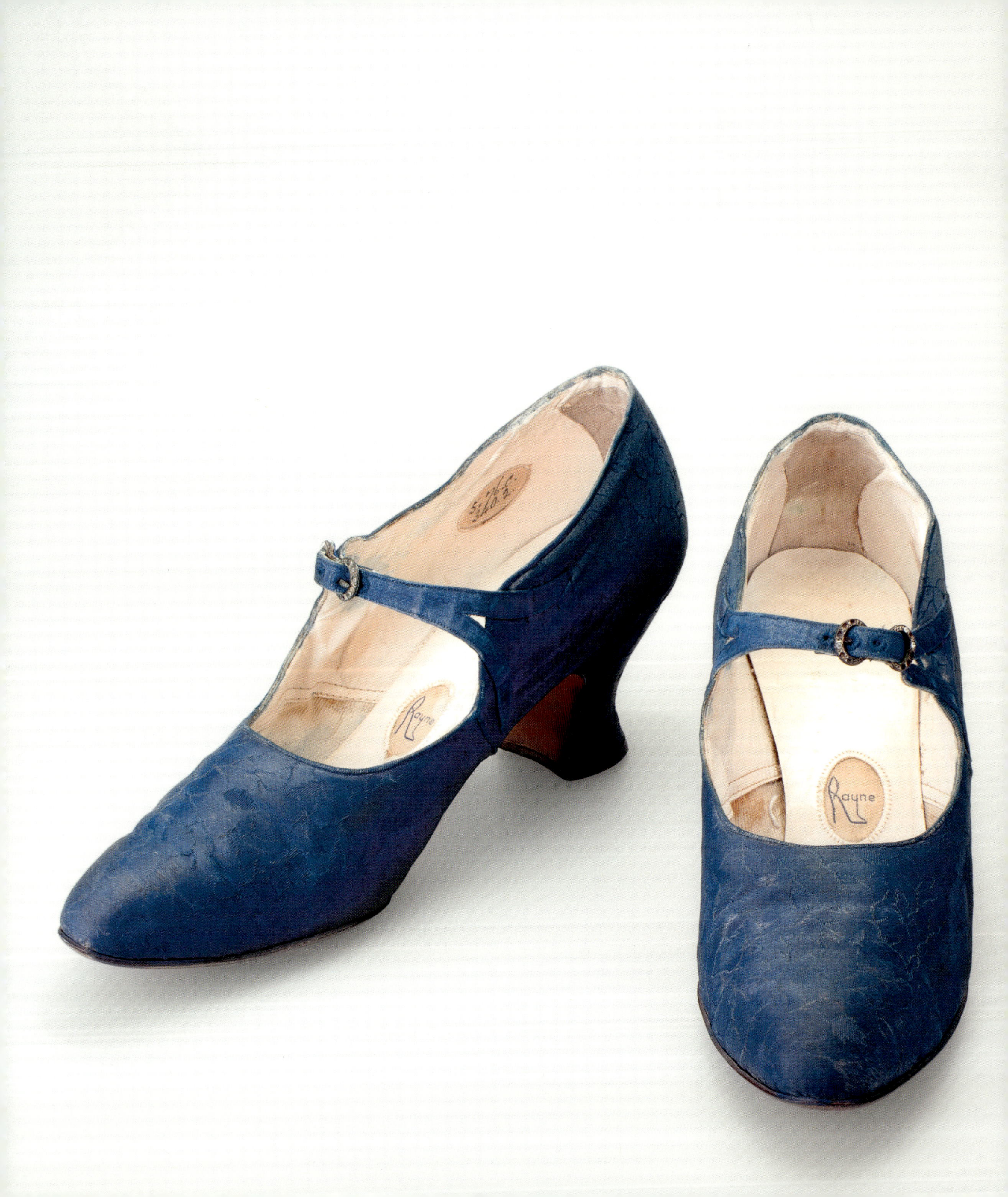
Rayne
Rayne

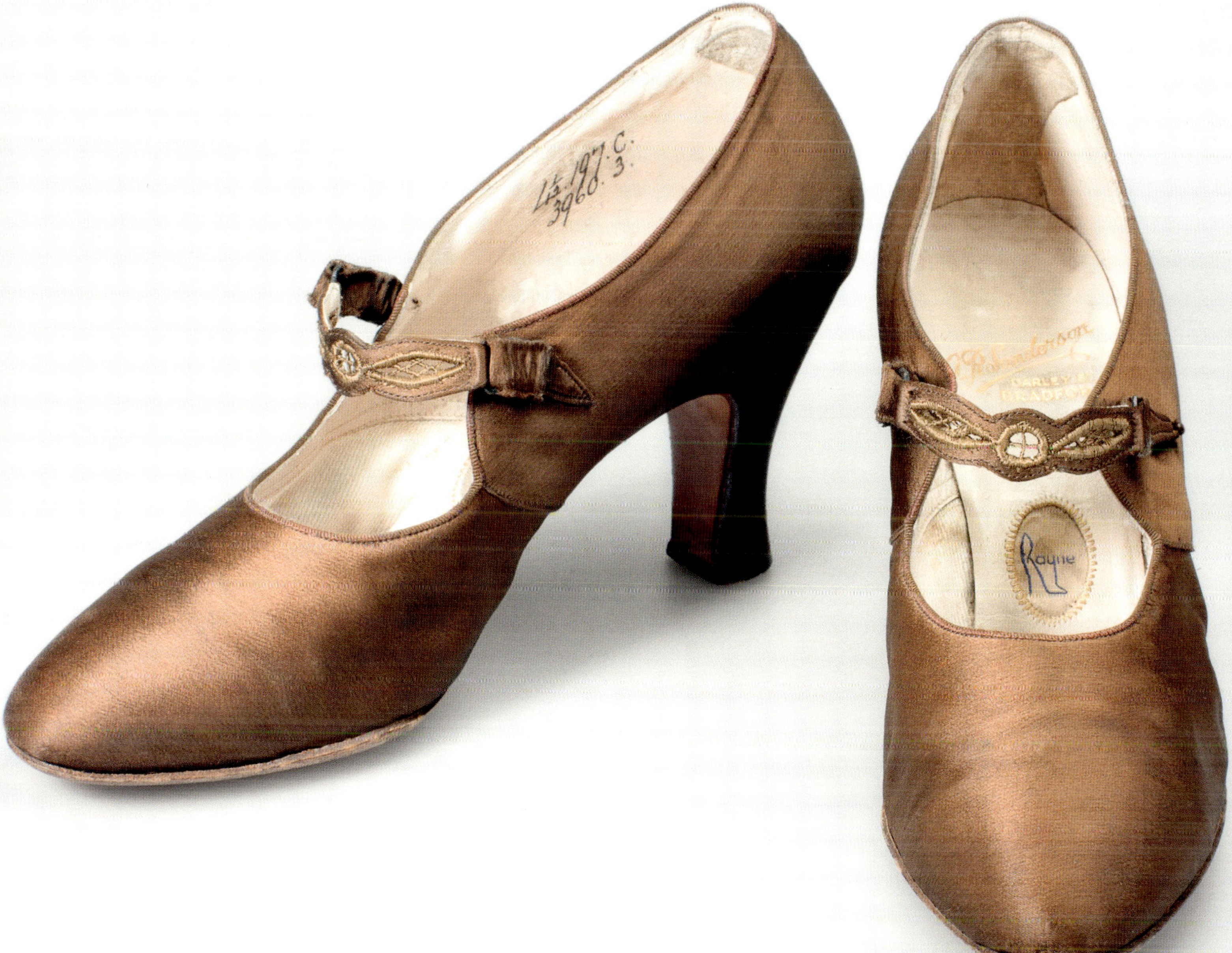
Rayne

Previous spread, left: These blue brocade afternoon or evening shoes employ a typically fashionable 1920s 'Jazz Age' fabric with an abstract motif. The low Louis heels remained in vogue for the first two decades of the twentieth century and the strap with its diamanté clasp gave retaining power needed for the more active dance movements of the period, such as the Charleston. c.1929.
COURTESY TRACY DOLPHIN COLLECTION

Previous spread, right: Straps and unusual fabrics formed a staple of Rayne designs throughout the century. These brown silk satin afternoon or evening shoes are heightened by the stitching of the central motif on the strap and, literally, by the use of the higher Spanish heel, which came to dominate 1930s shoe design. Both this pair and the blue pair display the feature on the inner sole of the distinctive Rayne logo evolved around 1928 and used in a *Vogue* October 1929 advertisement 'Inspirations of a Shoe Maker' showing the similar 'Charvine' model in '*crêpe-de-Chine with plaited straps with paste buckle ~ ~ 50/- ... also in white satin (suitable for dyeing)~ ~ 55/-*.' c.1930.
COURTESY TRACY DOLPHIN COLLECTION

Facing page: H. & M. Rayne Ltd did not rely entirely on their clientele for ultra-sophisticated afternoon or evening shoes. Fashionable day and sports shoes were constantly updated in their stock, many as novelties, such as the 1920 grey crocodile golf shoes advertised. Few survive, undoubtedly most were passed on as worn and unfashionable, then discarded. The pair shown here would have passed the test at many smart country gatherings, the long toes rely on excellent polished British hide for their impact with tiny punched detailing around the uppers and strap. As the inner sole proclaims, they have '*Hand Sewn Welts*', indicating that some processes were undoubtedly mechanised. c.1927.
RAYNE ARCHIVE

With J.E.R. as the driving force of the Rayne business, the New Bond Street shop brought challenges of its own. The shop now formed part of the southern section of Fenwicks store and was a prime location for Mayfair residents and those visiting the many Court dressmakers in the area. The premises of royal dress-makers Madame Handley Seymour were nearby at 78 New Bond Street. She was selected to design and make the wedding dress of Lady Elizabeth Bowes-Lyon on her marriage to Prince Albert, the second son of King George V and Queen Mary; both royal ladies visited the area and later became clients of Rayne. Rayne was also close to Bruton Street, where the Earl and Countess of Strathmore had a house and from which Lady Elizabeth left for her wedding in 1923. This was also the street in which a future Rayne collaborator, the young British dress designer Norman Hartnell opened his business on St George's Day in 1923. *Vogue* marked its thirtieth anniversary with an announcement on the title page of the January 1923 issue, 'Vogue, in reminiscent mood will recall to its old readers the modes, the manners and the pleasure of their youth and will amuse the younger generation with its memories of a time almost incredibly different from the present.' On the facing page was a striking photographic Rayne advertisement featuring four representative types of shoe including a 'Golf Shoe in Grey Crocodile'. Rayne was definitely *it*.

As J.E.R.'s son Edward later emphasised in the 1950s, London shoe-makers were better known for their fine craftsmanship than the design of the shoes. As with their clothes, many of the most fashionable women only sought Parisian designs and one of the first Rayne advertisements in both the early and late January 1920 editions of *Vogue* offers a variety of sophisticated designs likely to attract the attention of the most fashion conscious. At that date, Rayne's 47/49 Charing Cross Road shop sold what they termed 'The Smartest Footwear in Town'. Fashionable day and evening shoes of the early 1920s had medium to low 'Louis' heels with varied types of strap fastenings and fewer buttoned closures. Various forms of buckled fastenings became decorative features through successive decades and towards the end of the 1920s, pumps were more fashionable, as were the higher 'Spanish' heels.

By June, Rayne was emphasising its British credentials, advertising on a full page as 'Court Shoemakers' with 'Footwear for Ascot' and showing 'Shoes suitable for Ascot'. Eight elegant models are illustrated, including 'The Dandy... shoe in patent and grey, fawn and white Doeskin'. All models are of varied expensive leathers or cloths and named: crocodile for 'Langtry', black velvet for 'Melisande', side-laced bow-trimmed antelope for 'Washington' and bronze kid for 'Elegante'. 'Patricia', in patent and glacé kid leather, has a daring buckled ankle-strap; 'Chatham', also in patent and glacé kid leather, has two straps. 'Greek' is the most up-to-date of the designs with a patent upper and lizard toe rising to a point over the foot. Nothing else equates to these designs seen in *Vogue* at that time, they were advanced fashion and their designs sexy in a luxuriously subtle manner.

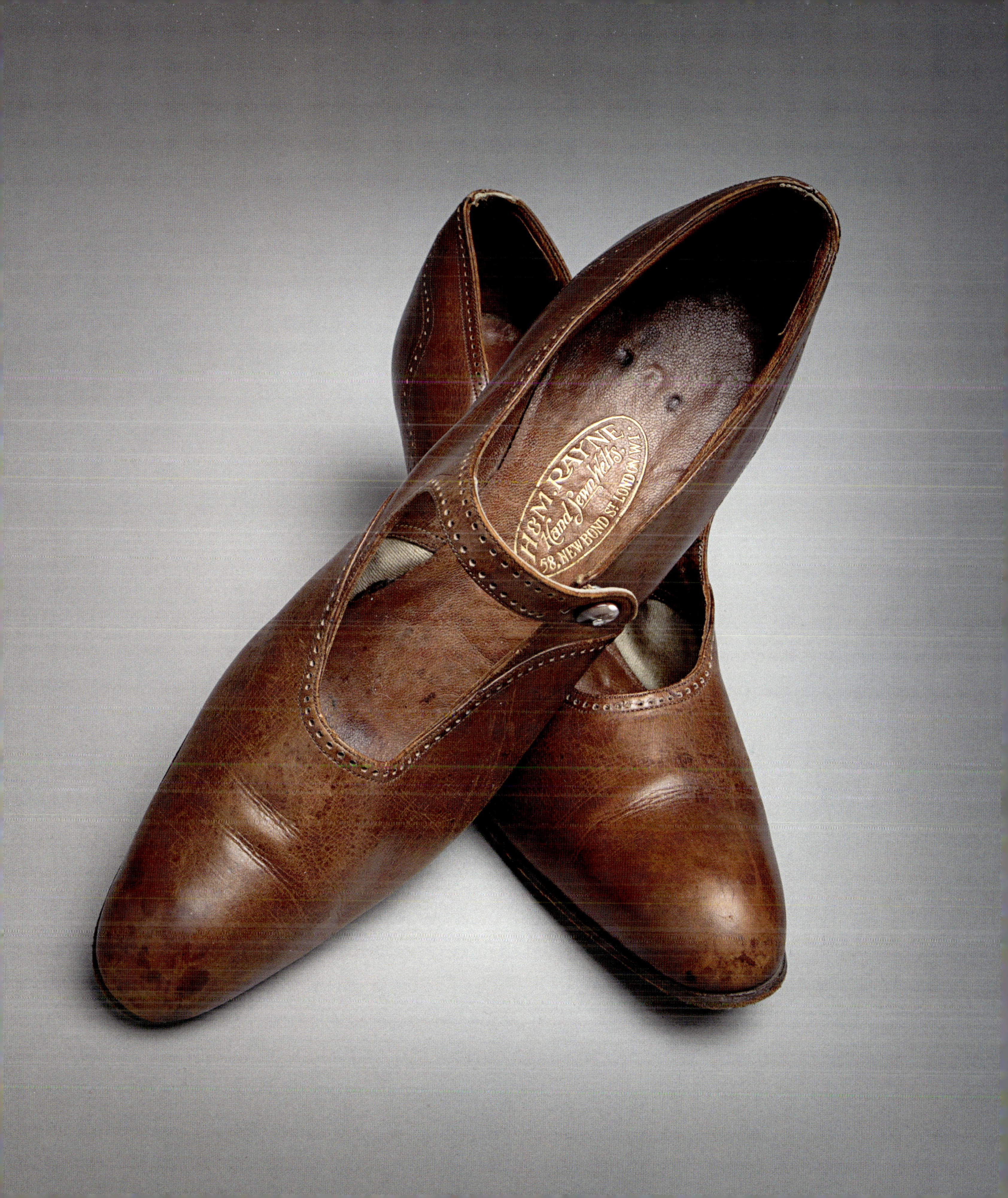
H&M. RAYNE.
Hand Sewn Welts.
58, NEW BOND ST. LONDON, W.

Below: 'Zabere', a Spring Model advertised as part of a composite page in *Vogue*, April 1931: '*In Black Doeskin trimmed Dull Kid. Available also in Navy Blue or Brown Doeskin with Strappings in self-colour. Made on entirely new shaped last. Prices from 55/-.*' Shoes with more pointed toes, low Louis heels and the higher Spanish heels are advertised together, giving a great variety of choice. The higher heels remained fashionable throughout the 1930s.   TRACY DOLPHIN COLLECTION

Facing page: By November 1931, the world-wide economic depression was depressing spending power. These elegant dark blue suede shoes with broad-woven ribbon decoration stranded into 'streamlined' flowing decoration on the toes and along the uppers are marginally more elaborate than Rayne's design 'Bezile', in a striking sketched *Vogue* advertisement bearing the caption '*With one eye on France and the other eye on United States, we continue making British shoes*'. The five models are sketched within a heart motif and beneath runs the 'handwritten' defiant message: '*The heart of the Empire LONDON where Rayne shoes are made*'.   RAYNE ARCHIVE

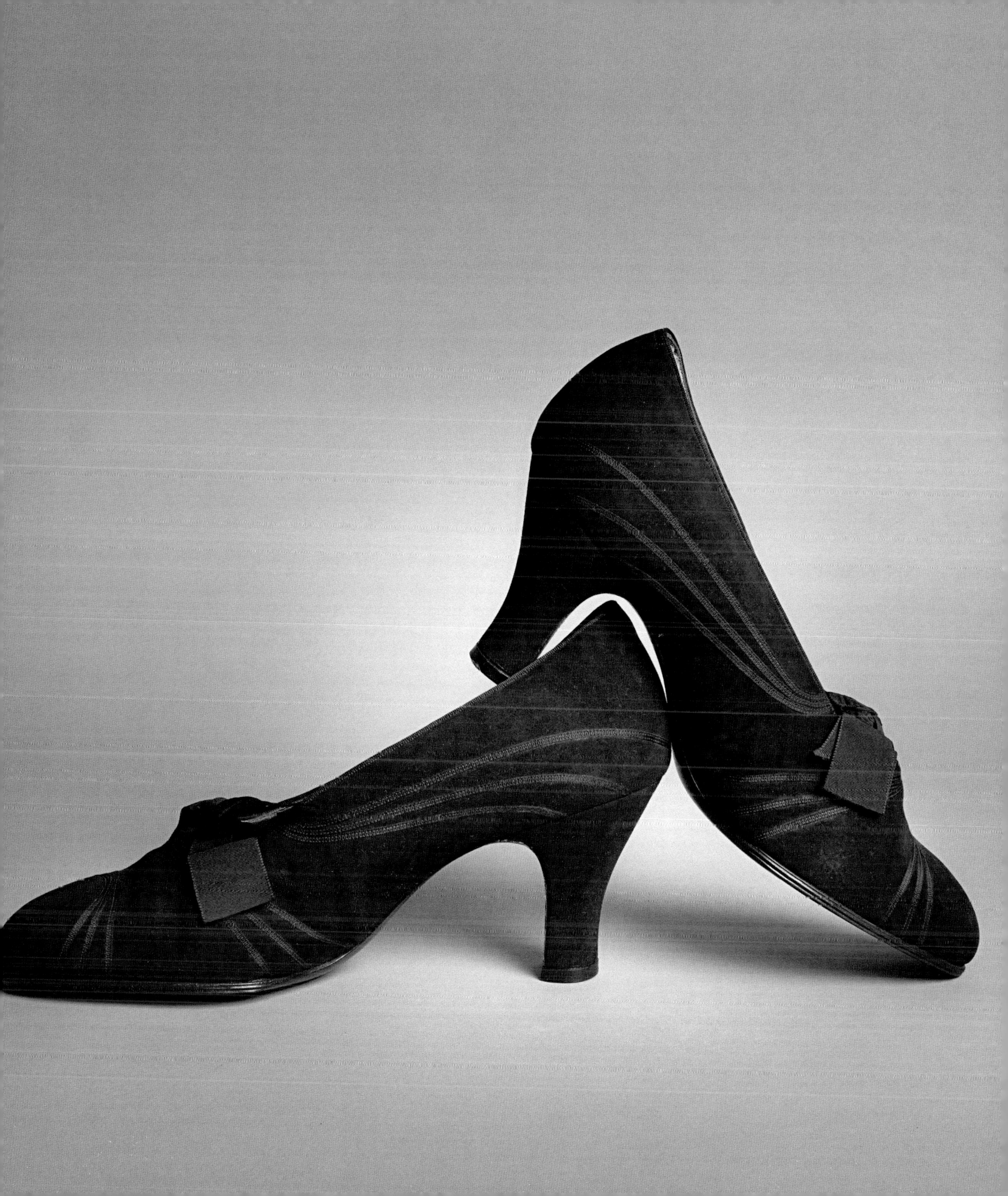

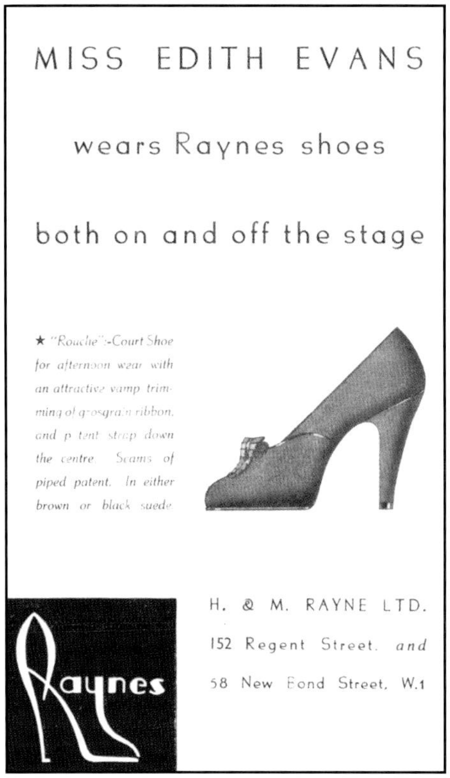

MISS EDITH EVANS

wears Raynes shoes

both on and off the stage

★ *"Roache"-Court Shoe for afternoon wear with an attractive vamp trimming of grosgrain ribbon, and patent strap down the centre. Seams of piped patent. In either brown or black suede.*

H. & M. RAYNE LTD.
152 Regent Street, and
58 New Bond Street, W.1

Raynes

Advertising augmented Rayne's much discussed presence in the great variety and quantity of London and provincial stage productions for most of the twentieth century. What smaller productions lacked in the quantity of shoes ordered for musical revues, such as those by C.B. Cochran or André Charlot, they made up for with the distinction of an acclaimed dramatic actress such as Edith Evans, here portrayed by Grant Macdonald as 'Sancia Carson' in *Robert's Wife* by St John Ervine, in a Rayne programme advertisement for the production at the Globe Theatre in 1938. RAYNE ARCHIVE

Vogue was certainly the most influential journal amongst the chic, though fashion reporting in the daily press grew more influential as printing processes advanced and the fashion coverage in the provincial press often augmented main advertising budgets. Rayne shoes were sold in a few of the best local department stores, which – acting as agents for Rayne shoes – would take out small advertisements depicting Rayne designs. Regional social life was centred around the major cities for many decades and local stores and stockists were patronised by the rich, for whom London shopping was less usual. J.E.R. promoted the development of a wholesale side to the business to include Harvey Nichols in London and the Marshall and Snelgrove stores around the UK, all selling the same designs available in the two Rayne London shops.

As well as the established families following the many events of 'The Season' – usually involving presentations at court and activities for debutantes and including dances and weddings – there was also a vast middle-class able to afford good quality shoes. In hotels and restaurants in many British cities and especially resorts, there was an expectation of sophisticated dressing and a use of a greater variety of clothes and accessories than we are used to today. Hats, bags, gloves and shoes were all a vital component of any woman's wardrobe; today shoes and bags have endured as accessories to a less complicated wardrobe. Cruises, holidays in sunny climes and great numbers of women who accompanied their husbands to all corners of the vast British Empire, helped spread the fame of Rayne.

In May 1923 Rayne boldly advertised their 'Florida' model as 'The Inimitable Quality. It has ever been the privilege of the House of Rayne to execute footwear for the woman of taste who must be exclusive. It is this experience and discrimination which gives to a Rayne shoe that natural, unstudied distinction which is yet to be successfully imitated.'

Facing page: Four extremely rare survivals of pen-and-wash designs for Rayne day shoes and sandals of the late 1930s. Designers would either send in unsolicited designs or be commissioned to create new models for the ever-discerning Joseph Rayne. The luxury of crocodile or reptile trimmings persisted as a house theme into the 1960s. A pair of Rayne grey suede high-vamped shoes tied with dusty pink ribbons, similar to those illustrated, is in the collections of the Victoria and Albert Museum London. c.1937-1940. RAYNE ARCHIVE

In 1929, editorial in *Vogue* illustrated Rayne's 'buttoned one strap sandals in blond satin, very fine stockings to match the skin. Evening bag to match sandals' and another on 13 November 'Rayne velvet shoes and bag to match are smart for evening'. The inclusion of bags in the shops, now at New Bond Street and also 15 Rupert Street, was a lucrative innovation that lasted for decades.

The 1920s had been a profitable decade for Rayne and on 19 August 1922 a potential Rayne dynasty was founded with the birth of J.E.R. and Meta's son Henry Edward at 13 Porchester Square, Bayswater. He would go on to create the truly enlarged global Rayne brand in the 1960s and 1970s. His sister Joan was born in 1920, to add to the excitement of that eventful year. However by 1929 the Wall Street Crash meant the beginning of difficult years for most businesses world-wide. In 1928, just before the crash, J.E.R. moved his family from their temporary home of 5 Porchester Terrace to a more convenient flat at Melbury Court, Kensington and on 21 August 1928 a new Rayne company was registered for the production and retail of shoes. J.E.R. was Chairman, James and Charles co-directors.

J.E.R. was exasperated with the way in which the four integral businesses were being run independently by his siblings. He consolidated his position and floated the new company on the Stock Exchange, though retaining 80% of the equity within the family. This gave him the means to control the company, whilst giving his brothers and sister financial independence, when and if they chose to go, as his vision was not shared by everyone.

J.E.R.'s comments recorded in the minutes for 24 January 1929 give us an insight into the state of the market, 'Although Rayne shoes command a somewhat higher price than the ordinary shoes, produced by purely mass production methods, there is a growing tendency for ladies of discrimination to pay a reasonable price for shoes of superior design and quality which our company produces.' If this reads like an advertising slogan, it underlines the fact that Rayne shoes were still largely handmade, even if there was a considerable amount of machinery involved in the process. This remained true of the British-made Rayne shoe until the 1970s. Interestingly, the Wall Street Crash is not mentioned in the 1929 minutes extracts, though the illness of George V is: it resulted in the 'curtailing of a certain number of social activities during the months of December and January, which had an adverse effect on retail sales.' The first year's trading figures were 'trading profit £23,436,00 19 shillings and 2 pence'. The pounds were mistyped and someone has in any case added 'maybe should read as turnover'.

55

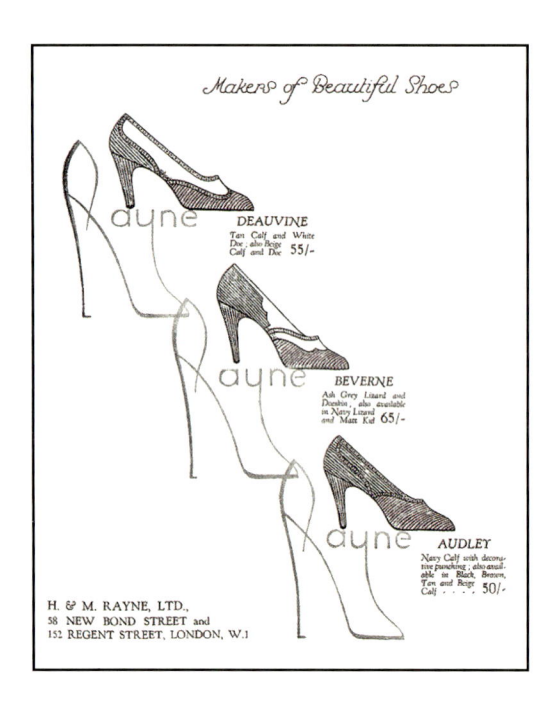

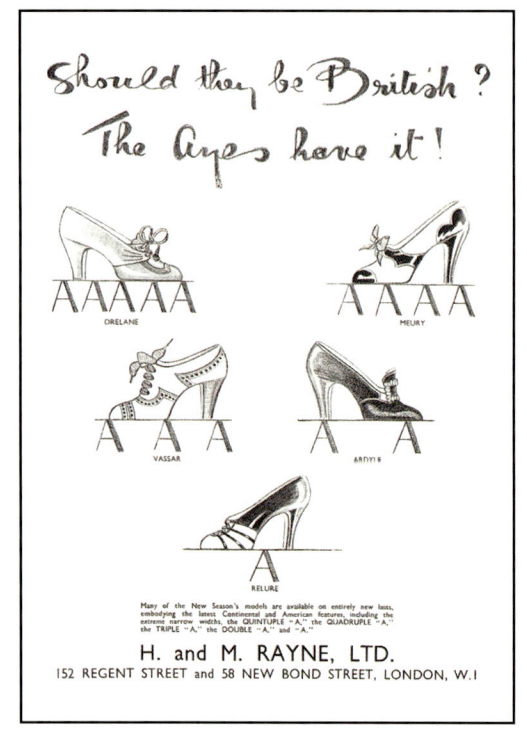

Whatever the actual figures, Rayne shoes were clearly a great commercial success and from May 1929 full page advertisements in *Vogue* often used the new Rayne logo representing a distinctive shoe silhouette formed from the 'R' and 'y'. The design of the logo is attributed to Charles Rayne, who also contributed designs for many shoes. The address of the additional shop at 152 Regent Street together with that of 58 New Bond Street is also used. Rayne emphasised the fact that the company was British. A full-page advertisement in April 1931 showing eight models states, 'With one eye on France and the other eye on the United States we continue making British shoes. The heart of the Empire LONDON where Rayne shoes are made.' Perhaps they were appealing to the concept of buy British during the financial crisis.

In 1935 – the Royal Silver Jubilee year, and the year that Rayne was awarded a Royal Warrant by Queen Mary – Rayne marketed themselves in terms of their reputation, with the words, 'A reputation earned through a firm refusal to compromise with quality'. The company report noted that they had 'a persistent demand for luxury footwear, particularly (evening) sandals in gold and silver.'

In common with most British businesses during the Depression in the 1930s, Rayne emphasised their British manufacturing base and this also formed part of J.E.R.'s sales strategy in pursuing the North American market. As a firm admirer of the technical processes, craftsmanship, stylistic invention and salesmanship of the finest shoemakers, J.E.R. was particularly impressed by Herman Delman, considered the manufacturer of the finest American shoes. The young Roger Vivier (1907–1998) was already selling designs to Delman. Delman had a concession at Saks Fifth Avenue, then moved to Bergdorf Goodman in 1937 where he took almost the whole of the ground floor and several windows. In 1937, Delman was in a position Rayne aspired to. American shoes were popular in London, not least because of their multiple sizing. Rayne took on the challenge – an April 1936 Rayne advertisement stressing, 'Should they be British? The Ayes have it ! Many of the New Season's models are available on entirely new lasts, embodying the latest Continental and American features, including the extreme narrow widths, the QUINTUPLE "A", the QUADRUPLE "A", the TRIPLE "A", the "DOUBLE "A", and the "A".'

Above left: This advertisement in *Vogue* (1 May 1929) typifies the Rayne policy of using non-photographic advertising to suggest the artistic nature of their designs allied to the superb quality of their manufacture. By 1931 the Rayne shoe logo was firmly established as part of the regular advertising undertaken by the company, especially in *Vogue* and established the company in the public's mind for the next half-century. 1929. Condé Nast

Left: As part of their recession-busting advertising campaign, Rayne emphasised their British origins and manufacture at a time when 'Buy Empire Produce' was a popular slogan. Rayne shoe fittings were always in American 'A' fittings, ever since they had imported American shoe manufacturing machinery, then the best in the world and resulting in supple, soft soles, amongst other processes. This 1936 *Vogue* advertisement stresses to customers that Rayne shoes give the best of both Old and New World skills. Condé Nast

The close ties forged between Rayne and Delman in the USA led to Rayne sometimes making shoes in London for Delman, who opened a shop at 16 Old Bond Street. Delman had a great section of the ground floor in Bergdorf Goodman, New York and this photograph shows a model wearing a pair of silver or gold mesh evening shoes similar to those seen in the 1937 *Vogue* advertisement 'with bands of kid and sparkling buckles'.
PHOTOGRAPH: RAYNE ARCHIVE; ADVERTISEMENT: CONDÉ NAST

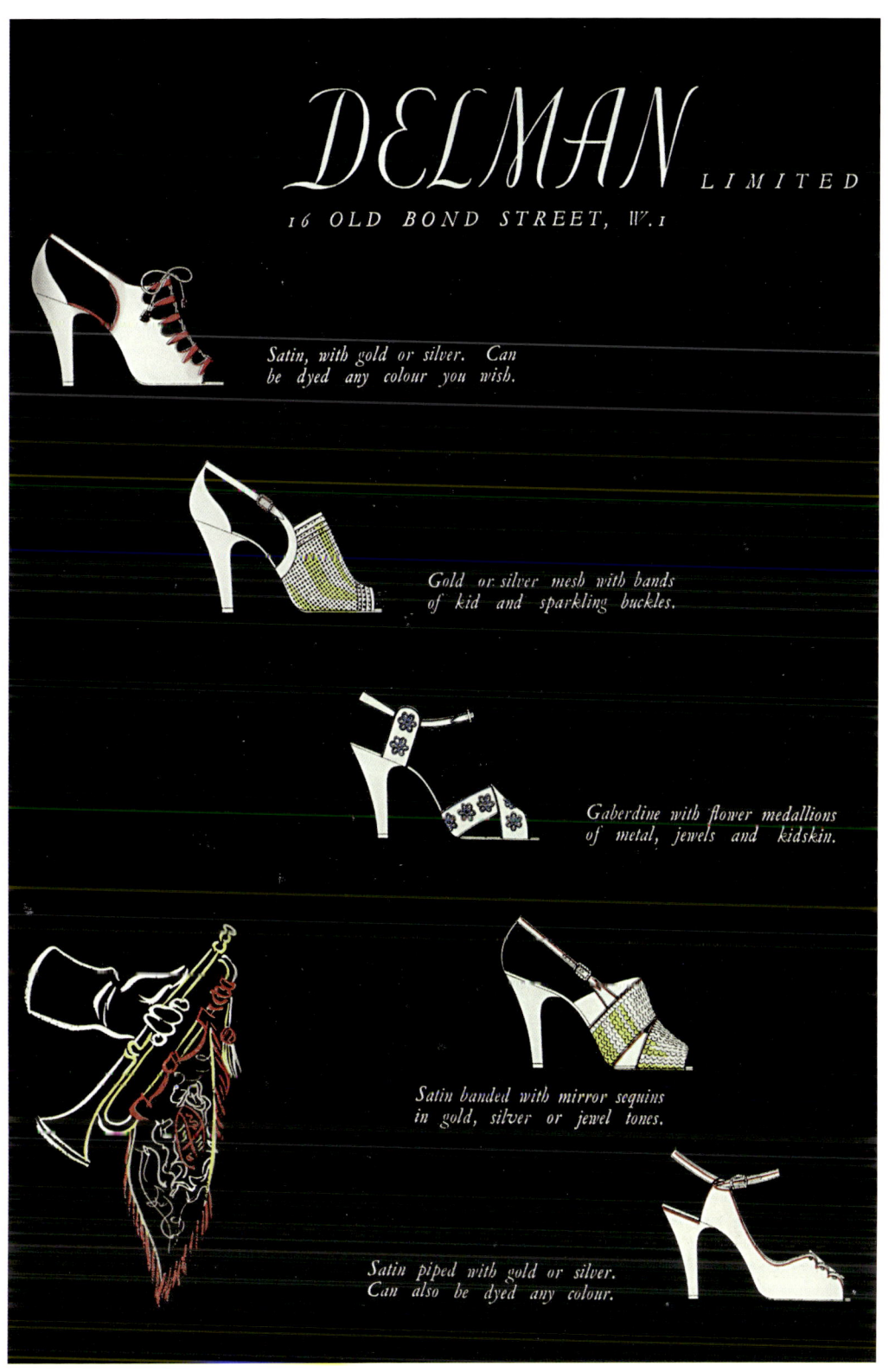

DELMAN LIMITED
16 OLD BOND STREET, W.1

Satin, with gold or silver. Can be dyed any colour you wish.

Gold or silver mesh with bands of kid and sparkling buckles.

Gaberdine with flower medallions of metal, jewels and kidskin.

Satin banded with mirror sequins in gold, silver or jewel tones.

Satin piped with gold or silver. Can also be dyed any colour.

A pair of Delman burgundy cloth court shoes with glacé kid trimmings to the toes and lined with white kid. Medium Spanish heels and the more rounded snub toe of the late 1930s. The trim around the toe suggests an open 'peep-toe' shoe, which, along with sandals, would later be condemned as unsuitable street-wear by *Vogue* editor-in-chief Edna Woolman Chase (1877-1957) in her autobiography *Always In Vogue* (1954). The insole is gilt-stamped '*Delman 16 Old Bond Street*'. These were probably made by Rayne for Delman's London shop around 1938. The marked AA fitting denotes the popularity of American fittings in London and the fact that Rayne always used them, having bought American machinery.

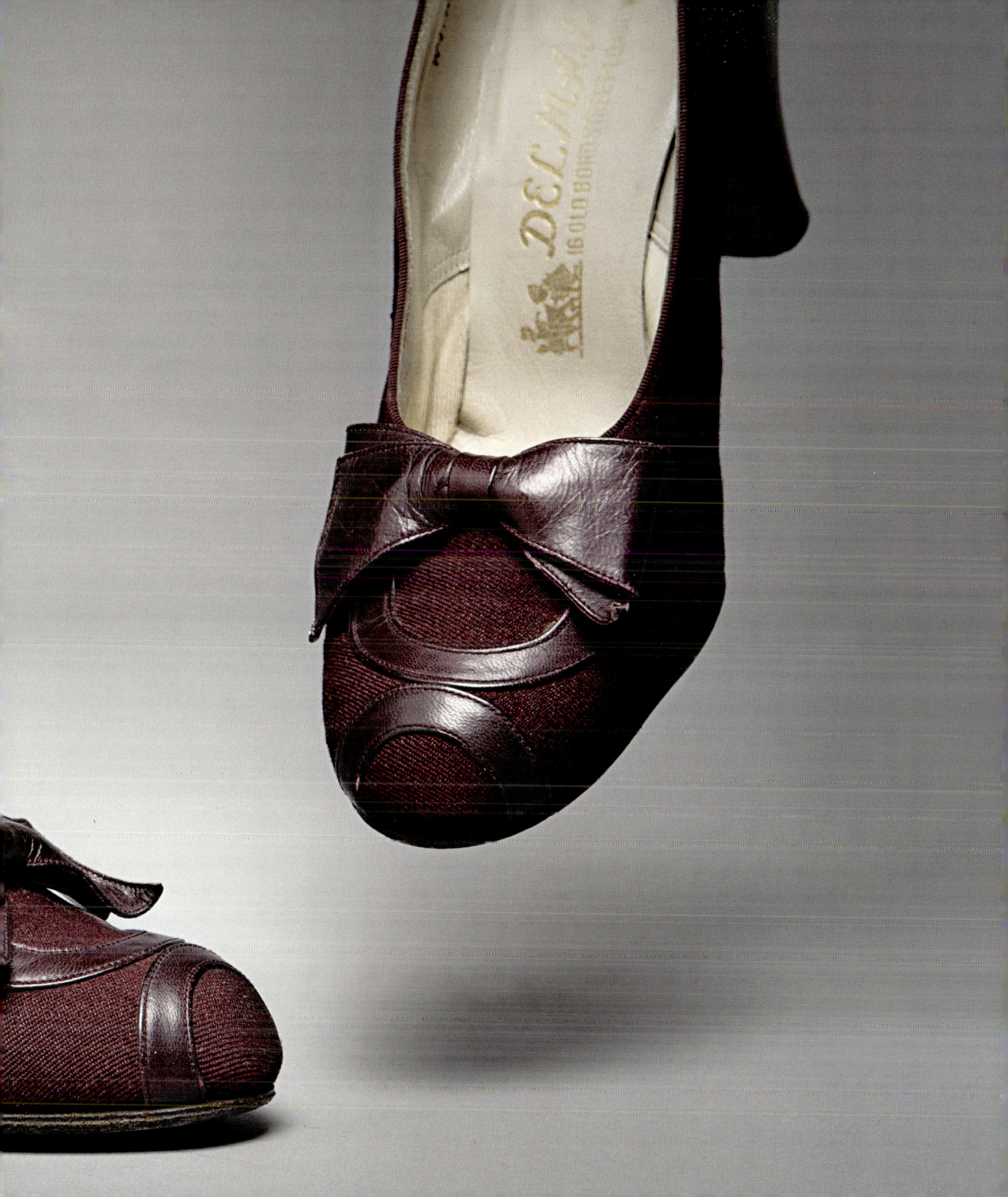

Rayne extended its factory in 1936 and J.E.R. and Herman Delman signed a remarkable agreement on 10 June, which gave Delman a seat on the Rayne board of directors and Rayne access to Delman's American enterprise. In return, Rayne received the right to represent Delman in the United Kingdom and British Empire in perpetuity.[6] Rayne opened the Delman London shop and took a colour page in British *Vogue* advertising their London address as Delman House, 16 Old Bond Street.[7] This negotiation and a further injection of capital persuaded Elizabeth, who had managed the first Bond Street shop, to retire to the South of France; Charles likewise moved with his family to California, where they opened their own business. J.E.R. and his brother James now held the remaining 20% of the equity in the company.

Rayne also had great expectations of the vast market formed by the United States of America, Edward taking a particular interest in the varied forms of last and the most advanced shoe-making machinery made there. He was late in this, for as he narrates in his autobiography, *Shoe Maker of Dreams*, Salvatore Ferragamo left Italy for America before 1914, wanting dollars and knowing that American women were increasingly shoe conscious. Many of the best American shoe artisans and factory workers were Italian immigrants or of Italian descent, and Ferragamo found the manufacturing skills and materials of great interest, as Rayne was to do.

American women came from a wide variety of immigrant stock and all had equally varied feet sizes and needed multiple shoe fittings, important to them in terms of comfort and style. This interest is summed up by the pre-1914 American master of the short story, O. Henry, who often refers to both clothes and footwear in a most detailed manner, '...it was Rosalie, in a loose, travel-stained automobileless coat, closely tied brown veil with yard-long flying end, gray walking suit, and tan oxfords with lavender over-gaiters.' (*The Memento*. 1908). The shoes mentioned here clearly reflect the current preoccupation.

Rayne responded to this by using American machinery and beginning to offer American fittings and the softer soles as favoured by American women. In 1934, Rayne acquired a new shoe-making plant with the Del-Mac process – the first in Europe. The factory attracted much attention abroad and J.E.R. temporarily employed Otto Pelz Junior, the son of a Viennese shoe manufacturer, who earned J.E.R.'s praise by learning pattern cutting and suggesting new designs.

In 1932 Meta had been presented at Court to King George V and Queen Mary, lending the name of Rayne some social distinction. Her daughter Joan was presented in 1938. Queen Mary by then patronised Rayne shoes and awarded Rayne their first Royal Warrant in 1935. Queen Mary was a dedicated theatregoer and would have noticed Rayne shoes on stage and their name in many programmes of the period, not least Noel Coward's *Cavalcade*, with a cast of over 400 – all shod by Rayne! Produced at Drury Lane Theatre by Charles Cochran in October 1931, partly as a riposte to the perceived threat of the Talkies, it included the famous patriotic toast 'Let's drink to the hope that one day this country of ours, which we love so much, will find dignity and greatness and peace again'. Words that reflected the economic and political problems of the day.

All during the 1930s, *Vogue* carried advertisements and editorial for an enormous variety of shoes and bags for all seasons and occasions. London was the destination and home of a remarkably diverse selection of elegant women, most of whom patronised Rayne. There was scarcely a famous actress not shod by Rayne. At least one, Gertrude Lawrence, had a new design of court shoe bearing a flat bow trim devised for her. Named simply 'Lawrence', the timeless design survived for decades and became a favourite of many women, including Queen Elizabeth II. The extension of the British studio system with Alexander Korda's glamorous London Films added film-stars to the client list: Marion Davies, Merle Oberon, Marlene Dietrich, Bette Davies, Valerie Hobson and Vivien Leigh all wore Rayne shoes. Even Mrs Simpson wore Rayne shoes.

By 1938 the business had outgrown the Waterloo Road extended factory, which was closed. The newspaper over-flow printing press building of the *News of the World* at Tileyard Road, Kings Cross was taken on and fitted as a model shoe factory, 'it compares favourably with any shoe factory of its size in the world. It is light, airy and spacious,' noted the Company Report. Rayne moved in on the very weekend that the Second World War was declared. The factory was then shared with one other shoe business, Joseph. Apart from planning for post-war times, output was regulated to however many pairs of shoes the Board of Trade allowed it make per week.

It was the worst time to start up a new shoe factory. After an initial flurry with the sale of flexible walking shoes, the company had a blip with the thinnest order books ever; undaunted, J.E.R. moved his family from Melbury Court to a fourth floor flat at Fountain House, Park Lane, overlooking Hyde Park, where after the 'Phoney War', anti-aircraft guns were soon booming at enemy aircraft as the Blitzkrieg began. They comforted themselves with the knowledge that the new block was of concrete and steel construction with an air-raid shelter in the basement. This proved useful. The 1940 Company report notes 'a sensational demand for evening shoes', presumably because they were allowed to continue making these luxurious specialities and ' a sudden change in footwear fashions due to war conditions', but the company made 'practical bootees and shoes with crepe rubber soles' following the orders of the Board of Trade.

Vivien Leigh trying on Rayne shoes and sandals wth Edward Rayne, 1945. RAYNE ARCHIVE

Most Rayne shoes displayed subtle fashionable designs unlikely to daunt even the most timid of purchasers. They sold tens of thousands of such quietly distinguished designs, of which few survive.

Below: An elegant pair of Rayne day shoes in dark blue suede with calf trim, simulated ribbon laces and low heels suitable for all ages. c.1935. Tracy Dolphin Collection

Facing page: An inventive pair of Rayne russet-red suede shoes trimmed with scalloped corded cloth to the uppers and down the toe with single bows to the toes. c.1937. Tracy Dolphin Collection

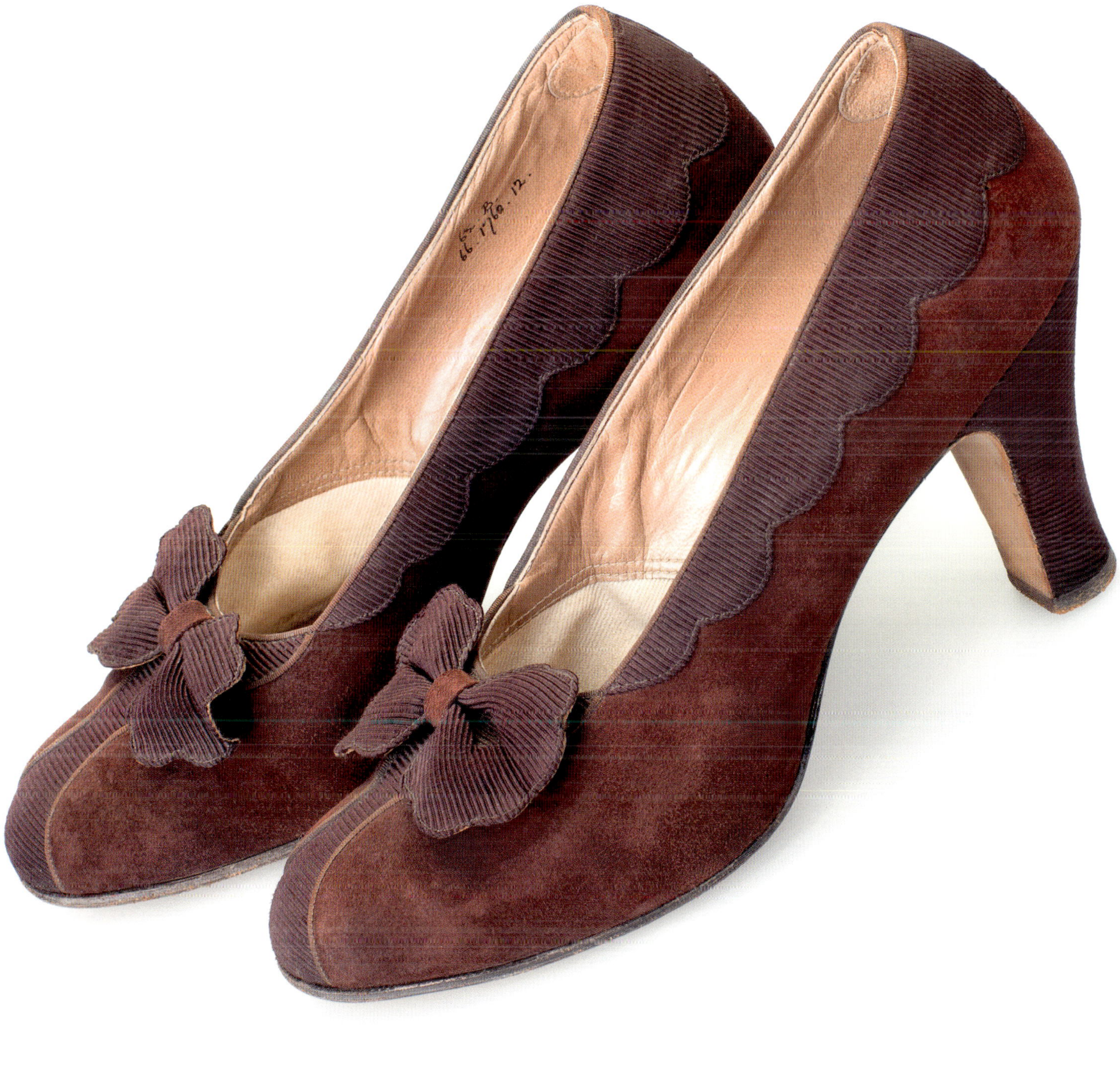

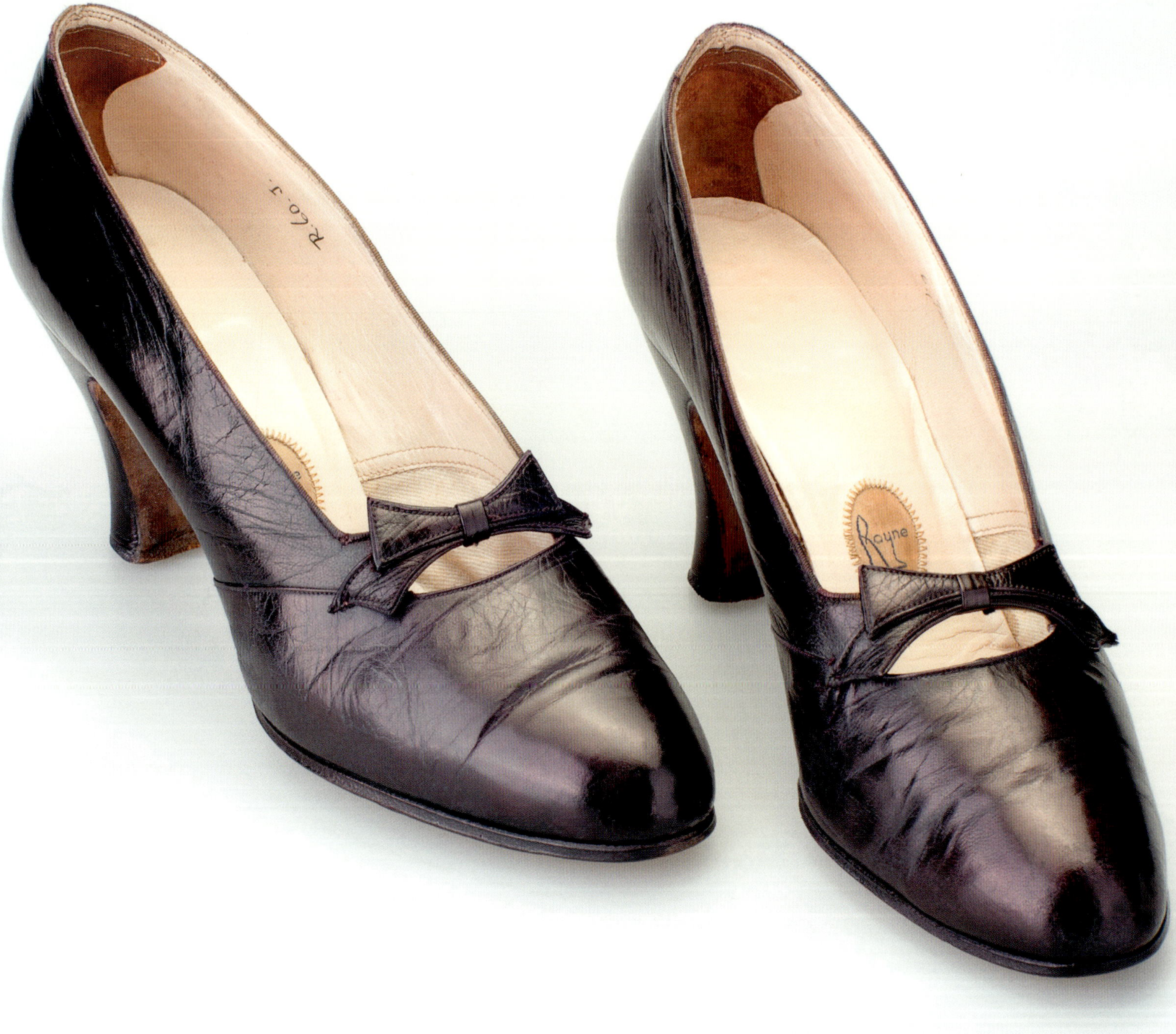
Rayne

Apart from incendiary bombs on the factory roof leading to four weeks' lost production in 1941, the company now faced the problem of losing male workers of call-up age; and manufacturing was doubly hit by rationing restrictions. J.E.R.'s son Edward, who had now joined the company, wrote that his father was, 'a compulsive pessimist and thought we now faced ruin', which seems at odds with his previous wartime and business experiences, although it is undeniable that a factory and three West End shops meant expensive outgoings. In May 1941 the Lambeth factory was also damaged and a claim put in for government compensation in accordance with regulations. Staff had to make the best of the situation and Edward later wrote of the high morale of the staff, who after spending the night in a shelter or sleeping on a table, still turned up for work. In 1944 J.E.R. noted 'the exemplary way in which the employees carried out their duties during flying bomb attacks.'

With no experience, Edward was assigned to help out in the Regent Street shop and was mortified when his first customer asked for a female assistant half-way through the fitting. His poor eyesight kept him out of the services and he was enrolled round the corner from Fountain House in the Mount Street, Mayfair ARP unit and fire-watching duties, where he met diverse local characters including the equally jovial Norman Hartnell, dress-maker to the Queen and to Queen Mary. Hartnell had been a significant figure in putting young British couture on the map in the 1920s and by the 1930s was joined by other designers, including Digby Morton, Hardy Amies, Victor Stiebel and Peter Russell. American stores and private buyers were no longer focussed simply on Paris and the success of London as a fashion centre benefitted other fashion suppliers such as Rayne. Until Hartnell's death in 1979, he and Edward enjoyed a particularly amiable business relationship; they also shared the same pre-War wit and sense of humour, undoubtedly useful during periods of tedium on firewatching duties.[8]

By 1942 customers had drifted back to London, after the worst of the bombing had eased off. Edward was put in charge of the Delman premises, considered by him the most beautiful shop in London, and then put in charge of ordering shoes for all three shops. As Austerity Regulations had come into force, his task was not arduous. Manufacturers were limited to one shilling's-worth of trimmings per shoe, heels no more than two inches high and leather that was black, brown or blue. The need for seven coupons per rationed pair of shoes made customer choice even more limited. As it turned out, business boomed: Rayne was the only truly fine fashion shoemaker in London and most of the production was sold in one of their three shops. Out-of-town wholesale buyers did not often make the journey to London, although some did and one Dundee shop advertised locally that it was retailing fashionable 'high wedge' shoes in September 1942. Fashion editorials, including *Vogue,* either mentioned or illustrated Rayne shoes throughout the war years; whether readers could obtain them was another matter. In 1942 Rayne acquired the share capital of Lesley, Rice and Co. Ltd, Shoe and Slipper Manufacturers.

Facing page: A pair of Rayne aubergine leather court day shoes with the medium Louis or French heels of the late 1920s to about 1940. Highly polished leather is given a distinctive small cut-out over the toe with a flat narrow leather ribbon as the only decoration. Neither ultra-fashionable nor out-fashion for all of the 1930s. TRACY DOLPHIN COLLECTION

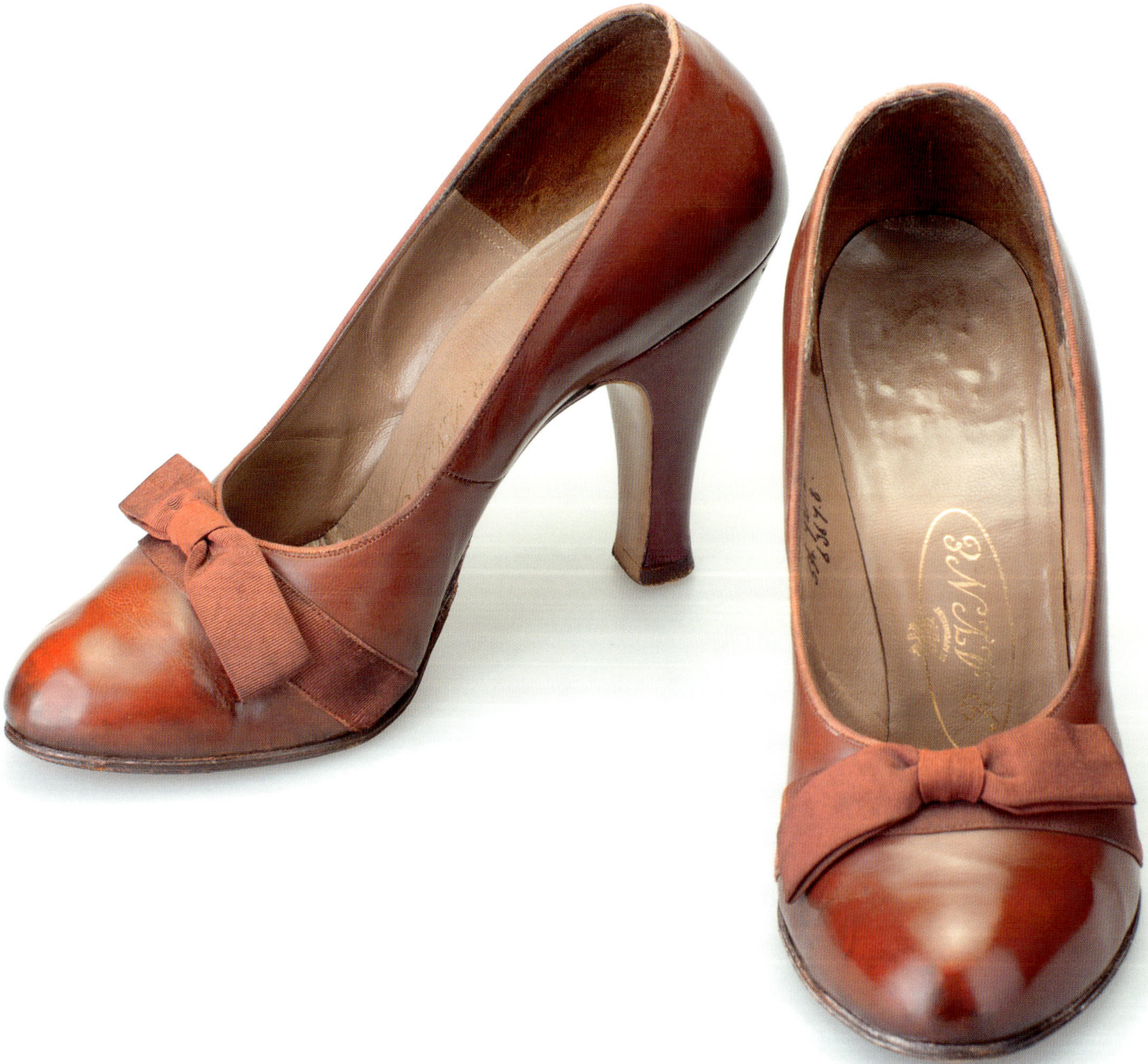

Unlike his father, Edward's taste for glamorous shoe design was honed by an interest in the theatrical side of the business. Board of Trade restrictions were lifted on shoes destined for use in the morale-boosting entertainment industry and so higher heels, a variety of colours and even greater variety of trimmings forbidden to the general public were permitted for theatrical use. At the age of nineteen, young Edward was sent to meet Cecil Beaton, the costume designer for the stirring British film, *Dangerous Moonlight* starring Anton Walbrook and Sally Gray and featuring Addinsell's evocative *Warsaw Concerto*. Edward was disappointed that the filming of *Dangerous Moonlight* rarely showed any of the 20 pairs of 'his' Rayne shoes and, of course, their use was scarcely ever credited in any film.

He had a happier experience with the 1945 film by Pascal of Shaw's *Caesar and Cleopatra*, for which Rayne made 20 varied pairs of sandals.[9] Edward had many meetings at Pinewood with Vivien Leigh, whom he first met in the Delman shop. The factory had not made such unusual footwear for some years and everyone was delighted with the results, which attracted much publicity for Rayne and showed Edward the advertising strength of unusually designed and glamorous shoes.

Facing page: By the late 1930s, heels had become as high and slim as in the late 1920s and were variously termed 'Louis' or 'French'. This pair of Rayne polished mid-red calf day shoes are enlivened by a discreet band of ribbon culminating in a flat bow across the toe. The insole reveals the newer gilt-stamped Rayne logo, which superseded the inlaid logo as a motif for insoles until the 1980s. c.1938. TRACY DOLPHIN COLLECTION

Below: The lower heels of these Rayne blue shoes are as discreet as the pattern of punched decoration executed over the toes and vamps, giving a sleek almost streamlined appearance. c.1936.

Cleopatra

Although Rayne shoes were continually seen on stage, their screen presence was seldom visible, to the particular distress of the young Edward Rayne. His two mid-1940s collaborations were with Cecil Beaton and Oliver Messel. He formed a lasting friendship with the latter over their work on the designs of the appropriate foot-wear to be used in the 1945 British Technicolor film version of George Bernard Shaw's play *Caesar and Cleopatra*. Messel carried out meticulous research and Edward Rayne had his designs made up in the Rayne factory. Vivien Leigh played Cleopatra and her shoes were a *tour de force* of shoe-making at a time of general shoe rationing, when all orders had to be passed by the Board of Trade. The film is still a visual feast, but there is a mere glimpse of one pair of Miss Leigh's footwear during the whole 123 minutes!

Above and below: Two designs of open ancient Egyptian sandals with appropriate decoration researched by Oliver Messel and apparently for Elizabeth Taylor c.1962. RAYNE ARCHIVE

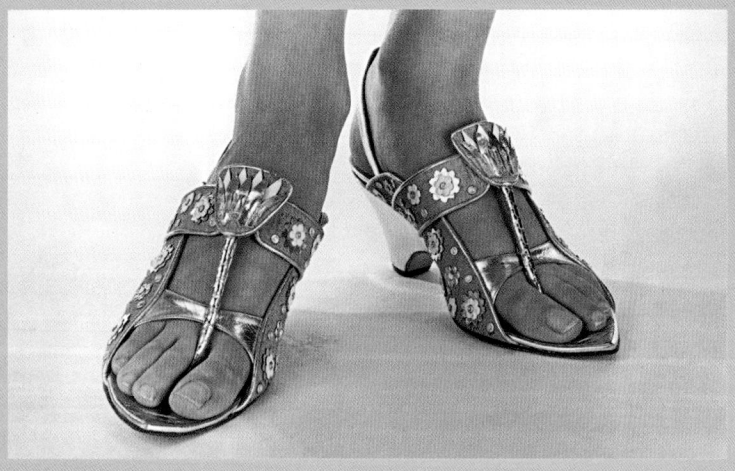

Sandals possibly for Elizabeth Taylor in the 1963 block-buster *Cleopatra*, on which Messel and Rayne collaborated, until the whole production was moved to Rome and re-designed. RAYNE ARCHIVE

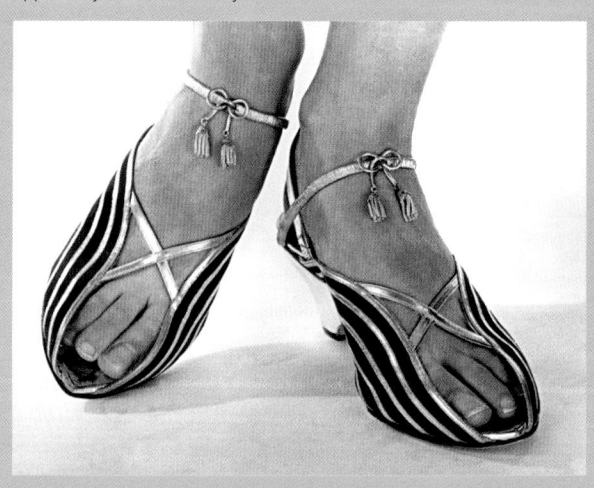

Far left: A pair of 1940s gilt kid Rayne wedge sandals made for Vivien Leigh. c.1945. RAYNE ARCHIVE

Left: Sandals made for Miss Leigh in *Caesar and Cleopatra*. 1945. RAYNE ARCHIVE

Facing page: Rayne military sandals and decorative leg protection designed by Oliver Messel, apparently for Stewart Granger playing 'Apollodorus', displaying the best of H. & M. Rayne's theatrical costumiers talents shortly before that side of the business was sold. 1945. RAYNE ARCHIVE

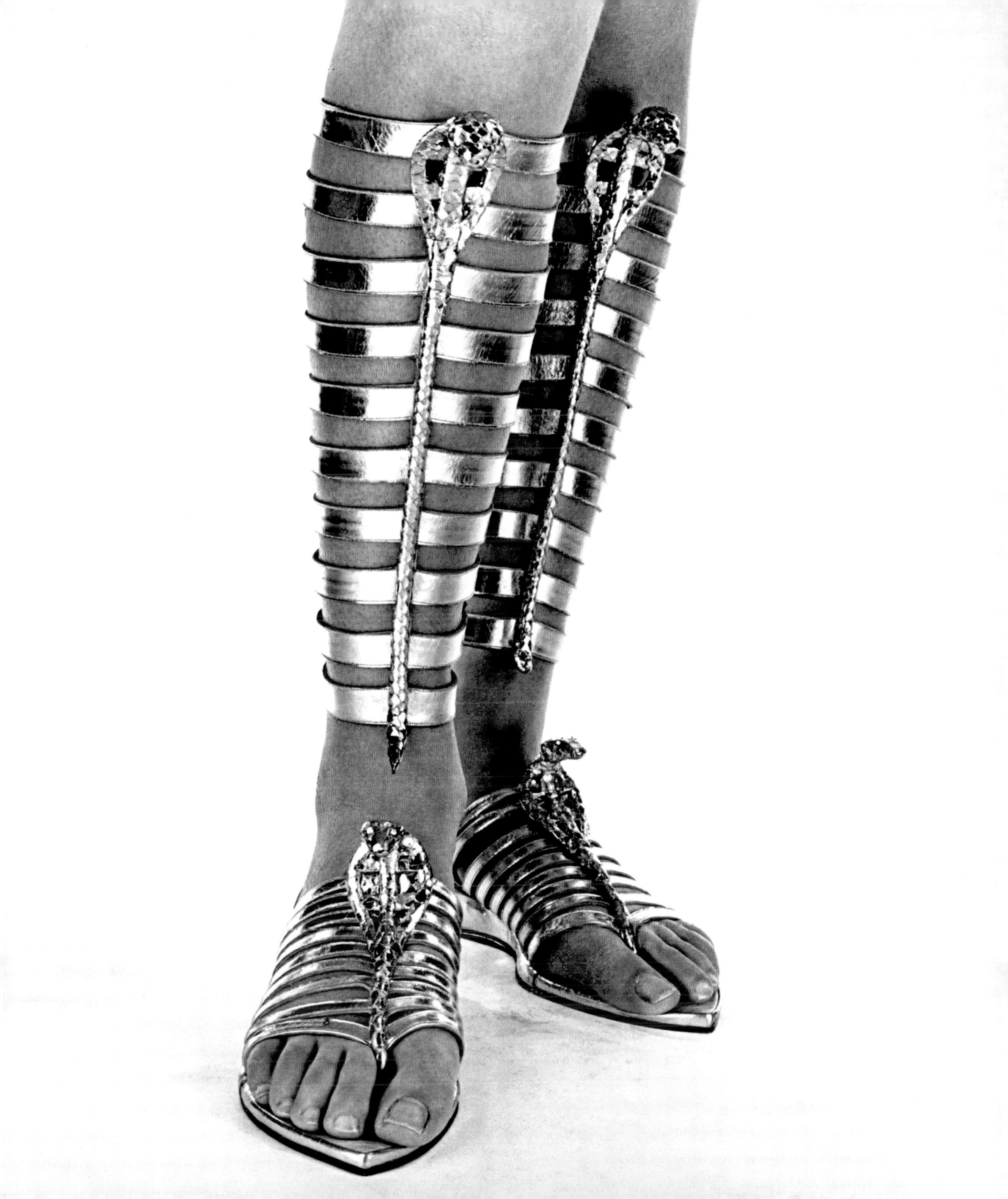

Below: The sun-ray motif was popular from the late 1920s to mid 1930s and is a form of *art deco* applied design that gave way to sleeker *art moderne* motifs. These Rayne summer day shoes were undoubtedly aimed at those taking sunny holidays or enjoying a cruise. The light structure and low heels depend upon a natural fibre net infill and a similar circular worked cotton or sisal roundel to the toe as a central decorative motif. c.1935. Courtesy Liz Tregenza

Facing page: White satin shoes were in constant demand for weddings, Presentations at Court or generally for dances and could be dyed to match the colour of the dress being worn. This example with the mid-height Louis or French heel and the Rayne inset logo to the insole, typifies a simple design popular and fashionable from the late 1920s to the mid-1930s. c.1934. Tracy Dolphin Collection

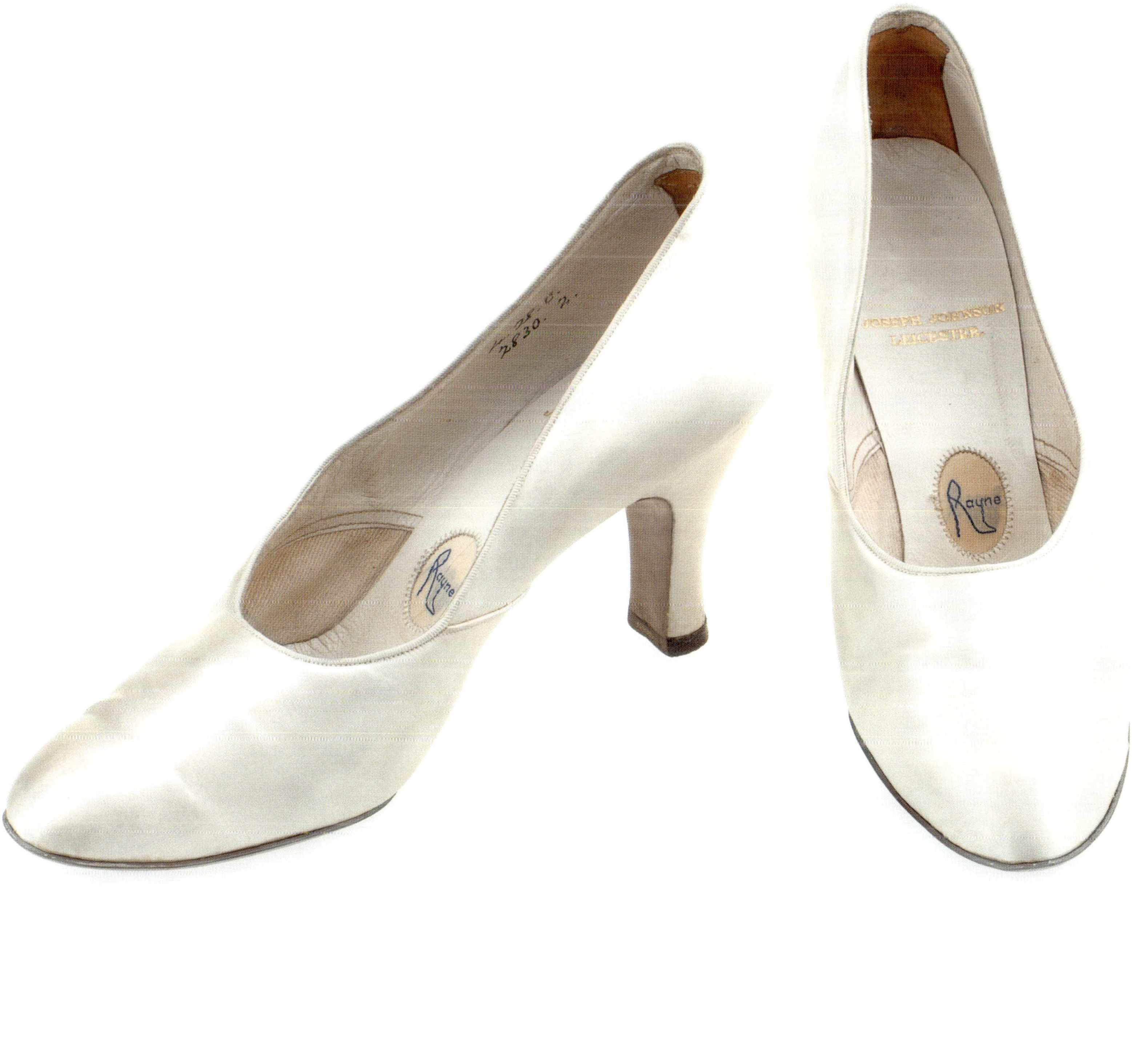

A pair of Rayne rose satin heeled evening sandals trimmed with intertwined satin-faced leather straps and with slim ankle straps. Lighter evening shoes with mid-heels were fashionable at all times throughout the 1930s and these sum up a last happy fling before the advent of the Second World War. c.1939. RAYNE COLLECTION

This pair of Rayne 'Coronation' evening shoes were advertised with other models for the summer season of 1937, during which King George VI and Queen Elizabeth were crowned. The high Louis heels are covered with the same fabric as the vamps, all with leather silvered trim, also carried out on the elaborate latticed decoration over the feet and toes. The diamanté highlights of this decoration run in a line to the toes. These could have been worn by Peeresses in full regalia over their dresses, or as evening shoes. At this date, it is most likely that Queen Elizabeth would have been aware of H. & M. Rayne's shoes, as her mother-in-law Queen Mary was already a client, but she had already used Jack Jacobus for many years as her trusted supplier of shoes. 1937. TRACY DOLPHIN COLLECTION

As he had time on his hands, J.E.R. joined the Hamilton Bridge Club nearby on Park Lane. He left the running of the business increasingly to his son and his colleagues, looking in at the factory at 2.30pm every day and then visiting the three shops, before leaving in the early evening for the Hamilton Club, where he played bridge or talked to interesting members. He seldom arrived back at his flat before 5 or 6am to sleep and would then go through the same routine day after day. This lifestyle and the fact that he smoked between 80 to 100 cigarettes a day, caused his health to deteriorate.

Edward spent increasing amounts of time with the joint managing Director, his Uncle James, in the Rupert Street theatrical premises, where he found constant interesting activity. J.E.R. found his brother boring, but they got on well enough in business. Edward said about Uncle James, 'My hardship was to have to lunch with him every day at Scotts...then in Piccadilly. It was a penance I was happy to endure.' (1985 interview) Apart from this, he considered himself lucky at his age to play such an important role in the family business. James died in 1947 and the theatrical costumier part of the business was sold to rivals Nathan.

After D-Day in 1944, it became clear that victory was in sight for the Allies. The outlook for the company was better after war ended, although rationing outlasted true Austerity Regulations into the 1950s. The factory continued to thrive, but J.E.R. became a worry to his wife, son and the staff. As his health declined, he belittled Edward's decisions, right or wrong, often quarrelling with him in complete contrast to the days when he encouraged young Edward at the beginning of the war. Like his father, Edward also sought solace in bridge, having joined the Hamilton Club. He became a world-class player winning important tournaments, whilst also trying to keep up with his father's moods. Nevertheless, the company prospered and made a profit of £40,336 in 1945 and acquired the share capital of Britten and Bannister Ltd. of London and Ipswich, makers of 'Britt Bann' shoes. Almost as a riposte to the changes his son was fighting for, the 1946 Company report includes J.E.R.'s comment that 'despite the highly mechanised nature of the footwear industry, the Rayne standard of design and quality did not readily lend itself to large scale mechanisation'. Young Edward's views soon won through. By 1948, the Ipswich factory was making 'Casuals' and, in 1949, Rayne bought Richard Ingram's latest patents for last construction, giving them the ability to make shoes of 'superior fit and quality'. This factory later made 'Rayne Casuals' and, from 1956, 'Miss Rayne' shoes for a younger market; it finally closed in 1963.

Post-war business was good for Rayne. Company reserves in 1947 exceeded £200,000 and a profit of £76,423 was made. Rayne shoes were now increasingly seen on the feet of the Queen and Princesses Elizabeth and Margaret. By 1950, J.E.R. had suffered a series of strokes from which he died in 1951 and young Edward then gave up his much lauded bridge career to devote himself fully to running the family company, which in 1950 was granted its second Royal Warrant by The Queen, later Queen Elizabeth, the Queen Mother.

Facing page: Rayne advertising was rarely found in colour until the often bleak days of Austerity Britain with its rationing and shortages at the end of the Second World War and into the 1950s. Joseph and Edward Rayne had the British optimism that characterised much of British life and manufacturing of the period and this advertisement from the late 1940s sums up the ingenuity of design following and reflecting the height of fashion. H. & M. Rayne had a global market throughout the Commonwealth and North and South America. The platform-soled shoes and sandals depicted in this advertisement with its Felix Kelly surrealism, represented the pinnacle of expensive British high fashion. There were rich customers able and willing to buy them. It was this successful optimism that propelled Edward Rayne into the 1950s after the death of his father Joseph. Summer 1949. The artist signing 'Rivett', created several 'dream' advertisements for various companies at the time.
RAYNE ARCHIVE

Rayne insists on All White

These models also in Black, Brown, Blue, Sepia, and pastel shades.

H. & M. Rayne, 58 New Bond Street.
H. & M. Rayne, 152 Regent Street.

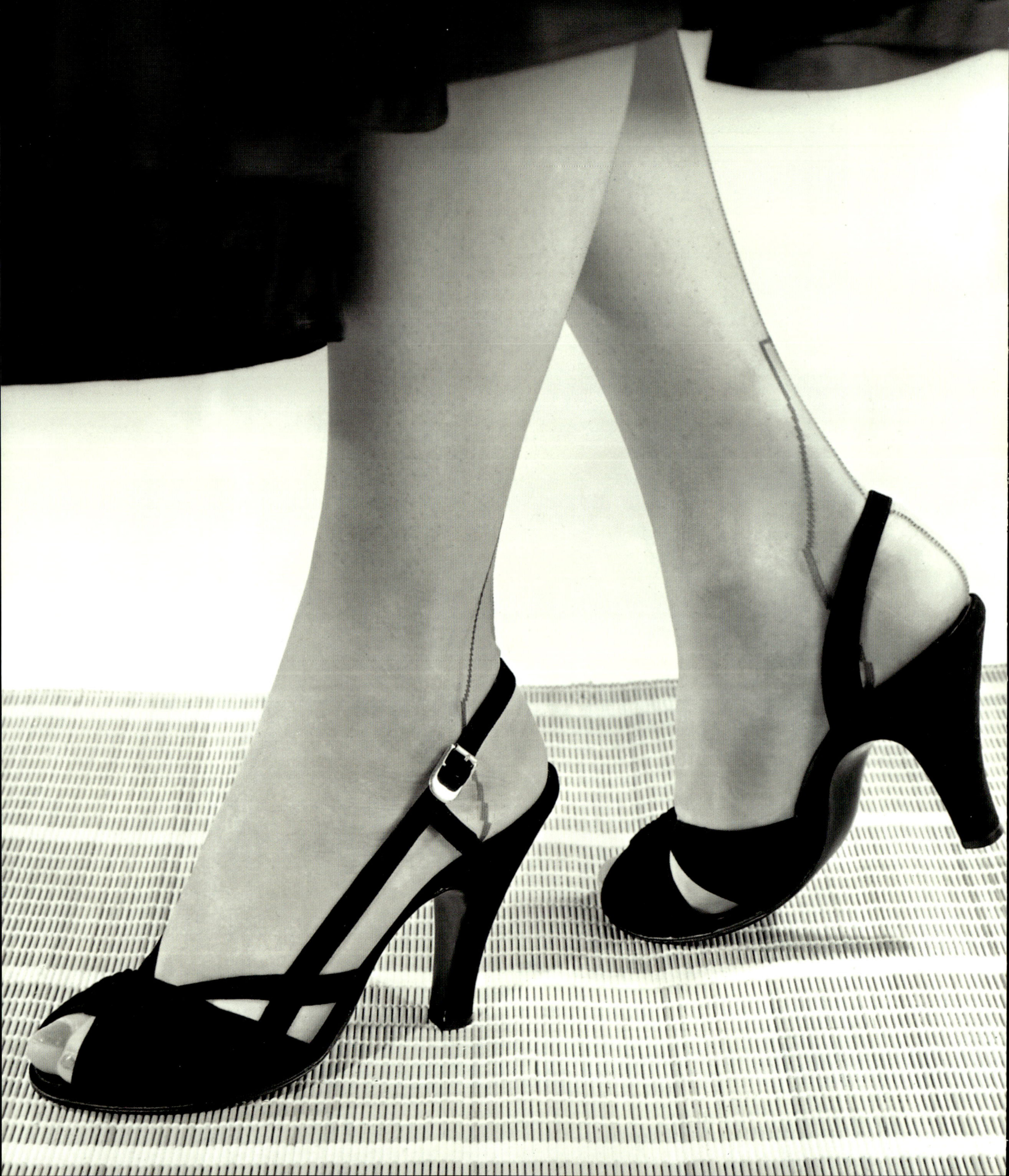

3

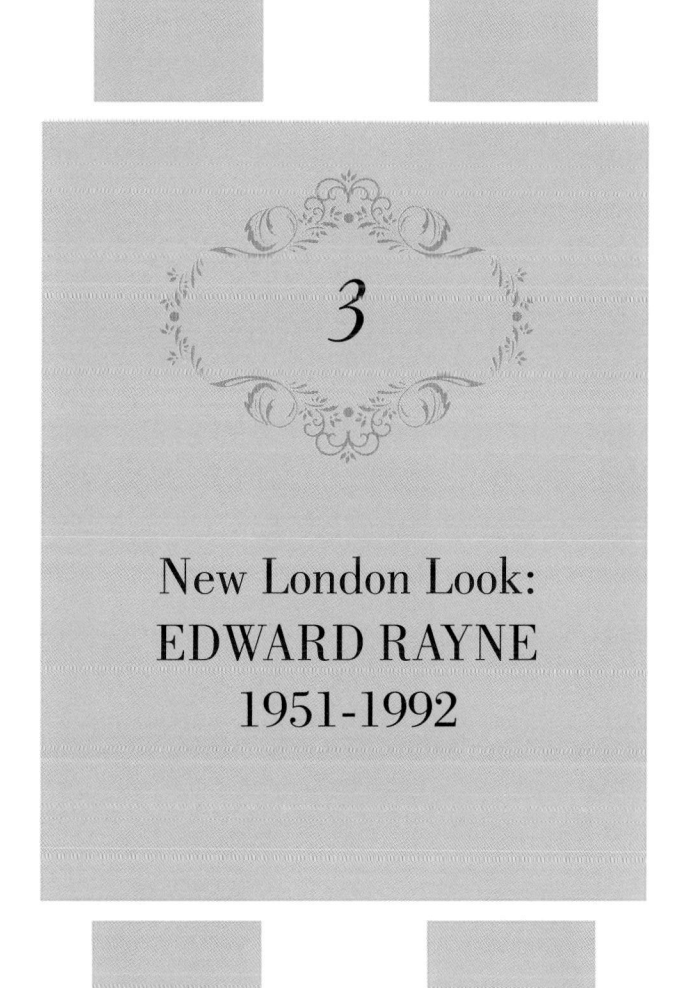

New London Look:
EDWARD RAYNE
1951-1992

Edward Rayne was one Britain's most successful twentieth century entrepreneurs. He turned a highly successful family company into a global brand on a scale envisaged by his father and never dreamt of by his Victorian founding grandparents. The third generation managing director of H. & M. Rayne Ltd began his in-house training in 1939 and became involved with planning and company acquisitions throughout the war and late 1940s, although he wrote of the frustration he felt at dealing with his ageing and increasingly irascible father. He first went to America in 1946 to learn 'all about PR and promotion. Shoe-wise, I was 100% educated here,' he told a *Washington Star* reporter on October 8 1980.

His father's pre-war purchase of advanced American shoe-making machinery and often more elegant American fashion shoe designs led to Rayne having more modern UK production methods and in turn a profitable contract with Delman shoes in 1936. There was very little pre-war competition from Europe. Germany had much of the mass shoe market in northern Europe and Central Europe was dominated by Bata's vast enterprise at Zlin in Czecho-Slovakia, occupied after 1938 by Germany. Italy's fashion shoe business industry was headed by the relatively smaller luxury brand Ferragamo and that of France by Hellstern and Perugia, amongst others; however, it remained usual for the affluent to have their shoes handmade. It was only after World War Two that European life changed dramatically and countries rapidly began to re-build industries and economies on the basis of the Marshall Plan with an eye to American business success.

Previous page: When Edward Rayne succeeded his father as head of H. & M. Rayne Ltd in 1951, post-war Britain was still struggling with some rationing restrictions and attempting to regain a better semblance of pre-war life. 1951 marked a public affirmation of a better future with the Festival of Britain indicating the way. London fashion had embraced the longer fuller skirts of Christian Dior's New Look, as far as possible, and with some government backing in the drive to gain foreign currency by exporting whatever was possible – fashion included. The lighter elegance of fashionable shoe design walked in tandem with the heavier platform sole and the now established nylon stockings lent a more alluring look to the fuller skirts, destined to last with seasonal length adjustments well into the 1960s. RAYNE ARCHIVE

Left and facing page: Two Rayne advertisements from the early 1950s continue to rely upon the graphic artist with the use of dense black and contrasting white imagery for a visual impact greater than exhibited in preceding decades. The September 1950 advertisement for pumps (top left) indicates the many variations offered on a theme with a lighter touch to the designs than seen during the 1940s. Anthony Denney's sensual *Vogue* cover of October 1950 (facing page) places the velvet pump next to the carefully applied velvety texture of the fashionable powdered make-up covering the model's face. From the 1900s onwards, velvet was a recurring favourite amongst Rayne designs, which lost none of their ingenuity, as the 'up or down' vamp of the slightly earlier design (left) illustrates. CONDÉ NAST

VOGUE

PARIS COLLECTIONS

SHOES · ACCESSORIES

OCTOBER 1950 · PRICE 3/-
overseas (except in Australasia,
S. Africa and Eire) 3/6

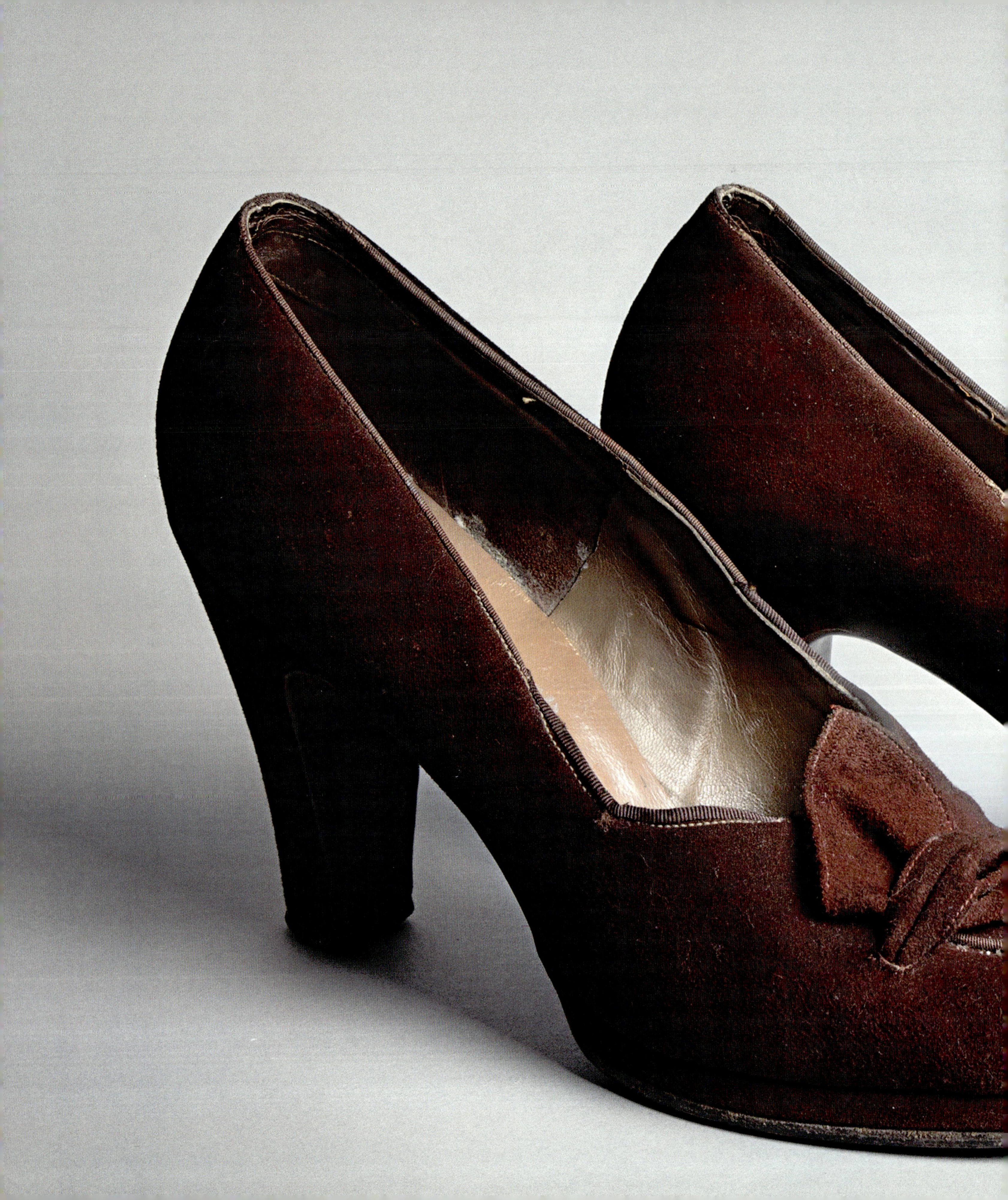

Platform soles are usually thought of as a staple shoe design statement of the 1940s, but were popular throughout most of the 1950s and were revived again in the 1970s. These post-war Rayne russet suede peep-toe shoes have a simple suede tie motif above the toes and apart from the platform sole, vary little in design from similar shoes of the mid to late 1930s. RAYNE ARCHIVE

Facing page: Satin evening shoes of the late 1930s varied little until the early 1950s and the most elegant showed small developments in the design. The multiplicity of straps and the elaborate ruching of the satin on this pair are more staid than many of Rayne's surviving designs, but have a pleasing effect. These were suitably retailed by Bobby of Bournemouth, one of the many nation-wide department stores with which Rayne had successful commercial relationships, catering for an affluent local community not necessarily keen to be in the vanguard of fashion.
MICHAEL PICK COLLECTION

Edward Rayne became equally adept at evolving new shoe styles and company strategies to counter the rapidly increasing post-1950 competition. From the days of Henry and Mary Rayne, keen awareness of high fashion has always been a constant factor in the success of the Rayne business. Pre-war journals such as British *Vogue* rarely put together a complete ensemble of couture clothes with named high quality accessories. A March 1937 editorial page showing a sketch of a Digby Morton suit with Rayne shoes was unusual, but this became the practice from 1940s onwards. The interdependence of clothes and accessories became a popular feature of press editorial. Edward Rayne's interest and knowledge of world fashion trends and designers' ever-changing seasonal collections led to many of his greatest successes. In his 1955 autobiography, *Silver and Gold*, Norman Hartnell, a world-famous leading British couturier of the time, wrote of his design processes leading to a complete collection, emphasising, 'my friend, Edward Rayne, most obligingly designs special shoes'.[1] They collaborated most spectacularly on shoes for both Queen Elizabeth II and Queen Elizabeth The Queen Mother. Hartnell was also one of several notable dress designers to design shoes for Rayne.

The post-war revolution in dress design came in Spring 1947 following the opening of Christian Dior's business and the world-wide influence of his 'New Look'. Parisian and New York designers and manufacturers reacted swiftly to create the lavish use of fabrics utilised in the full-skirted look, which was completely different from the prevailing fashions that were still based upon 1939/1940 styles. In London, members of the Incorporated Society of London Fashion Designers (INCSOC) and wholesale trade struggled to compete due to crippling government Austerity regulations delineating the quantities of fabric and types of decoration allowed. Most commodities including fuel and energy were heavily rationed at this time. The government had allowed the continuation of war-time easing of regulations and supplies for Export Collections, but this did not mean that women could easily copy the new full, long-skirted fashions at home. Rationing coupons could be saved and used to buy Rayne shoes in the latest styles, very often platform soled with leather and colour variations, when they were available. The latest designs naturally complemented the new fashions and, by 1951, were being exported to twelve countries.

Overleaf: For the affluent and avid follower of fashion, this selection of Rayne platform sandals dating from 1946 to 1953 exemplifies the variety of colours and designs available. Although favoured as a shoe design by The Queen and the Princesses Elizabeth and Margaret, whose dress designer Norman Hartnell collaborated with Edward Rayne to create a heightening of their smaller statures, such shoes were more generally worn by a younger clientele. Studs, plaiting and the use of reptile skins lent the shoes as much fashion drama as an elaborate hat. The sandals second from the right were selected in white by Princess Margaret for her trip to Italy in 1950 (see p.166) and the design was featured in the 1947 shoe orders for the Royal Wedding (pp.150-151), as are those on the far left of this image, a less elaborate version of the 1947 design 'Zarine' selected by the Queen for The Royal Wedding of 1947 (p.152). Acutely fashion-conscious women could thus capture some of the glamour of a royal event by acquiring similar Rayne shoes. RAYNE ARCHIVE

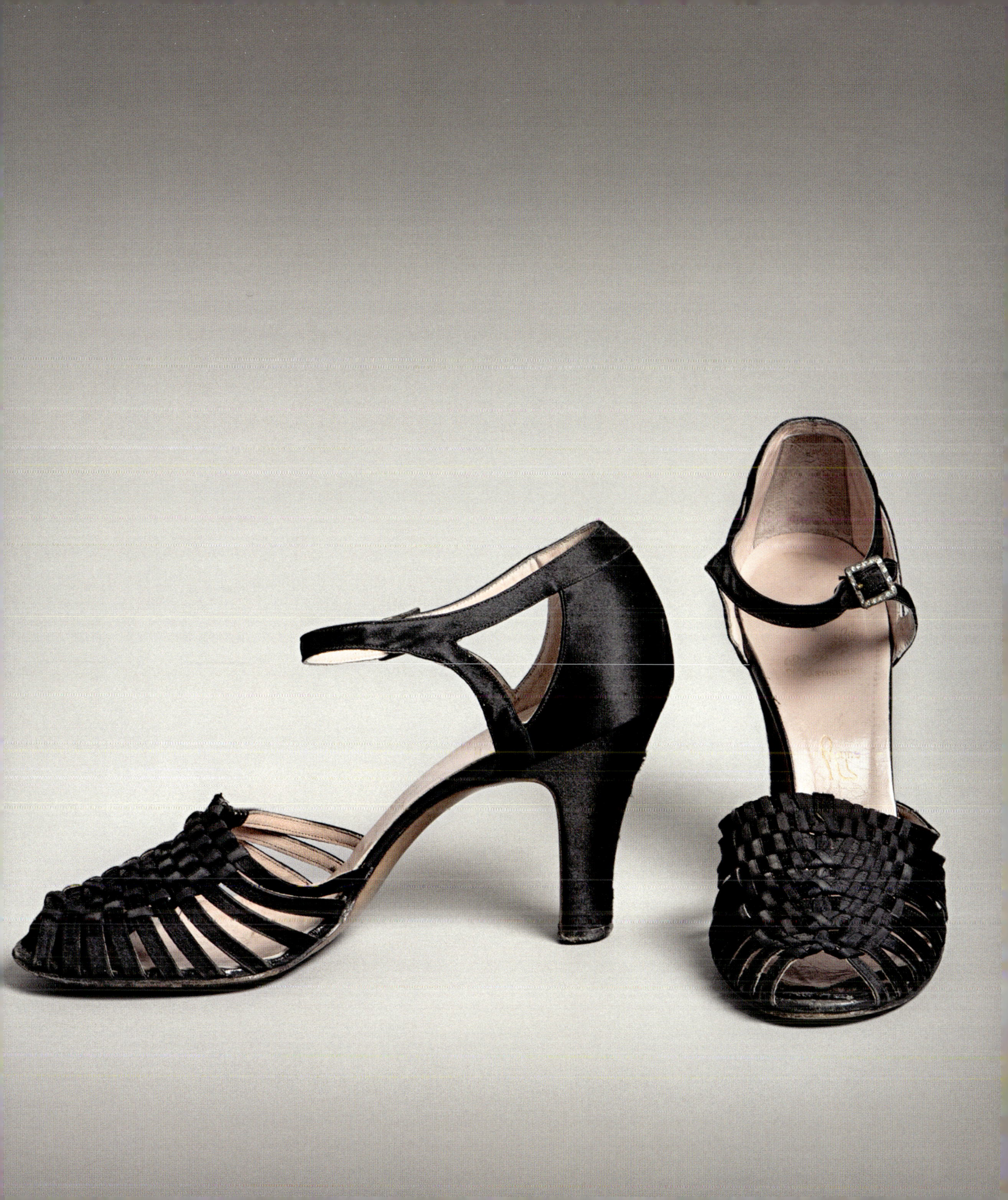

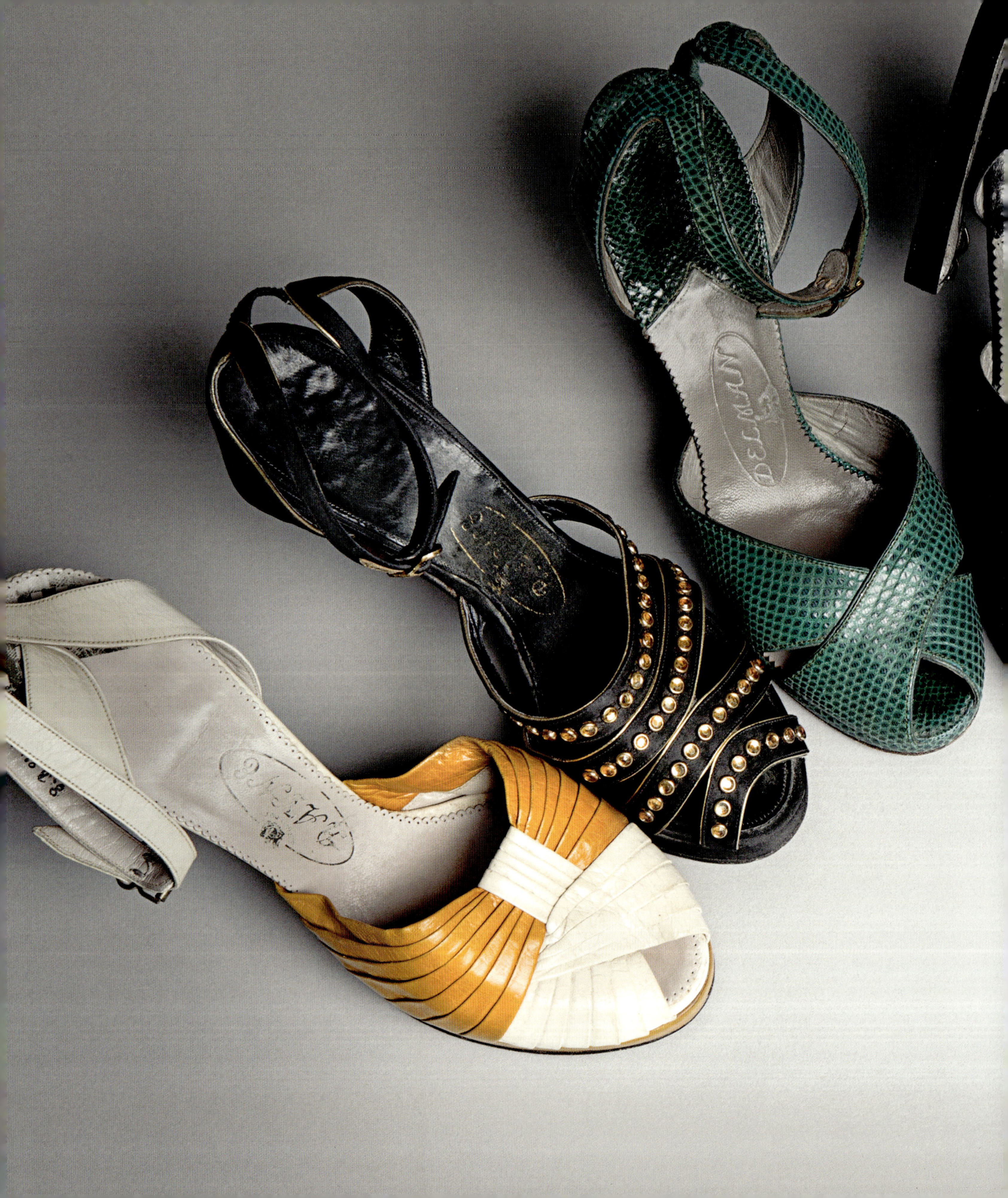

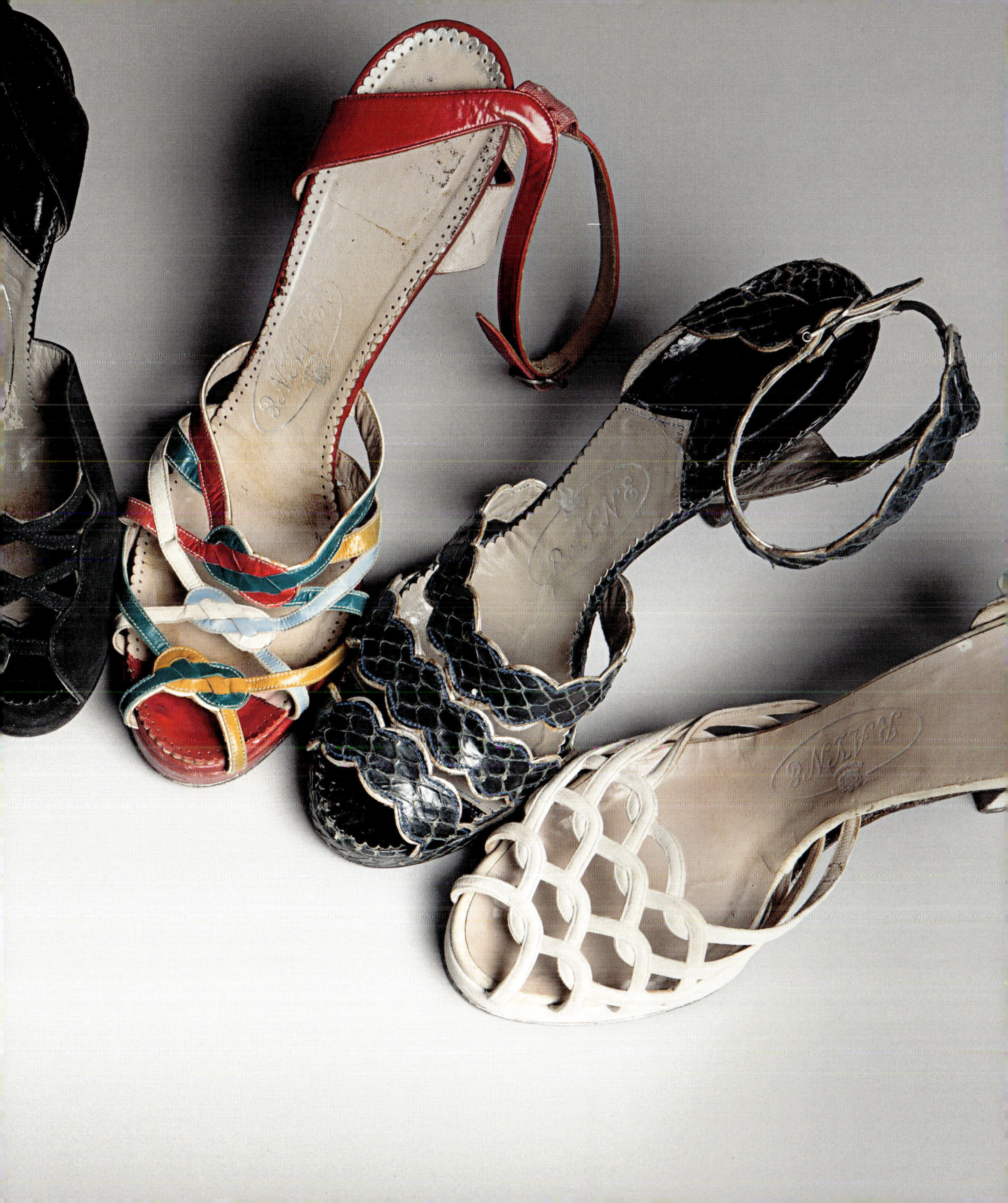

Above: Before wild-life preservation became an issue, reptile skins were used to cover expensive shoes and bags, amongst other things. Left: Two pairs of high-heeled Rayne shoes with thick heels indicate their origins in the full-skirted fashions of the post-war 1940s and date from c.1946-1952. The sheer weight of wool used in the top coats, suits and the weight of fur coats worn in a country without much central heating and experiencing bitter winters, explains the stability sought in the thicker heels of what are essentially autumn or winter shoes. A matching hand bag would usually be worn with such shoes.   RAYNE ARCHIVE

Facing page: A variety of shoes utilising dyed reptile skins of varying shades, the very pointed toes dating from the 1950s into the 1960s, even including 'Miss Rayne' less expensive variants. Those with the rounder toes and gilt-metal trim date from the late1960s and early 1970s.   RAYNE ARCHIVE

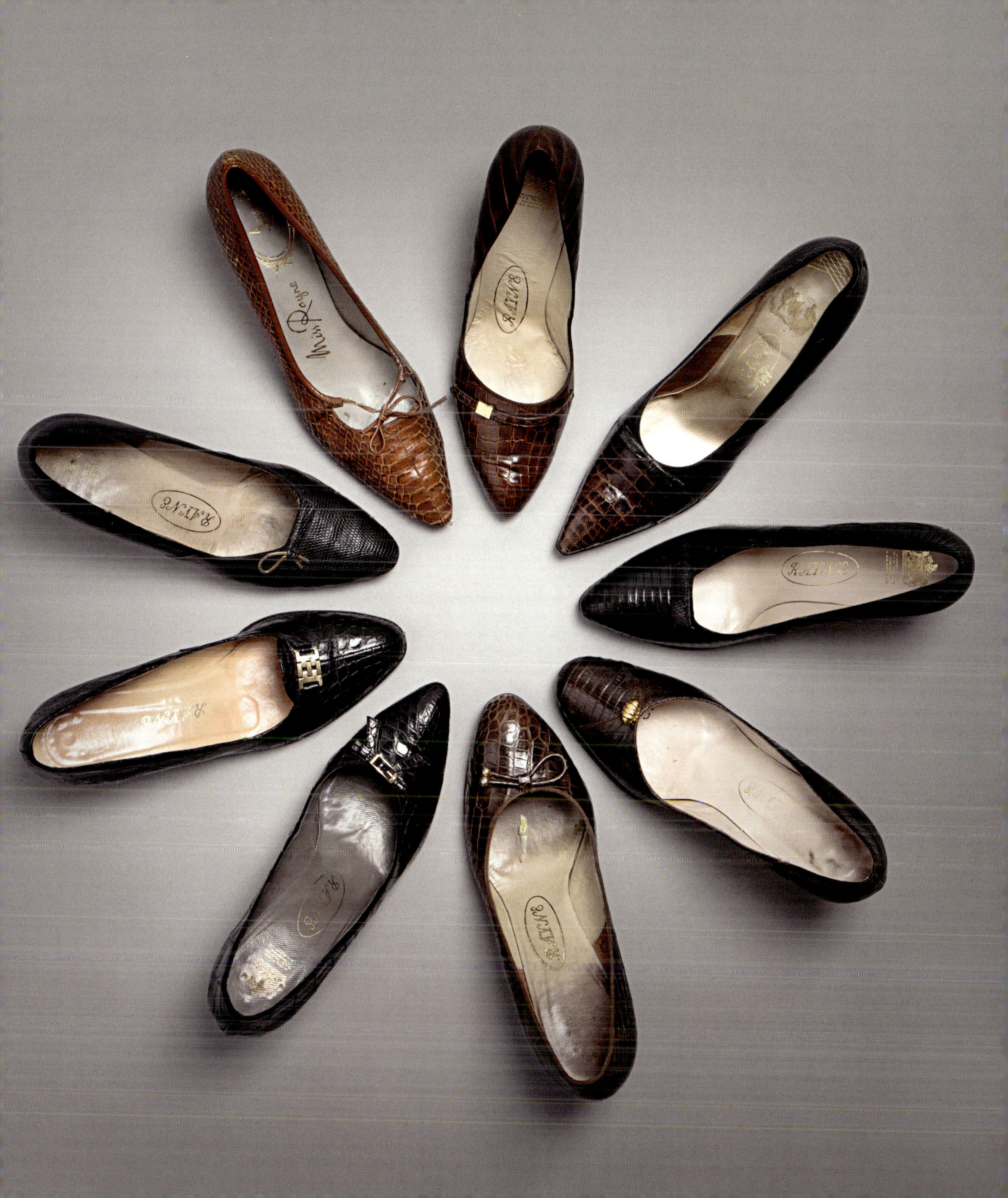
Miss Rayne
RAYNE

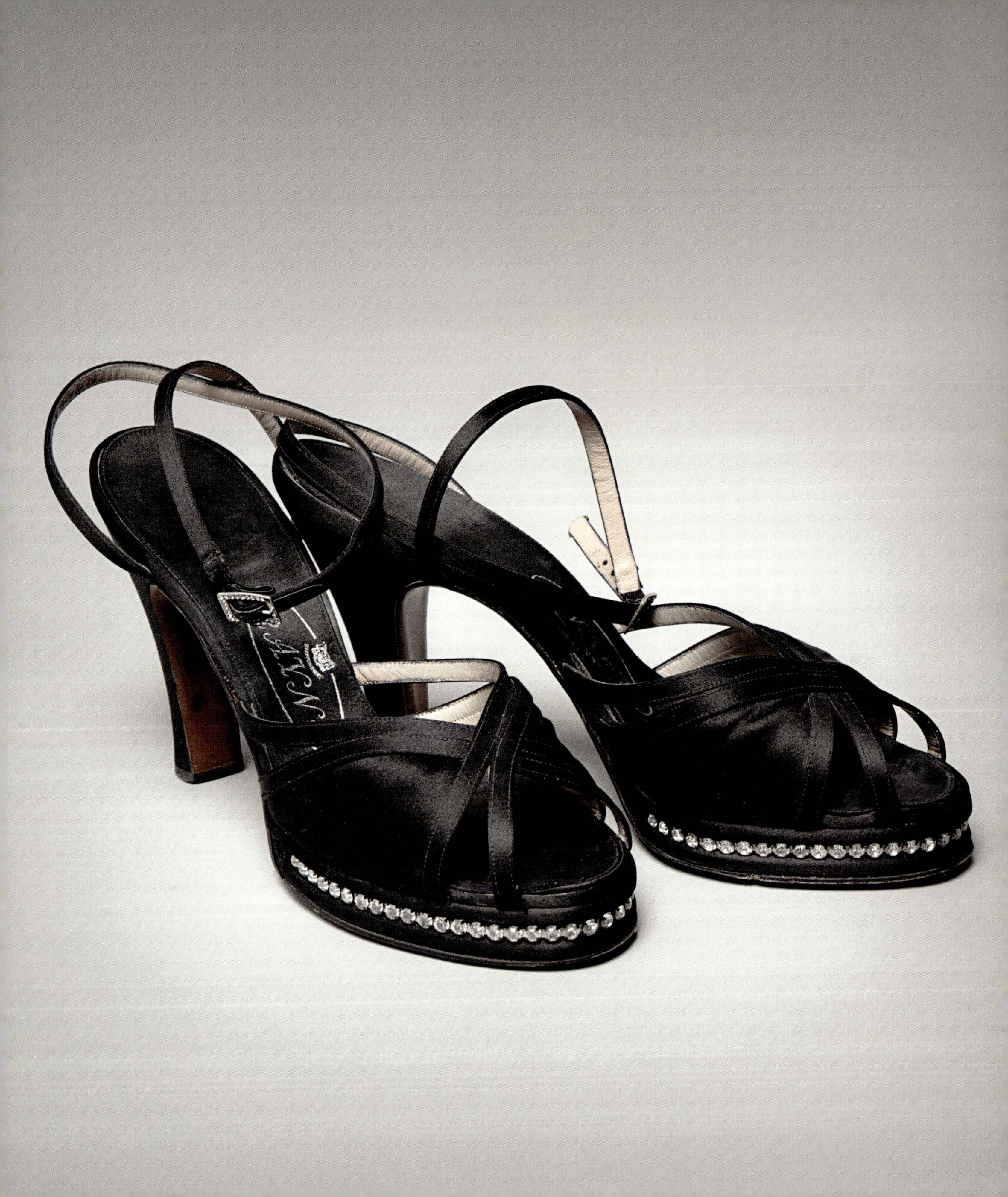

Facing page: This example of black satin-covered platform-soled evening sandal dates from the early 1950s. The diamanté-studded platform is intended to highlight the feet of the wearer beneath her long evening dress and was a design also selected by the then Queen, as demonstrated by an example given to the collection of royal shoes held by Historic Royal Palaces. c.1952. Rayne Archive

Below: A pair of Rayne platform-soled evening sandals in silver and gold kid with central diamanté clasp fastenings on the parti-coloured ankle straps, the glamour of the dual-coloured design is heightened by the ingenious way in which the overlapping halves are joined. c.1950-1952. Tracy Dolphin Collection

At the same time, Edward built on his father's success with in-store shops in the best provincial department stores, such as the 1951 circular 'Rayne Salon' opened in Griffin & Spalding's, Nottingham and in Daly's, Glasgow. As early as 1952, a Rayne department was opened in a Stockholm department store; neutral in the war, Sweden was enjoying a much higher standard of living than the UK, as was Germany in 1956 when Rayne was to be found in-store at 'Schopp' in Stuttgart.

Edward's visible commercial drive and vision was backed by continual advertising and editorial coverage augmented as before by the continuing use of Rayne shoes on stage and in films by notable stars, although it was nearly always the case that film shoes remained uncredited and largely unseen, unlike those supplied to the various ladies of the Royal Family. The latest Rayne shoe designs worn by The Queen and the two glamorous Princesses, Elizabeth and Margaret were seen in the extensive world-wide media coverage given to their every activity. The 1947 Royal Tour of South Africa and Southern Rhodesia and then the November marriage of Princess Elizabeth displayed Rayne chic to perfection complementing the clothes by Hartnell and Molyneux and hats by Aage Thaarup. Rayne shoes were sought after in South Africa, Australia and Canada and more so during Coronation Year, 1953, and the subsequent Royal Tour of the Commonwealth from 1953-1954, for which Rayne provided the shoes to accompany the many remarkable dresses by Hartnell, Hardy Amies and Horrockses. In short, Rayne shoes were often universally the stuff of many women's dreams.

1952 brought Edward a happy marriage to Morna Cort (1918-2010), who had been an aspiring actress under the name Morna Leigh and then a West End stage manager during the war. To Rayne's PR man Peter Hope Lumley she became known as 'Thumper' for her habit of rigorously testing the many pairs of Rayne shoes she selected for her own use. Edward and Mona took a lease of Norman Hartnell's elegant London house in Regent's Park, where they began to entertain with style and became a popular couple in an era when cocktail parties were highly fashionable.

Edward was a convivial host and surviving Rayne expense accounts from the 1940s reflect the period flavour of an affluent businessman's round of restaurants and hotel visits, with expensive cars (often undergoing bodywork repairs as Edward's sight was very poor – the reason he left school early and was exempt from war-service) and first-class voyages to and from New York on the RMS *Queen Elizabeth* in the company of glamorous fellow passengers, all busy making useful business and social contacts. In keeping with their fashionable London life, they subsequently had flats in Portland Place and latterly Grosvenor Square, Mayfair.

In an era when the middle-aged and older woman still dominated fashion purchasing power, elegant yet sensible comfortable shoes were in constant demand. The navy suede shoe with supple lattice vamp and low heel (facing page, top) was advertised nationwide in Marshall & Snelgrove's Rayne pages and every year had variants on this theme (above). Similarly, everyone's mother or aunt would have looked smart in the peep-toed ribbed-fabric afternoon shoes with their perky bow decoration (facing page, bottom). Such shoes were a staple of shoe merchandising. This shoe had its design origins in those of the 1930s. c.1950.
Above: RAYNE ARCHIVE;
Facing page, top: NORTHAMPTON MUSEUMS;
Facing page, bottom: TRACY DOLPHIN COLLECTION

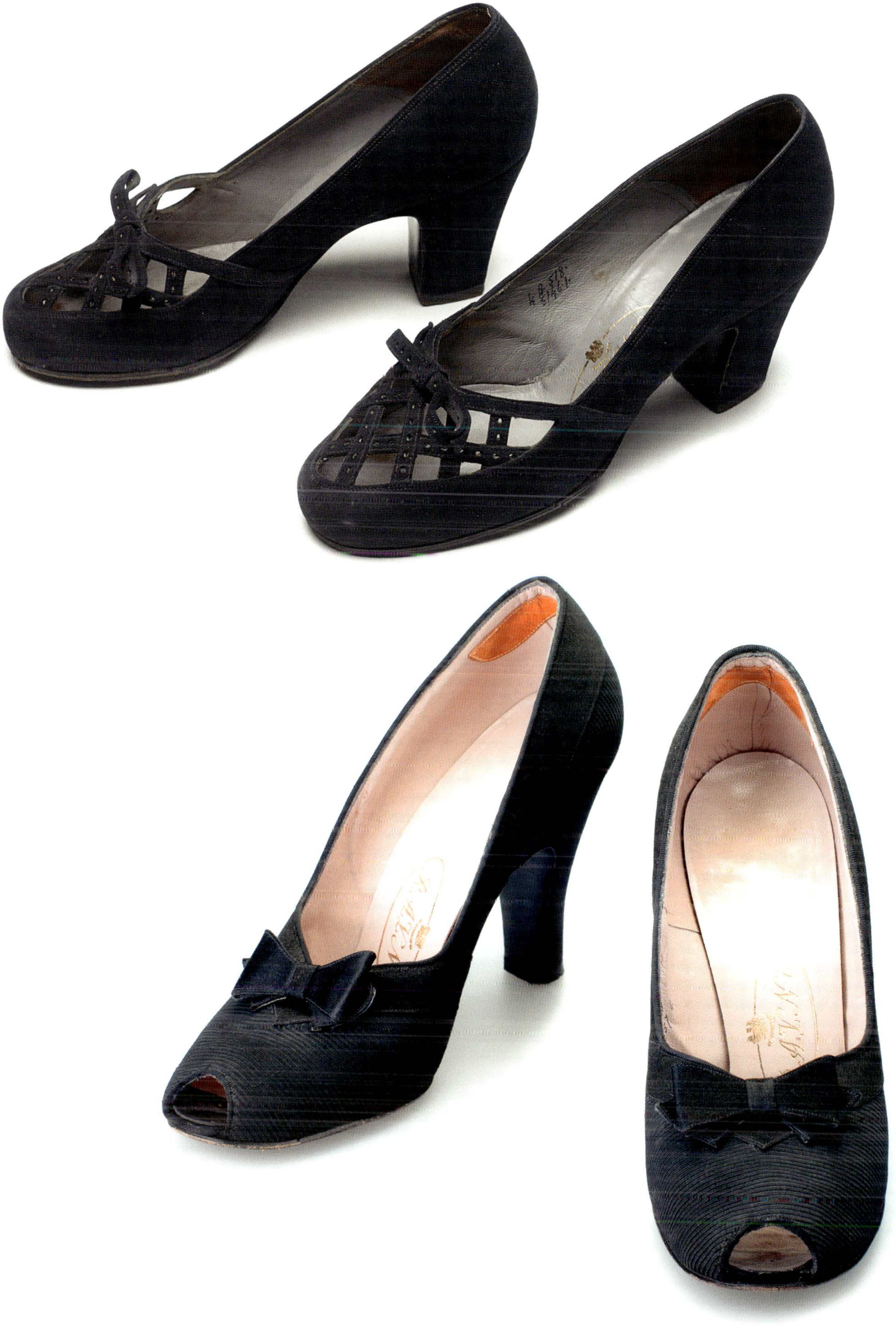

Countrified calf pumps or court shoes were a staple of Rayne's market, usually sold in their Regent Street shop, which had come to specialise in 'county' ladies and their daughters needing rather wider fittings. This shop differed from the more expensive Bond Street shop and was on the established route of out-of-town shoppers alighting from the tube at Piccadilly Circus and then visiting Swan & Edgars department store. This had one entrance directly from the station booking hall, and also stocked Rayne shoes. From there, shoppers could progress up Regent Street via a then remarkable variety of different shops (including a Rayne store), as far as Peter Robinson on Oxford Circus and nearby John Lewis – or beyond.

Above: A pair of tan peep-toe high heeled pumps with discreet trim suitable for country or suburban wear. MICHAEL PICK COLLECTION

Right: The slimmer heels date the shoes to c.1953/55. The darker calf pumps with lower heels by 'Miss Rayne' with stitched detailing were aimed at the younger teenage or young married market. c.1958/9. MICHAEL PICK COLLECTION

Much lucrative business and many good connections were made this way. Expansion of the business followed and in 1953 Rayne acquired H.E. Randall Ltd with two factories in Northampton and 69 shops, selling fine shoes and formerly holding the warrant of The Prince of Wales (later the Duke of Windsor). Edward Rayne consolidated this policy further, buying the Cantilver Shoe Company in the same year. The business was further augmented by the appointment of Jean Matthew, one of the Royal College of Art's first students in what was then called the Fashion Department, and the only one at that time who wanted to design shoes. In 1954 at the age of 26 she was working at the Kings Cross factory, 'she designs and adapts models and sees them through to production. And she is in charge of advertising and publicity. Her office which she shares with two men and hundreds of shoes at all stages of manufacture looks out over the factory floor. During the day, she will probably discuss new leathers, fabrics and designs; draw and adapt to the Rayne last and market some fabulously elegant kid pumps from Italy; modify another already in the making; and hurry through a special order for a couture house. She will consider next season's advertising campaign with the agents; rush a prototype pair of shoes to *Vogue*, or *Harpers*, for photographing; visit the main Bond Street store, to talk over sales and styles with the head buyer; and, in her spare moment, punch studs into a new model, because someone has to get it done by that evening. She is a slightly unexpected figure on a factory floor. And, to judge by the greeting she gets, a welcome one. "You certainly couldn't have picked a better personality feature girl," said Mr Cook, who has been with the firm 35 years.'[2]

Jean Matthew's Rayne connection came through the sale of sketches to Peter Jellinek of Dolcis and the influential Geraldine Stutz, then with *Glamour* magazine. Initially, Jean Matthew was employed as 'fashion co-ordinator', but as she explained, 'after all, the shoe industry is something of a plagiarist industry. But it gradually grew into a job.'[3]

This included devising advertising and supervising its implementation, until Edward later realised the potential of her design skills and appointed her to design two shoe collections a year. She was filmed working on a shoe design in the Rayne London factory.[4] He appointed professional agents to take care of the advertising and Peter Hope Lumley to run the PR for Rayne; Hope-Lumley represented many clients and models in the fashion world – Hardy Amies remained a client until his own retirement.

Jean Matthew, seen here at her work-table in the Rayne factory near Kings Cross Station, had a long and productive career with H. & M. Rayne Ltd., becoming a major designer of many of their most beautiful shoes. c.1954. JEAN MATTHEW ESTATE

Possibly one of the most beautiful pairs of Rayne sandals ever made; these hand-embroidered platform-soled examples would have been worthy of a royal wearer and certainly contain motifs included in the 1953 Coronation dress of HM The Queen designed by Norman Hartnell (see rose detail). They did have their moment in the Queen's proximity, as they were sold in 1953 from Georges Department Store in Melbourne, Australia, to a frequent client, Mrs. Elsie Mcintosh. She wore them with a beige dress of guipure lace and a tiara to the City of Melbourne Ball held during the Royal Tour of 1953-1954 in honour of the visit of Her Majesty Queen Elizabeth II and His Royal Highness the Duke of Edinburgh at the Exhibitions Building on 2 March 1954. The diapered or trellis gilt design on the heel section of the insole only appears on the very finest Rayne shoes of that period.
NATIONAL GALLERY OF VICTORIA, MELBOURNE, AUSTRALIA. GIFT OF DAVINA MCINTOSH IN MEMORY OF HER MOTHER, 2011

For the next decade Rayne supplied many shoes for fashion shows and commissioned exclusive designs from the leading London designers Norman Hartnell, Hardy Amies and John Cavanagh. Remarkably, the Rayne London factory could manufacture these within five to ten days. But by 1973 couture demands had dwindled; the process now took just one day to create a sample. At this date the aim was to create shoes for women without any particular age in mind, although Matthew considered that the 30-35 year old woman was an ideal.

The fashionable American market was directly opened up for the company in 1955 when Rayne shoes were sold in the Delman shoe department of Bergdorf Goodman, New York.[5]

Edward's keen business sense was displayed in a 1983 lecture, '...nothing is sold until a member of the public buys it' and with the expensive investment in 850 factory hands, staff, plant, materials and shops Rayne could never stand still. In 1956, for example, sales of 'Rayne Casuals' made in the Ipswich factory were too weak for the investment involved. The factory became the base for the new 'Miss Rayne' label offering Rayne quality at a lower price to the younger growing consumer power becoming a force in British commercial life, at a time when younger women were gradually ceasing to dress like their mothers. Quality and design were not compromised and depending on factory volumes, 'Miss Rayne' shoes were also produced in London factory.

Many of the older British and foreign clients continued to buy many pairs of shoes at a time when couture collections often changed radically from season to season. An extreme example of this 'necessity' was the amazingly newsworthy former dancer Norah Docker. Her husband was Chairman of Daimler and she designed their show-stopping car interiors and sometimes exterior details such as gold sprayed metalwork, for the Earls Court Motor Show. Lady Docker had a keen eye for press publicity and often ordered ten pairs of shoes of one design in varying colours for each of the many new outfits in her new season's wardrobe, mainly from Norman Hartnell. Buying in such quantity was not usual, but affluent British women were not unlike their American counterparts and annually increasingly bought a greater variety of shoes.

In 1957, another contract with the General Shoe Corporation of America resulted in the right for Rayne to make shoes in London bearing the Christian Dior label and designed by Roger Vivier in Paris. Vivier designs had been bought by Rayne over many years, as had those of Perugia. Adding to the fame of the prestigious Rayne-Delman collaboration, Rayne also made shoes for the equally exclusive I. Miller and Millerkin companies. Fostering links to famous designers played a crucial role in Edward Rayne's business plans.

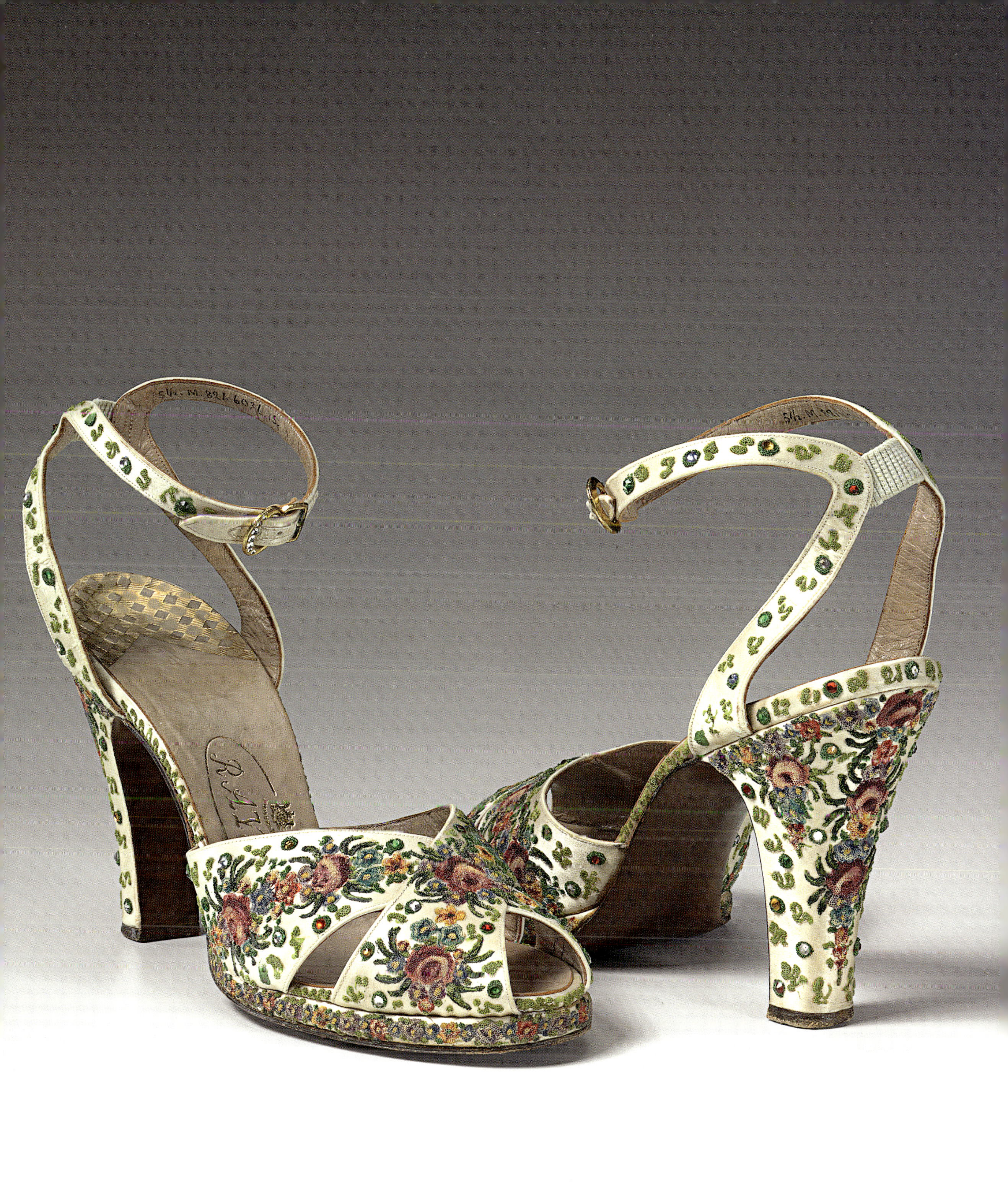

The evolution of the Rayne sandal during the first half of the 1950s:

This page: A black suede heavy platform-soled version with a cut-out vamp and the gilt heel decoration to the insole denoting Rayne's best quality (above), echoed in the insole of the black shallow platform-soled design (left) with a latticed gilt edged vamp. Both c.1950/53. Tracy Dolphin Collection

Facing page, top: A flat-soled evening sandal with gilt-metal florettes – typical mid-century motifs. c.1953/4. Rayne Archive

Facing page, bottom: Soft-blue velvet frames the foot with a minimum of necessary support with the interlaced velvet straps across the toes and high-lighted with tiny glass brilliants. c.1954/5. Tracy Dolphin Collection

97

Facing page: A pair of off-white Rayne calf shoes from the mid-1960s echoing the designs of 1930s shoes in the form of the decorative gathered and clasped motif across the toe. Not everyone wanted shoes with stiletto heels and these shoes formed one of the alternatives.

Below: A pair of Rayne steel blue-grey low court shoes with peep toes enlivened by a corded applied ribbon around the vamp and centred with a decorative button. The overall design and heel are not too dissimilar from Rayne designs of the 1930s. c.1952/54. TRACY DOLPHIN COLLECTION

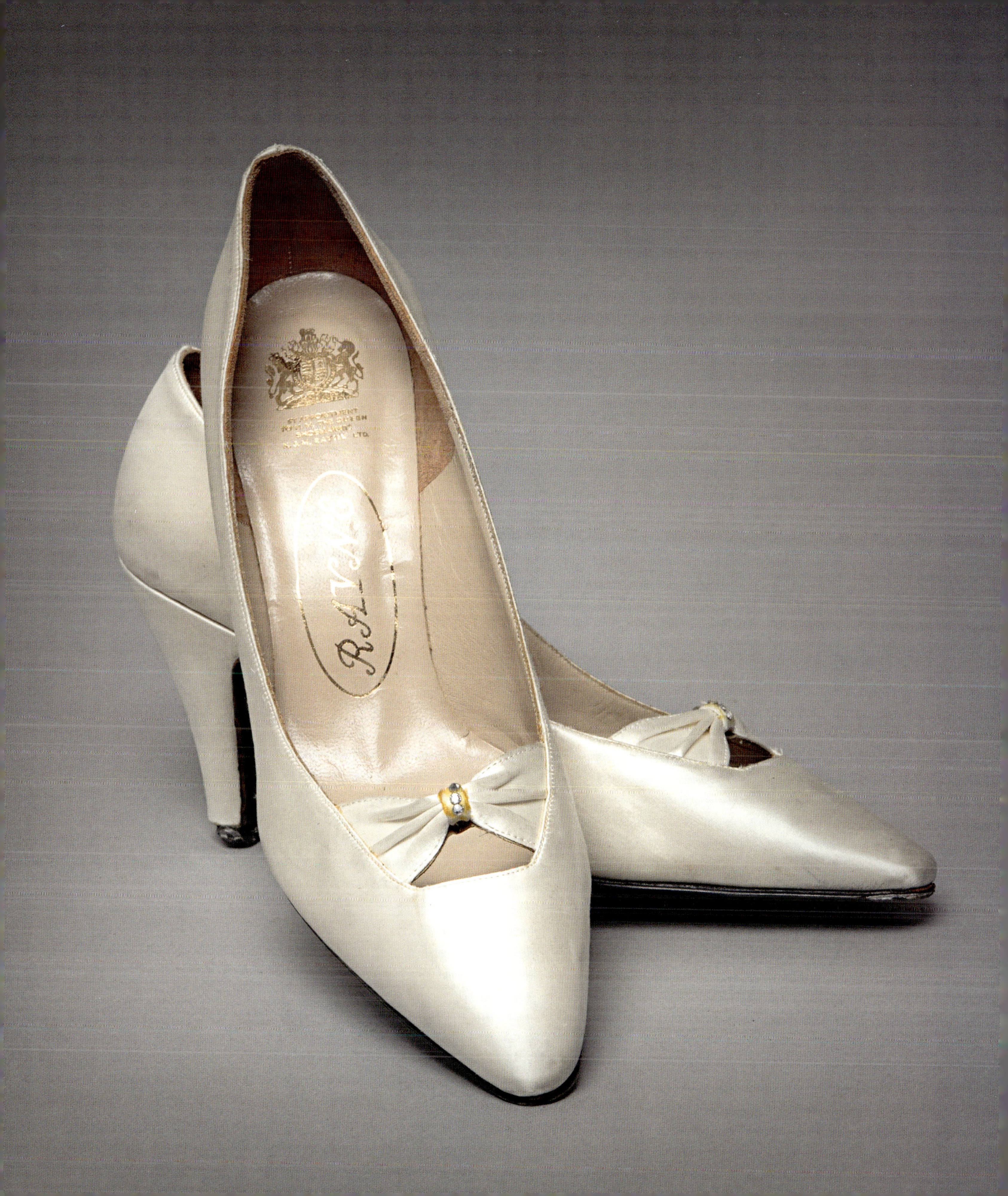

The Stiletto: the greatest mid-twentieth century innovation in shoe design rapidly evolved from the substitution of thicker heels – predominantly of wood, or even horizontal sections of leather for country shoes – with the strong steel 'stiletto' heel. It was first popular in Italy. As with many innovations in shoe design, it is considered to have evolved from 1940s designs by André Perugia (1893-1977) for the French star Mistinguett. As so often, the widespread adoption of the revolutionary style is attributed to Roger Vivier (1913–1998) for Christian Dior's 1954 collections. Vivier had previously worked for Delman in New York and in 1950 began a business association with Dior. Both Perugia and Vivier sold designs to Rayne, who also made shoes for Dior in the 1950s.

Above: A Rayne elegant pair of black shoes with a simulated broad satin ribbon tie over the toes terminating in a bunched ribbon bow to one side. c.1956. These shoes are similar to ones designed by Beth Levine (1914-2006) for famous wife and husband company Herbert Levine (1916-1991). Edward Rayne had business dealings with them and utilised some of their designs, occasionally selling Levine shoes in London. As Jean Matthew's stock books reveal, designs of all periods were scrutinised by shoe-designers and ideas adapted. This design is akin to one of the mid-1930s by Dolcis, seen as a colour advertisement in *Vogue*.
TRACY DOLPHIN COLLECTION

Right: A pair of Rayne two toned *cafe-au-lait* extra svelte pointed shoes of fine caramel nylon mesh with minimal thin leather trim and bows balancing on thin stiletto heels. c.1958.
RAYNE ARCHIVE

Facing page: A selection of Rayne high-heeled stiletto shoes made from a variety of lace and other nylon reinforced fabrics, the pointed toes of the late 1950s giving way to the chisel and then rounded toe of the early to mid-1960s. The strength of the man-made steel heels had its counterpart in the strength of man-made fibres and new glues holding the various component parts of the shoe together. RAYNE ARCHIVE

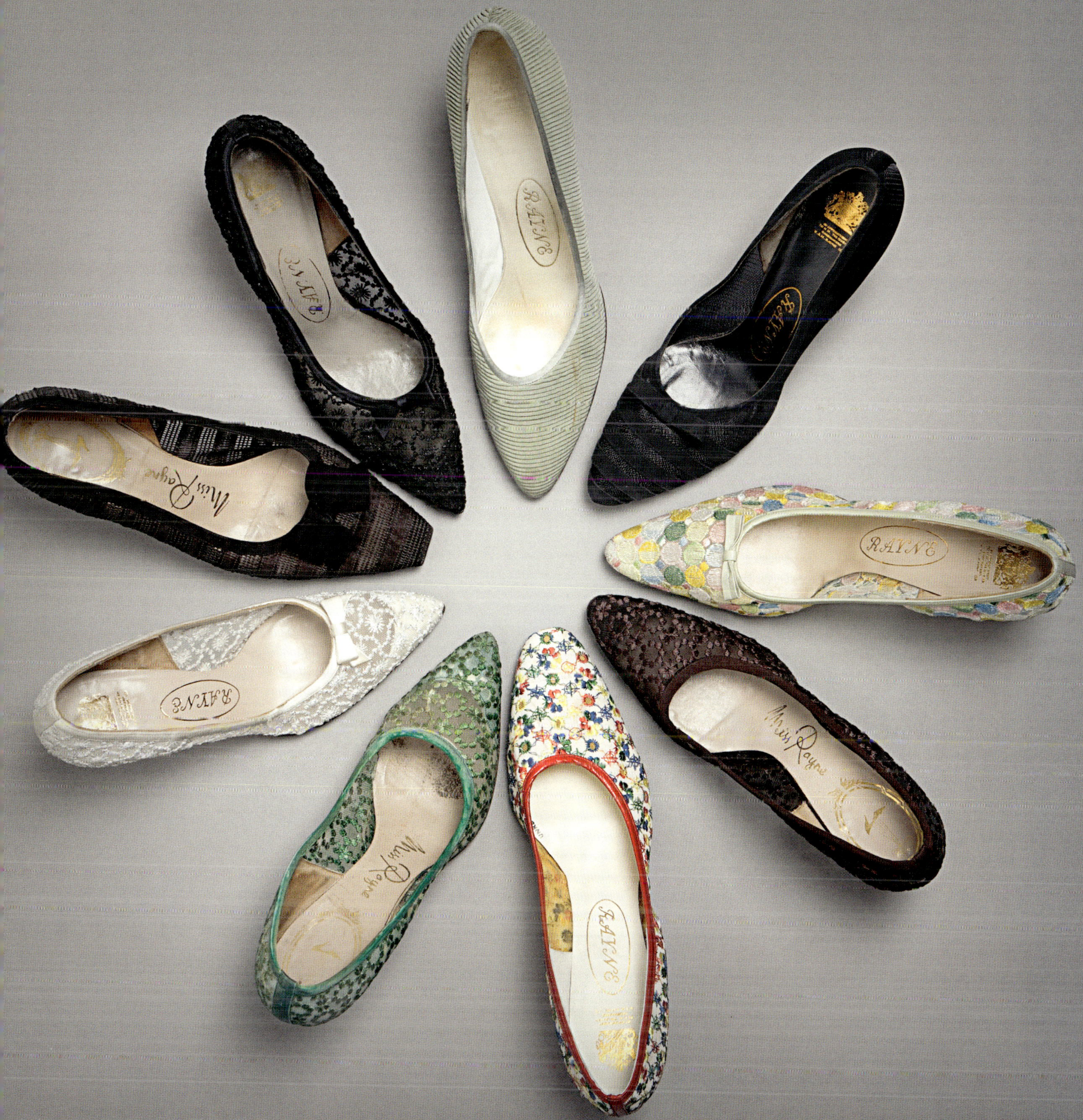
RAYNE
Miss Rayne
RAYNE
RAYNE
Miss Rayne
Miss Rayne
RAYNE

At Number 58 in this World Famous Street, is the World Famous House of Rayne.

Left: This brocade shoe with ribbon trim typifies Rayne's attitude to luxurious design and the use of graphic artists for advertising. This is a precursor of André Perugia's notable 1956 innovation called the 'disappearing pump' or 'vanishing vamp', but with its total absence of retaining structure between heel and toes, it most resembles a sandal without any ankle strap and with slimmer heels was only for the most sophisticated wearer. Rayne was known to buy designs from Perugia, but there is no evidence that this was by him. c.1952. Michael Pick Collection

Facing page: A black suede Rayne shoe evolved from the Perugia design is given a flat satin ribbon tie and full bow similar to the one on p.100. c.1956. Rayne Archive

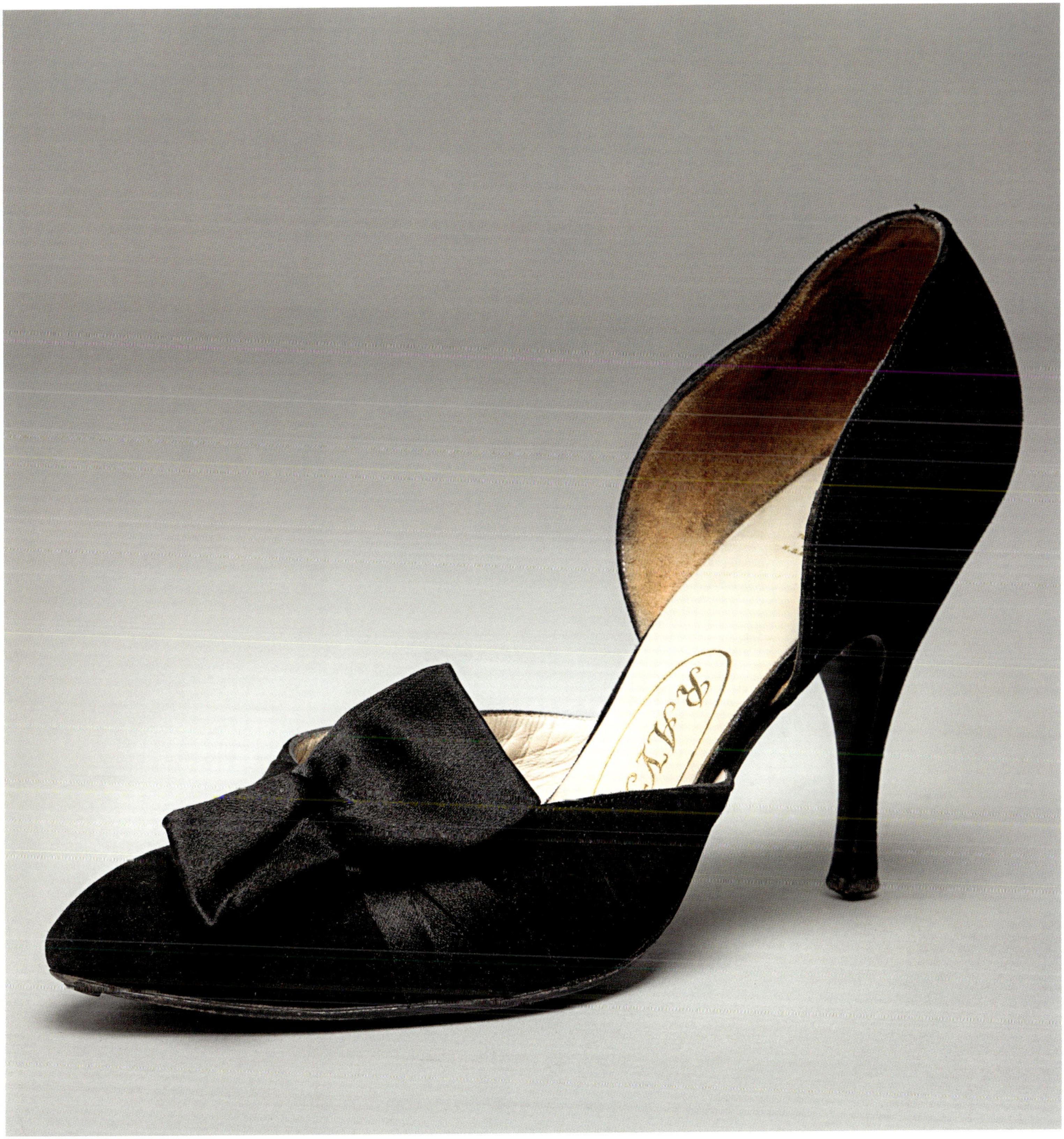

Facing page: This image by Caradog Williams appeared in *Vogue*, March 1958 on p.143 with the caption:

'Flowers at your feet
As if your toes had suddenly blossomed into spring flowers;
these lovely shoes in brilliant cut velvet, satin-backed, charmingly Victorian in effect.
By Rayne, 15gns. a pair from Rayne 58 New Bond Street., and Delman, 16 Old Bond Street.'

CARADOG WILLIAMS/*VOGUE* © THE CONDÉ NAST PUBLICATIONS LTD.

Below: A pair of Rayne red floral velvet low-heeled shoes in the tradition of popular Rayne velvet shoes of the 1920s and 1930s, but bolder and more dashing with the slipper-effect of the flower and leaf-patterned velvet fabric. c.1958. RAYNE ARCHIVE

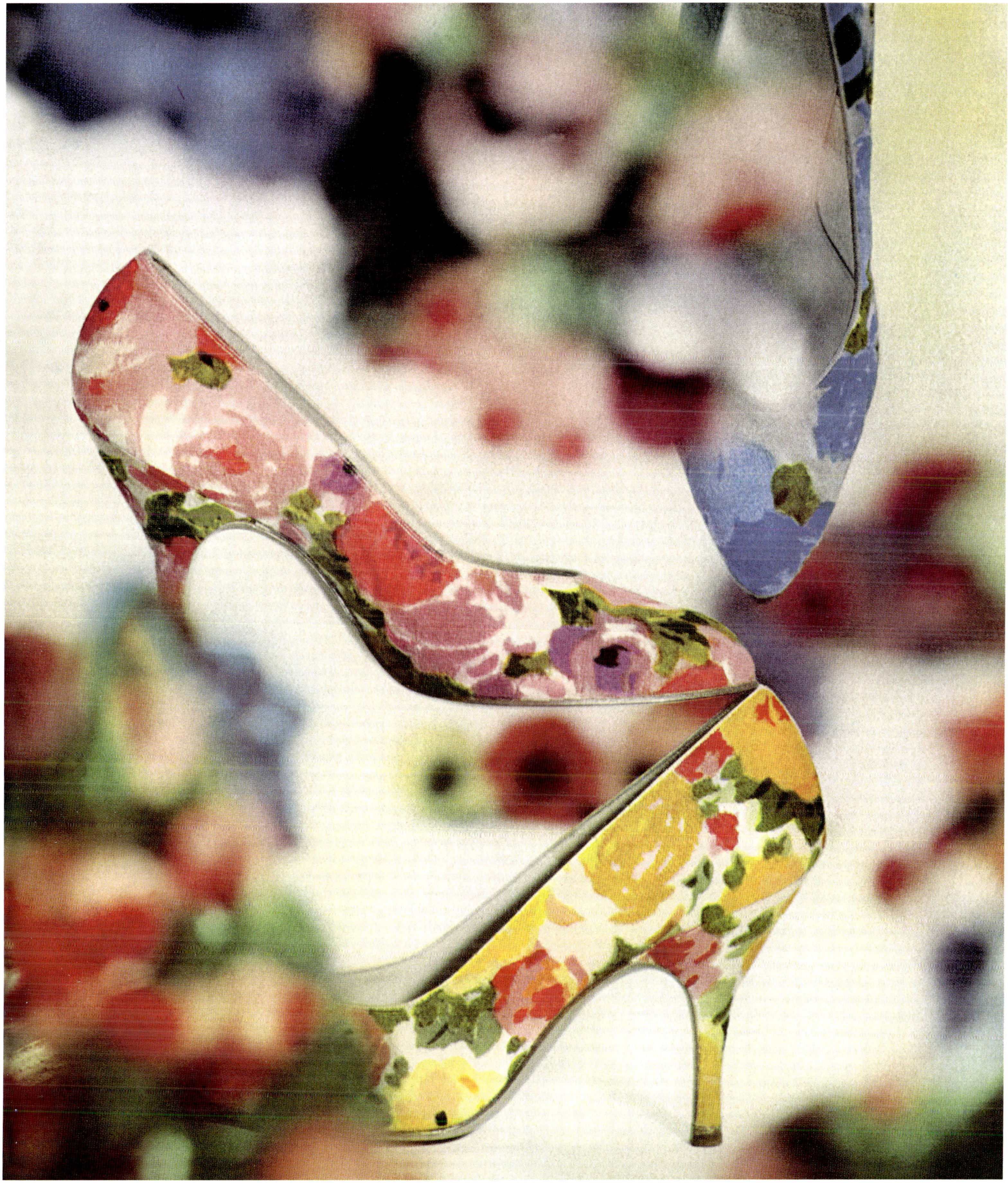

This page: Possibly as a reaction to the limited design possibilities of the stiletto or 'needle' heels as they became, Rayne designed more conventional Louis heels with a variety of exotic motifs. This example features what appears to be crushed mother-of-pearl, but is an overall application of tiny brilliants. c.1955.
RAYNE ARCHIVE

Facing page: The famous Wedgwood heels introduced by Rayne in 1957-1958 had a small vestal figure surrounded by an ornamental wreath in blue and white jasper wear, but were varied with the less usual daisy motif on a green jasper ground, here attached to low pumps (left). The idea was successfully revived again in 1977-1978 with a more elaborate draped dancing figure and in a variety of colours, here seen in green. Many shoes of the 1950s did not have stiletto heels, which were increasingly frowned upon by those with fine wooden floors, leading to the sale of plastic caps as temporary 'finials' to avert the crushing weight of the heel pock-marking floors and often said to have the concentrated impact of a small elephant's weight.
RAYNE ARCHIVE

In 1958 a collaboration with the world-famous quintessentially English Wedgwood company – one of the co-founders of the British eighteenth century Industrial Revolution – resulted in, 'a surprise ... with heels made of jasper and some trimmed with Wedgwood cameos ...exhaustive trials, long to be remembered... were necessary before the first perfect batch was delivered hot from the oven to H. & M. Rayne. Within a few days they had been made up and were on their way to a special fashion show in America.'[6]

The first batch depicting 'Hebe and the Eagle' were made in pale blue, sage green and lilac and the new Rayne Wedgwood Collection was shown to great acclaim in October 1958 at the Plaza Hotel in New York and the National Shoe Fair in Chicago. An eye-catching advertising campaign featuring trick photography depicted a London bus with all four wheels improbably perched on Rayne-Wedgwood heels. There were even matching handbags, court shoes, flat shoes and sandals and such was the success of the style that it was repeated twenty years later in many new colours, though with a differently shaped wide toe in the 1970s style.

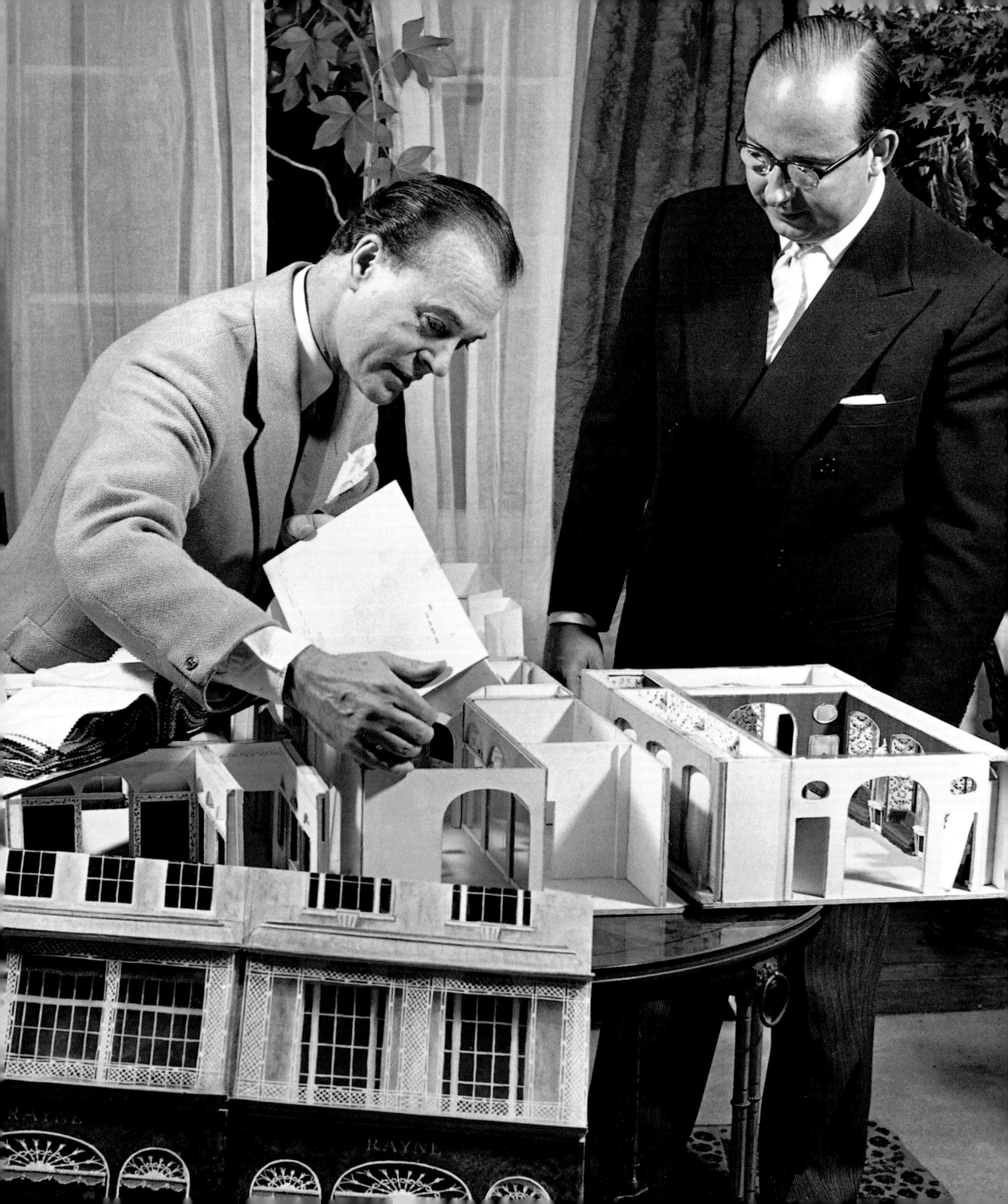
RAYNE
RAYNE

Oliver Messel and the Bond Street Shop

In 1957 further interest in Rayne was aroused with plans for expanding the Old Bond Street Delman shop into a visually stunning new Rayne shop. The lease of the bank next door was bought and by 1959 nos 15 and 16 Old Bond Street had been transformed by Britain's leading stage designer Oliver Messel, acting on Edward's instructions to 'make it as beautiful as possible' on a then lavish budget of £100,000. A year later, Edward wrote to Messel, 'Our turnover was almost exactly 50% up on the previous year, and I do not think one can have any more positive recognition than that of the wonderful job which you did for us. It is a most gratifying thought to think that the general taste and appreciation of the public can still be affected to this extent by the creation of what I sincerely believe is the most beautiful shop in the world.' (9 December 1960, TM archive). Edward considered the result so prestigious and successful that it was completely renovated in 1984, when he stated that it would cost £1,000,000 to reproduce it from scratch.

Facing page: Edward Rayne and renowned stage and film designer Oliver Messel (1904-1978) examining the models of the new Rayne shop at 15-16 Old Bond Street, London W1. 1959. THOMAS MESSEL ARCHIVE

Above: The new 'Regency' façade of the 'most beautiful shop in the world' complete in 1959, and seen left as a model. RAYNE ARCHIVE

Edward first met Messel during the war and helped to translate his shoe designs into reality at the Rayne factory for Vivien Leigh to wear in the 1945 film *Caesar and Cleopatra*. Much later he stated that, 'those were the most beautiful Rayne shoes ever made'; unfortunately, because of Austerity restrictions, commercial production was impossible. Famous since the 1920s, Messel designed stage sets for leading impresario Charles Cochran, who used quantities of Rayne shoes in his productions worn by many of the most beautiful actresses of the period. The all-white bedroom set for Evelyn Laye as 'Helen' in Cochran's acclaimed 1932 Messel-designed production of the comic opera *Helen!* was more instrumental in making the art moderne neo-Baroque style fashionable than the designs of his friend, the decorator Syrie Maugham; it was much illustrated and seen by many thousands of theatre goers. Many films extended this style and the luxurious Penthouse Suite at the Dorchester Hotel designed by Messel in 1953 echoed the theme in a polychrome magical manner, attracting Rayne clients such as stars Marlene Dietrich and Elizabeth Taylor. Messel evolved a muted version of this style for the new Rayne shop in close collaboration with Edward, used to discussing his own views on shoe design with Jean Matthew and the factory hands.

The publicity for the new shop was enormous; it embodied glamour and the sense of elegant luxury that Edward achieved with Rayne shoes. The shoes were complemented by a range of bags, often made by other companies such as Launer, or made in France, although a hand-bag section was opened at Kings Cross in the 1980s. Accessories sold included scarves, belts and Rayne stockings (made from 1957 into the 1960s) – all displayed on Louis XVI-inspired painted furniture, in subtly-lit niches and show-cases, some imitating bird-cages. Messel also designed new shoe boxes, including ones for 'Miss Rayne', although the famous yellow and black ones continued in production, offset by the yellow and white striped carrier bags.

The seductive fantasy of the design appealed to customers used to the various imaginative boutiques installed in the major couture houses of Paris and London. Shoes appeared as covetable items, more valuable displayed in the windows and these surroundings than they were. This style of selling was already going out of fashion and as 1960 chairman of INCSOC (Incorporated Society of Fashion Designers) he could gauge the changes. In a few years the Messel-Rayne interiors certainly seemed out-dated to the young women of the Swinging Sixties, but it personified an enduring taste for those with money, much as the popularity of the decoration of the Ritz Hotel, or the ever-popular and timeless chic of the Dorchester Penthouse Suite survive. The Rayne image was also continually refreshed with PR through Peter Hope Lumley's agency (Edward's best man at his wedding) and advertising using the Colman, Prentice, & Varley agency from 1956 until the '70s.

Facing page and above: Two partial views of some of the elegant shop interiors. The drawing-room atmosphere was one much admired by Edward Rayne in the Messel-designed Penthouse Suite at the Dorchester Hotel on Park Lane, a firm favourite with such Rayne clients as Marlene Dietrich or Elizabeth Taylor.

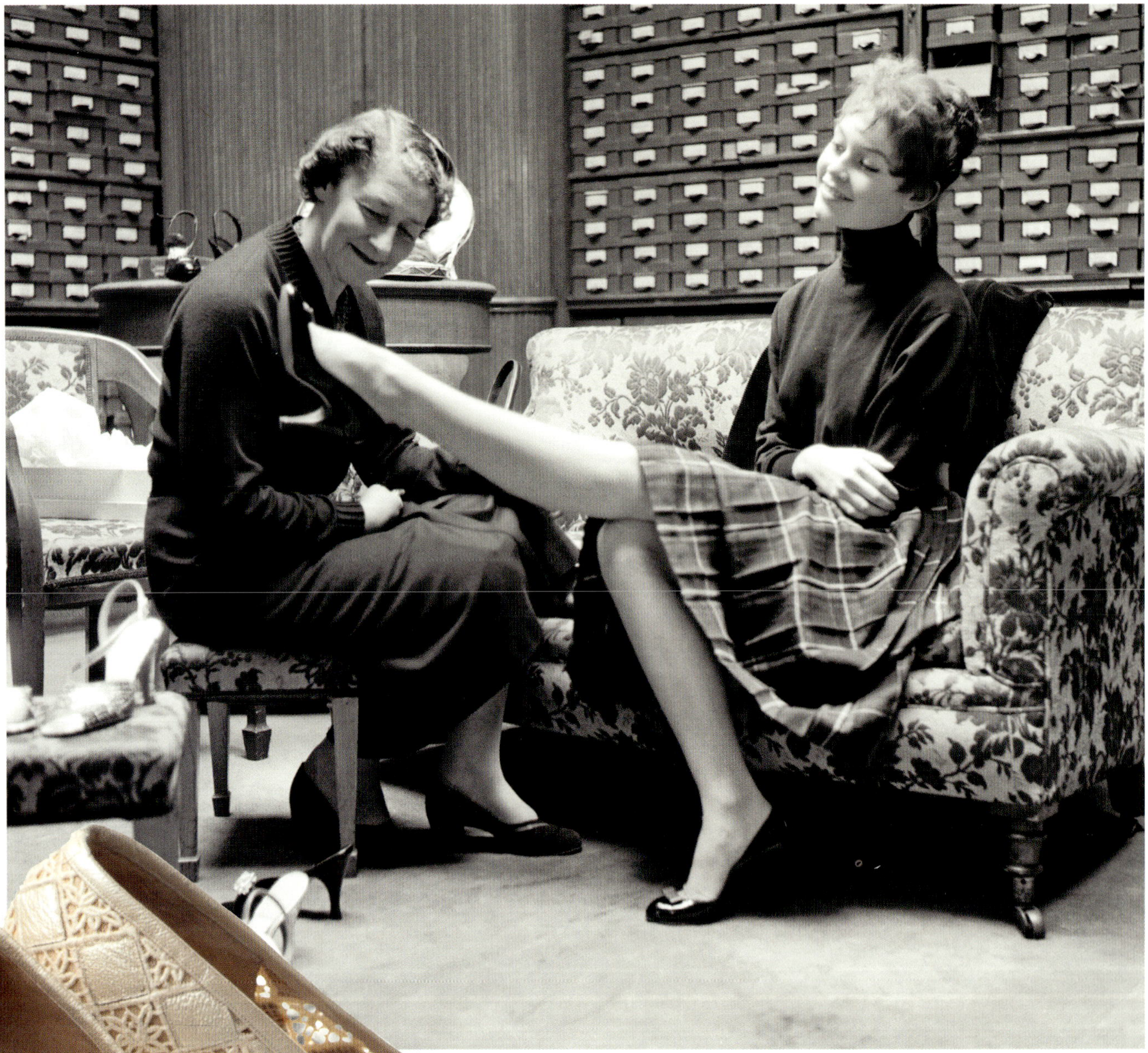

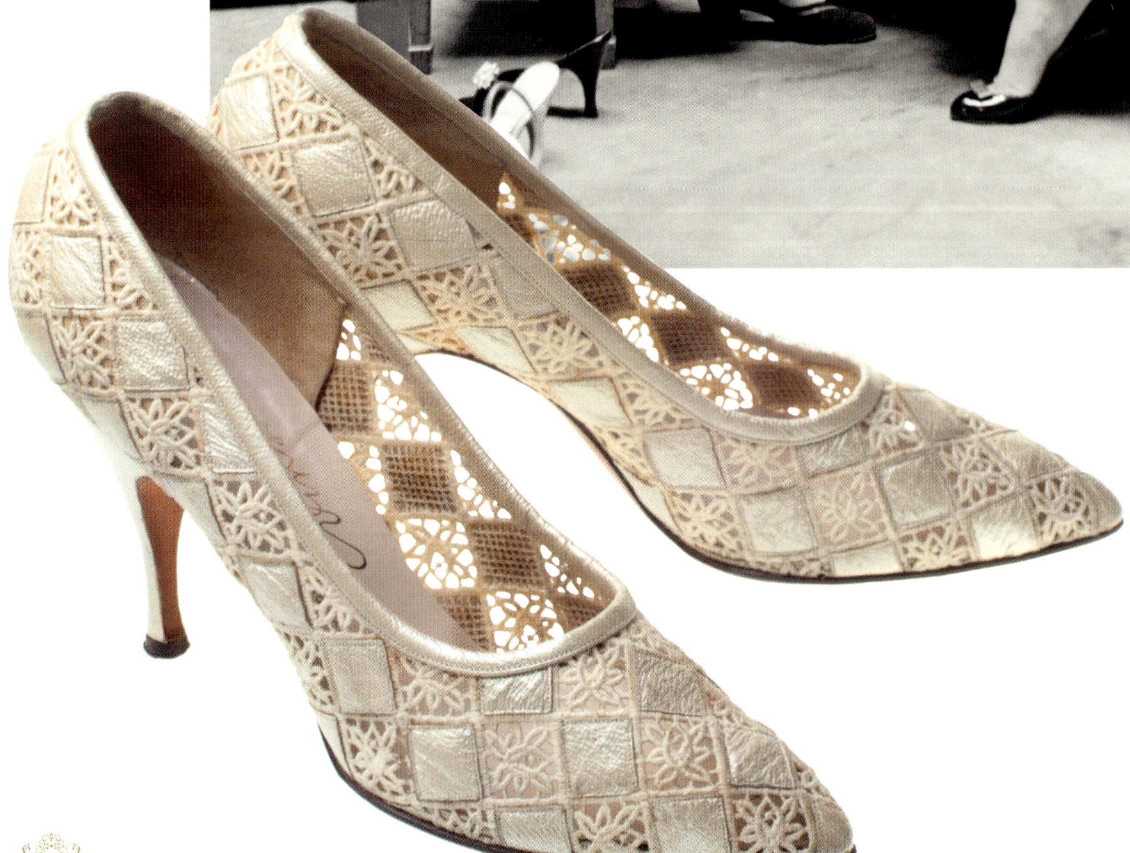

Edward Rayne's success continued and in 1961 he fostered the creation Rayne-Delman Inc in the USA under his control and acquired two other UK businesses: John Plant Ltd and Butlers Bootmakers Ltd. His inherited interest in the theatre and film world continually bore fruit. The 1961 beginnings of the extensive press campaigns around the filming of the epic *Cleopatra*, eventually released in 1963 starring Elizabeth Taylor, resulted in excellent publicity for Rayne, as they re-invented and supplied the Egyptian footwear designs for the overall designer Irene Sharaff, much like Edward had done with Oliver Messel for the 1945 British film *Caesar and Cleopatra* starring Vivien Leigh.

The new Messel-designed shop was equally popular with American visitors to London as well as journalists. The distinguished fashion columnist of *The New York Herald Tribune*, Eugenia Sheppard, syndicated to 80 newspapers and credited by Andy Warhol as 'having invented fashion and gossip together' gave an upbeat Trans-Atlantic view of London fashion in January 1962:

'... best time to look at London couture fashions is a weekend soon after Italian fashions and mid-way through the Paris fashion follies... a plane load of American and Canadian retail store buyers, manufacturers and press, flown over to look at eleven collections in two days by members of the Incorporated Society of London Fashion Designers. London is probably the only spot in the fashion world where designers still think of clothes, first and foremost, as something to improve a poor benighted female. With so many clothes designed as dazzling ideas or something to mass produce and make a million dollars with, you can't help hoping London fashions will keep the sympathetic, personal quality that, even in the mad dash from showroom to showroom, came through this weekend.

Hartnell's show was a real production with hair styles by the famous Rene who was present, in person, behind the scenes. Though everybody expected big, baroque ballgowns, Hartnell has switched to long, slinky, glittering sheaths like the gold one checked in gold crystal beads, or the green one framed in an enormous boa of pale green and white ostrich. One of Hartnell's prettiest is a white crepe dress worn with a white feather hat and Edward Rayne white feather evening pumps and handbag.

Edward Rayne opened his beautiful little boutique, decorated by Oliver Messel on Old Bond Street for a buffet luncheon, and it's almost too bad such a big crowd turned up. The Rayne news in colored patent leathers, especially white, blond and olive green, is rounder toes and liberal heels coming in strong.'

Facing page, top: Brigitte Bardot in 1955 trying on Rayne shoes in the New Bond Street shop, which was opened in 1920, as the fittings clearly indicate. Miss Bardot was in London filming *Doctor At Sea* with Dirk Bogarde as the male lead and her youthful approach to fashion was a clear sign of how things were changing. Daughters no longer all dressed like their mothers and with the demise of Presentations at Court in 1958, formal dressing in everyday life rapidly went out of fashion over the the next six years.
© POPPERFOTO/GETTY IMAGES

Facing page, below: The use of hand-made textiles in Rayne shoes was a well established tradition by the late 1950s when these white stiletto shoes were made, although the fabric used on these shoes may not be hand-made. The intricate lozenge pattern includes applied details of soft leather squares. c.1959. RAYNE ARCHIVE

Below: A similarly labour-intensive luxurious shoe covering is the black lace applied to the pink satin of these Rayne black stiletto-heeled evening shoes. c.1960. RAYNE ARCHIVE

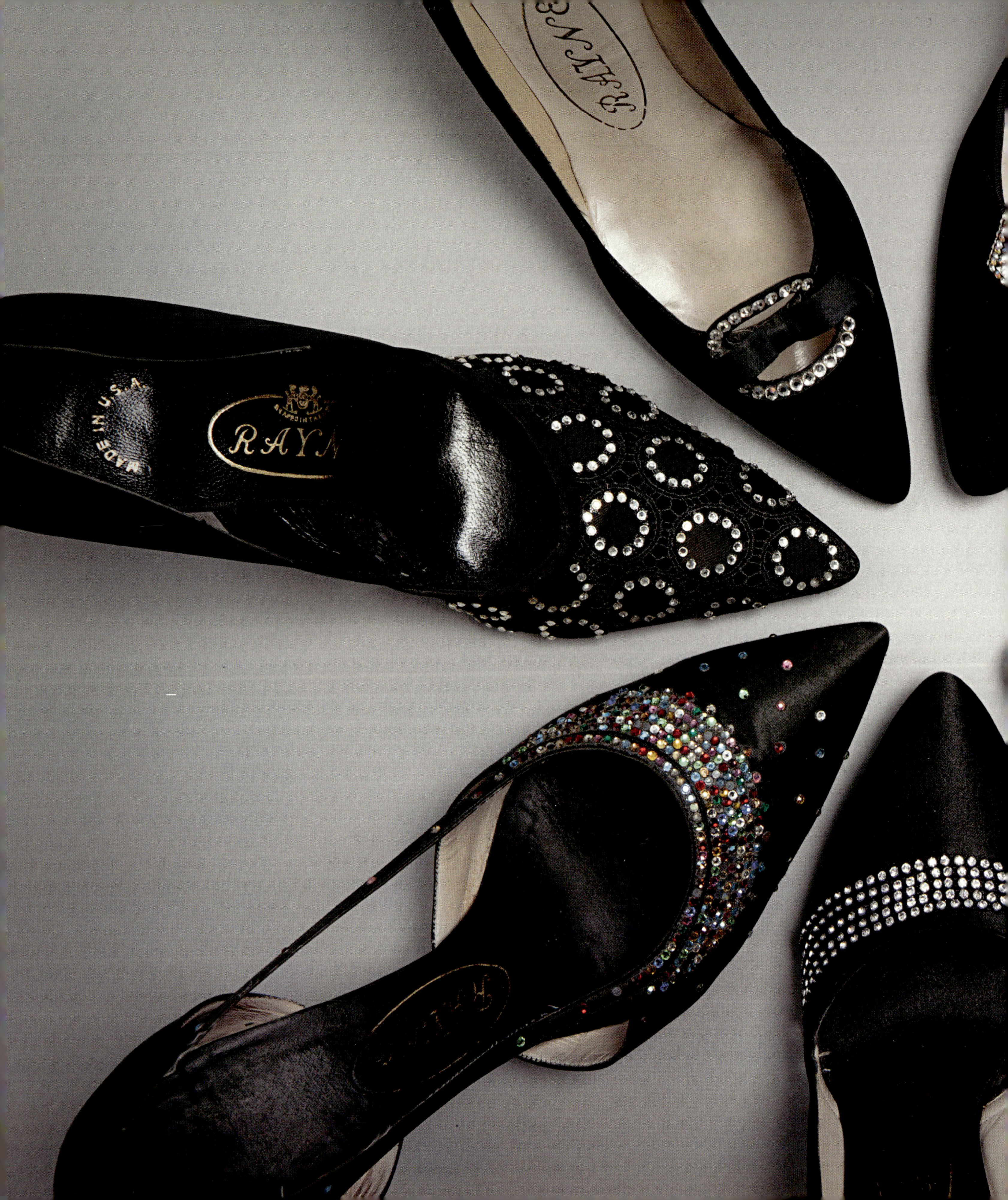
MADE IN U.S.A.

A cluster of black silk, satin and fabric-covered evening shoes illustrating just seven ways in which applied glass brilliants, diamanté trim and ingenious patterns were used by Rayne to create a variety of different styles for varying tastes on what would otherwise be 'little nothing' shoes. c.1955-1985. RAYNE ARCHIVE

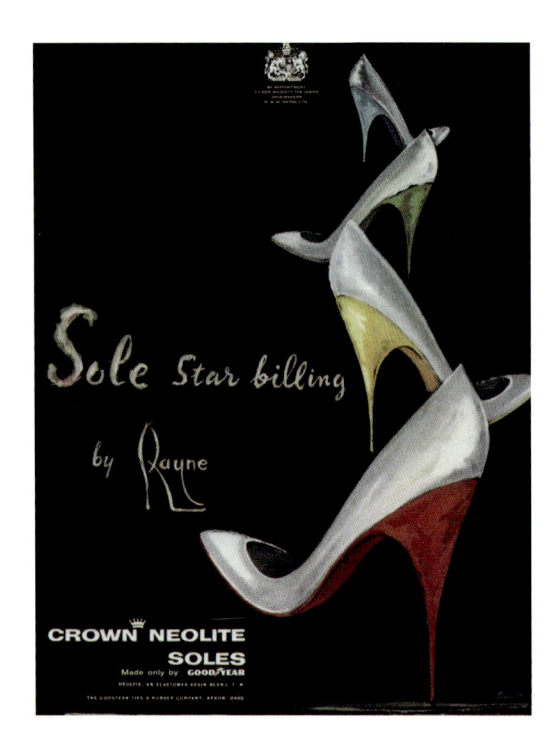

Above: Rayne always sought innovations and new processes for their shoe design and manufacture. The import of sole-softening machinery from the USA had been one of the earliest manufacturing benefits applied to Rayne shoes. American Crown Neolite soles had the full weight of considerable American advertising power behind them – these copywriters' samples of 1953 are compelling: *'Photo shows how flexible buoyant these amazing new soles are – they actually float!'* or *'Now lift a ton less every day by making each step ounces lighter! CROWN NEOLITE SOLE see how much lighter!'* Edward Rayne was convinced. c.1955.   Rayne Archive

Right: As with new processes, so with innovative designs, as demonstrated by the single adjustable gilt kid strap for these pink sandals. c.1958.   Rayne Archive

Facing page: Although Rayne shoes sometimes utilised lace-like fabrics for the uppers, these summery afternoon shoes in pink leather have a striking white leather simulated lace ornament applied to the toes. c.1960.   Rayne Archive

All his working life Edward was in the thick of the fashion world at home and abroad and it was this valuable experience that was later so influential in re-creating a new form of PR for British fashion during his tenure as Chairman of the British Fashion Council.

As fashion never stands still and British taste in most things was rapidly changing by the end of the 1950s, so the structure of British society was changing. In 1958 The Queen abolished Presentations of debutantes at Court, already scaled down to garden parties. The introduction of the Morris and Austin Mini cars and popularity of the universally admired variety of British sports cars meant that the structured more formal way of dressing was no longer necessarily the height of fashion, nor compatible with everyday life. Since the war, younger women of all backgrounds were quite usually seen in trousers or jeans for casual wear and casual shoes took on a new importance in the wardrobe.

In 1960 Mary Quant designed her first leather stacked stiletto shoe and a grown-up version of the round-toed strapped shoes known as 'Shirley Temple' style. Quant's influence on 'street fashion' had an impact on clothing worn by younger people typified by the huge popularity of Quant's mini-skirt in 1963, named after her favourite car. She later wrote, 'It was the girls on the King's Road who invented the mini. I was making easy, youthful, simple clothes, in which you could move, in which you could run and jump and we would make them the length the customer wanted. I wore them very short and the customers would say, "Shorter, shorter".' As she wrote in her autobiography, lunching with Edward Rayne in New York, he gave her an introduction to Geraldine Stutz of the influential Henri Bendell store – 'the chic-est'. This was a characteristically generous gesture on Edward's part.[7]

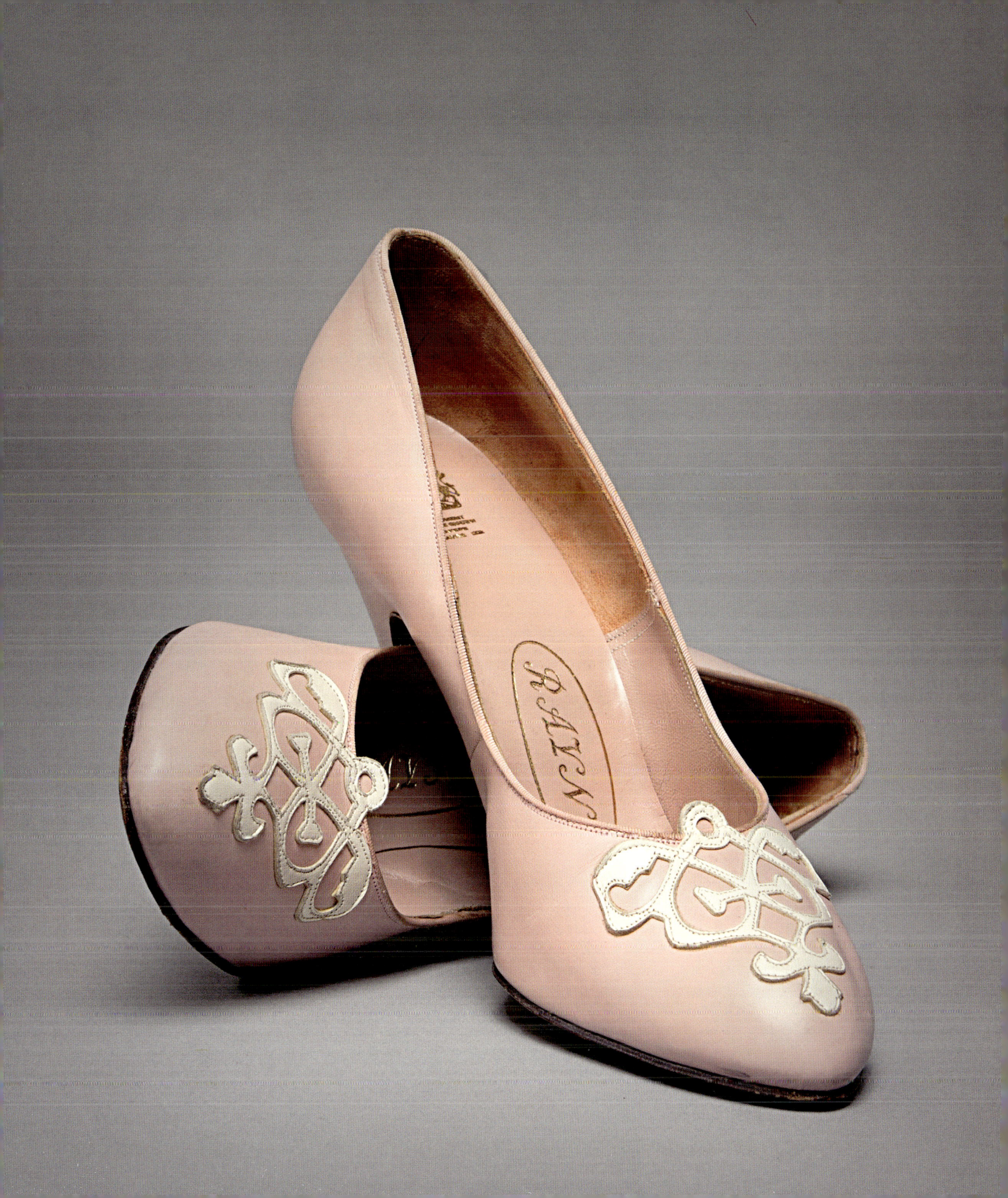

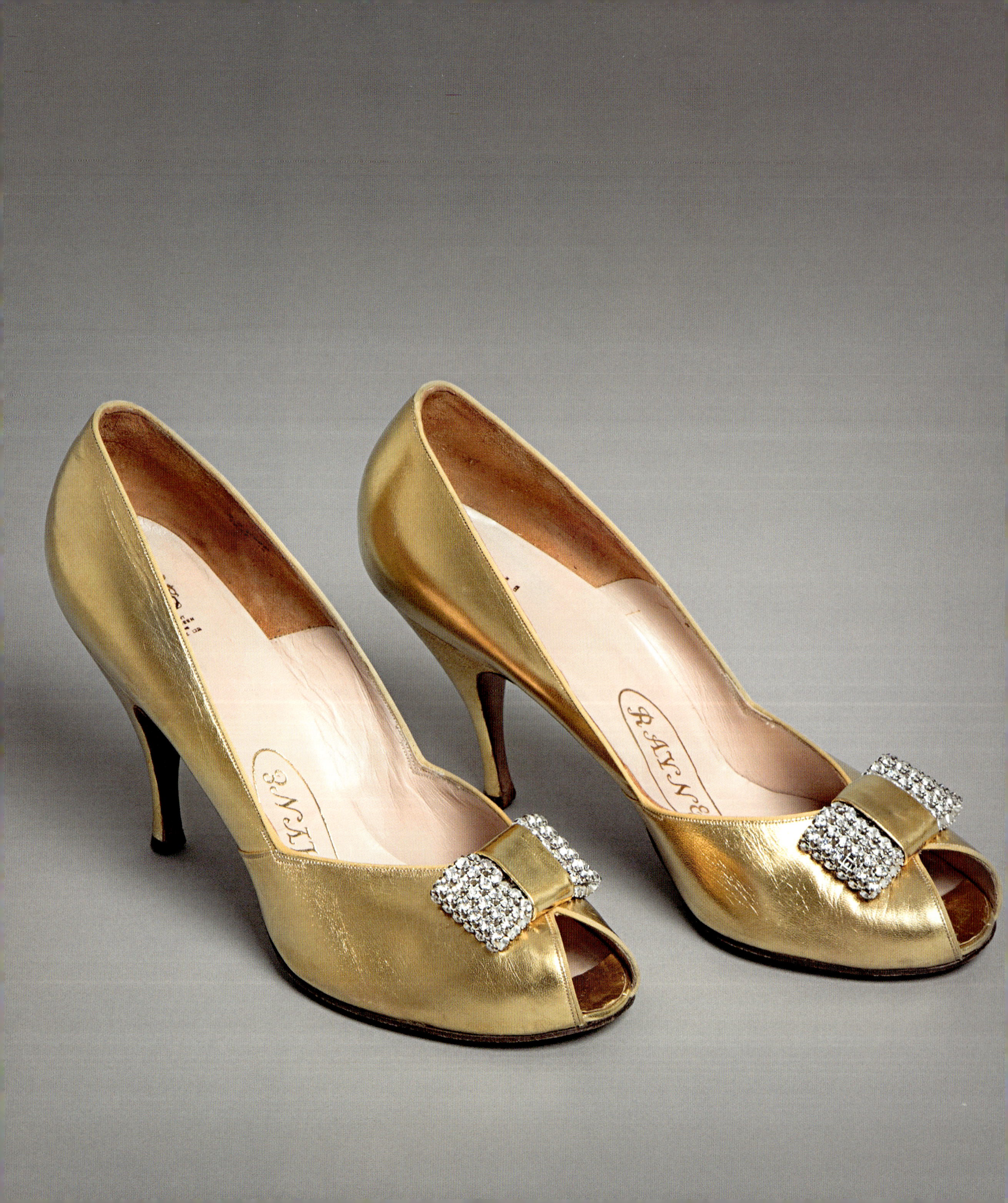

Two contrasting exercises in personal Rayne flamboyance.

Facing page: A pair of gold stiletto-heeled peep-toe cocktail or evening shoes with a bold simulated ribbon bow of glass brilliants with a gilt leather clasp. c.1962.   MICHAEL PICK COLLECTION

Below: A pair of Rayne pink satin-covered boudoir slippers with clear vinyl uppers and swans-down trim. These are made in France and form part of the tradition begun in the 1930s of buying in some novelties for the Rayne shop not made in the London or Ipswich factories. c.1974.   TRACY DOLPHIN COLLECTION

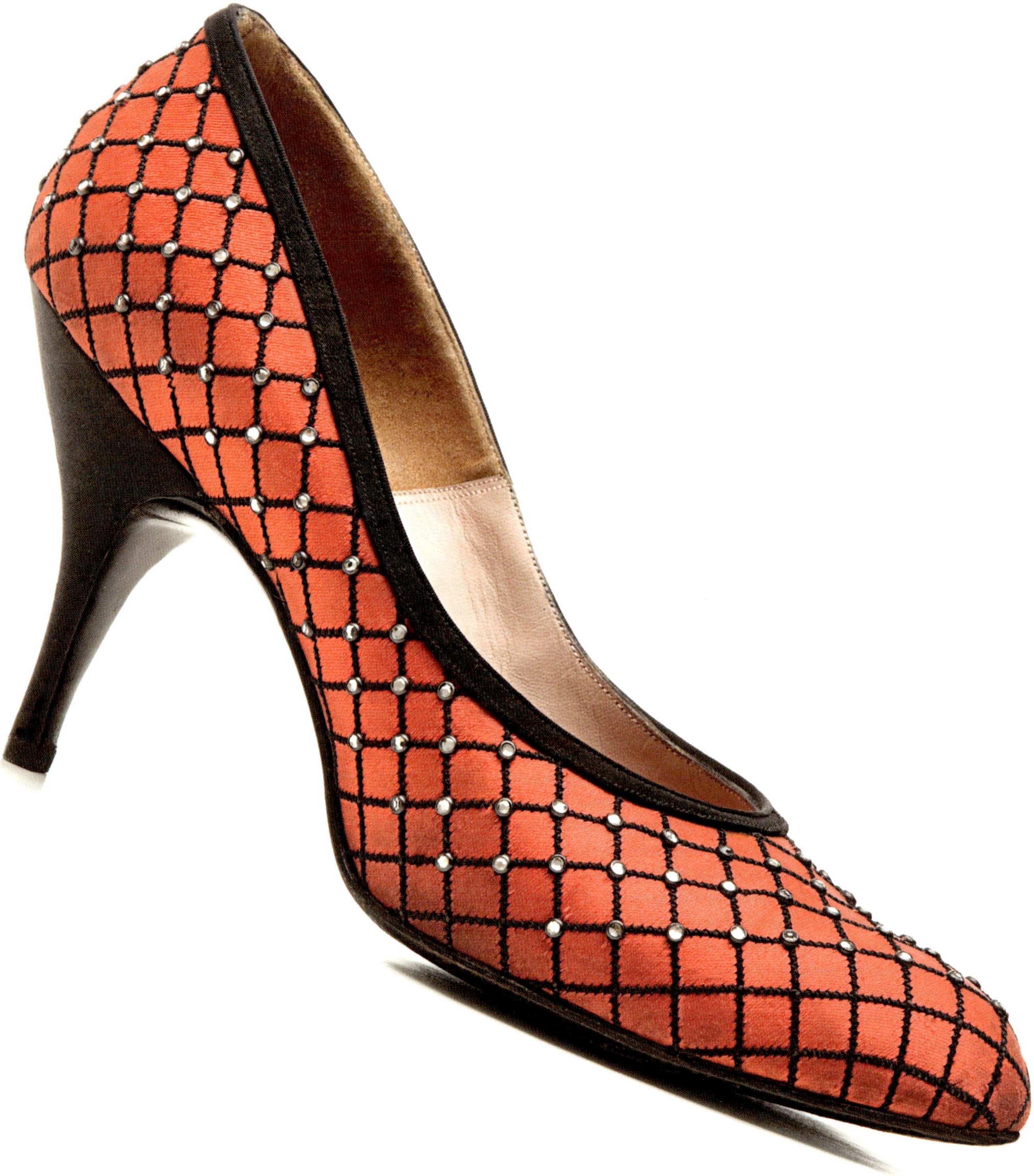

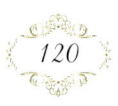

Unsurprisingly, 1963 was a poor financial year for Rayne and the 'Miss Rayne' factory in Ipswich was closed in March followed in November by the Northampton enterprise. It was some form of recompense that Edward's contribution to fashion and retailing was recognised by the award of the *Harper's Bazaar* trophy in that year. At the same time, the growing popularity of the broadsheet press new weekly colour magazines focussed attention on the latest design and fashion with articles by influential younger correspondents and photo-essays by the leading photographers of the day. Fashion was no longer the preserve of the up-market glossy monthly magazines and lifestyle was presented in a radical new youthful manner.

Ever pragmatic, Edward Rayne fought back with a variety of new designs including those commissioned from Mary Quant. By 1967-1968 he had acquired all the issued share capital of Rayne-Delman Inc. with a view to further American expansion, whilst selling the Randall Shoe business. His business friendships with American shoe designers and manufacturers included David Evins, and Herb and Beth Levine, although she maintained that he – and others – copied some of her designs, an habitual hazard in the shoe manufacturing industry. Edward and David Evins were good business allies as Eugenia Sheppard underlined in her syndicated column 'Summit on Shoes' (29 September, 1964) describing a walk taken by both men along upper Madison Avenue to observe what women were wearing. Rayne said that the American look had influenced the whole world, whilst Evins counters with the compliment on lighter structure coming from Europe. The two men then went to hold a telephone conference with Roger Vivier, 'The summit concludes with a sigh of relief, feet are here to stay.'

The part transparent vinyl uppers or Lucite heels used by Rayne and Delman in the 1950s and '60s had been very successful and Edward found advertising backing for the use of DuPont's 'Corfam' as synthetic patent leather and Jean Matthew considered the Rayne Corfam shoes to be excellent. The process was scrapped after the competition led to lower real leather prices. Amongst the many eye-catching components of Rayne shoes in the 1960s, were colourful snake-skins sold by Teddy and Arthur Edelman. Many affluent women bought shoes made of these skins, including the Maharanees of Jaipur and Baroda, who in 1961 bought about 50 pairs of brilliantly coloured Indo-China gold-lined crocodile court shoes.

Above: Glass brilliants or rhinestones were often used as decoration on Rayne evening shoes from 1946 onwards. Seldom were they as lavishly applied as on these chisel-toed pair with the cross-over straps. These were almost certainly made to be used as part of a special window display or for an advertising shoot. c.1962. RAYNE ARCHIVE

Facing page: The subtle use of reflecting glass points is seen here applied to the intersecting strands of the black trellis design covering the rose ground of the black stiletto-heeled Rayne evening shoes. The toes are left bare of the glass decoration at a point where damage would occur from scuffing. c.1958. TRACY DOLPHIN COLLECTION

Below: Two colourways of the same Rayne design with minimal trim and decorative bows all utilising one of the many synthetic fibres of the period to give an iridescent effect. The novelty of these developments in such fibres was fully exploited by designers of the period. c.1960. TRACY DOLPHIN COLLECTION

Facing page: By the 1960s, fashion was rapidly becoming youth-orientated and the established dress designers were beginning to lose ground to what became termed 'street fashion' in the newly styled magazines of the period, notably *Queen* and the *Sunday Times Colour Magazine,* launched in February 1962. New decorating ideas, such as that for *art nouveau* patterns, were featured in the pages of the magazine from the mid to the late 1960s and the shoes shown here – utilising a fabric based on an *art-nouveau* design in muted shades – typify the era and the advent of the mini-skirt. RAYNE ARCHIVE

By the late 1960s changing London shopping habits led to the closure of the 1920 Rayne New Bond Street shop. A new one was opened in Bruton Street near Norman Hartnell in 1967. This location was unsuccessful, but sales to the emerging Japanese market and in the new Rayne salon in Harrods were successful. The increasingly youthful chic of the Knightsbridge/Chelsea shopping areas resulted in a new Rayne shop with interiors by theatre designer Carl Toms at 157 Brompton Road, not far from Harrods. This was closed in 1987, when the business world of takeovers and asset control meant that Rayne was effectively sidelined as a brand.

In Regent Street, the Rayne shop opened in the 1920s continued to flourish, and was particularly aimed at county or provincial ladies wanting wider fittings. Here too a completely modern re-fit in 1966 gave it fresh appeal with the designs of celebrity interior decorator Kenneth Partridge,[8] which lasted until it was closed in 1982 to maximise the value of a very long lease. Edward had been impressed by the sets designed by Partridge for the INCSOC annual shows for Queen Elizabeth The Queen Mother and for Hartnell's ground floor Bruton Street boutique, Le Petit Salon. Partridge was also asked to produce window and other sets for the interiors of the Bond Street store and the youthful designs were echoed in the famous advertising campaigns, some by the fashionable *trompe l'oeil* artist Martin Battersby, and latterly featuring the bespectacled face of Edward himself.

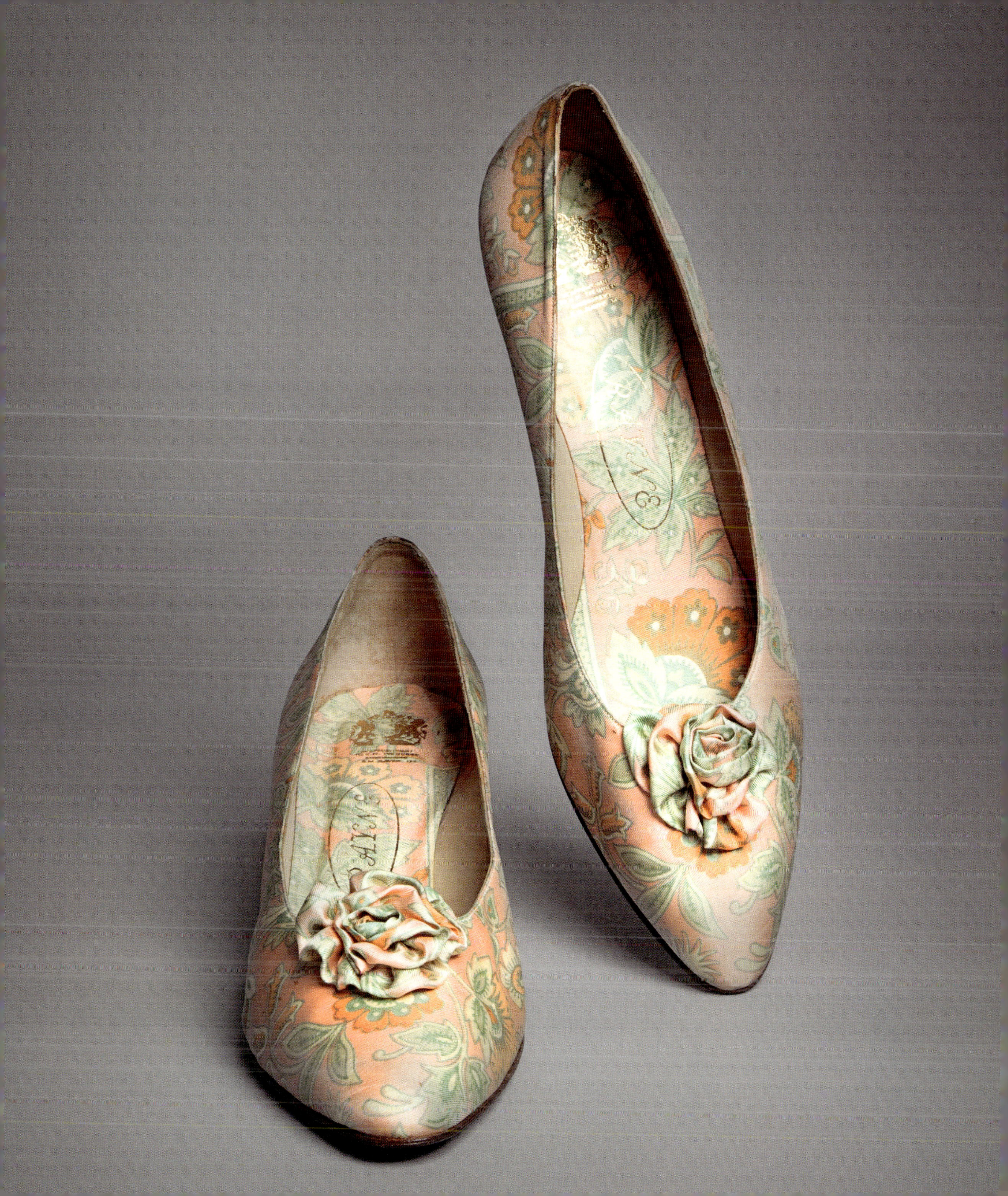

This page: The lower-heeled, sling-back design in coral red and black versions features a moulded 'glass' roundel clasped above the toe. There was also a 'horse-shoe' variant and these sophisticated shoes were ideal for evenings out for clients of all ages. They evoke the new youth trends in fashion and dance. Discos were an established feature of 1960s nightlife and the shoes worn reflected the simplicity of women's dress with an emphasis on legs and mini-skirts. RAYNE ARCHIVE

Facing page: A pair of silvered gilt-laced evening shoes capturing the spirit of 1920s Rayne designs in a mid-1960s idiom, as still seen on the feet of Mrs Peel played by Diana Rigg in early surviving episodes of *The Avengers*. RAYNE ARCHIVE

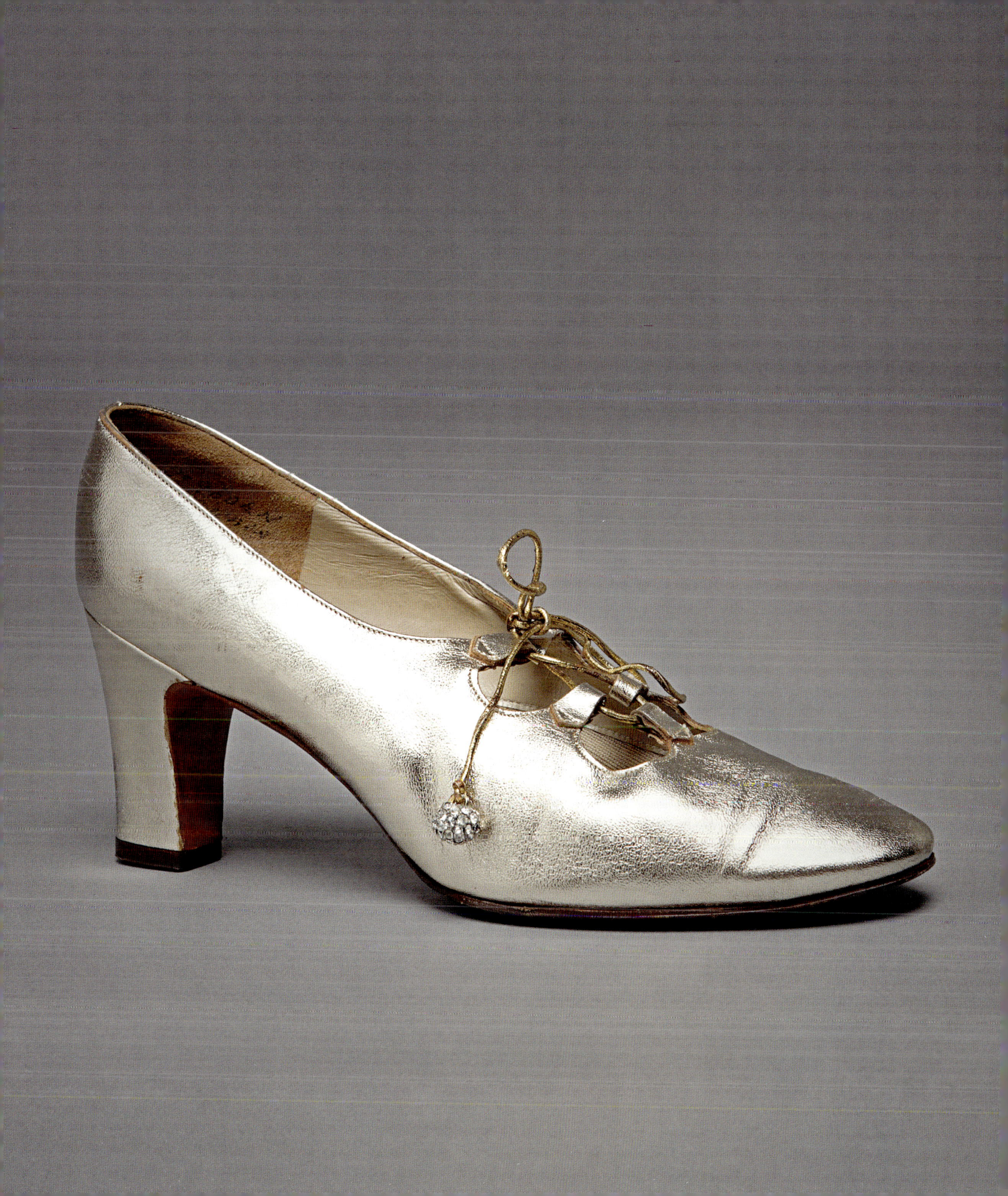

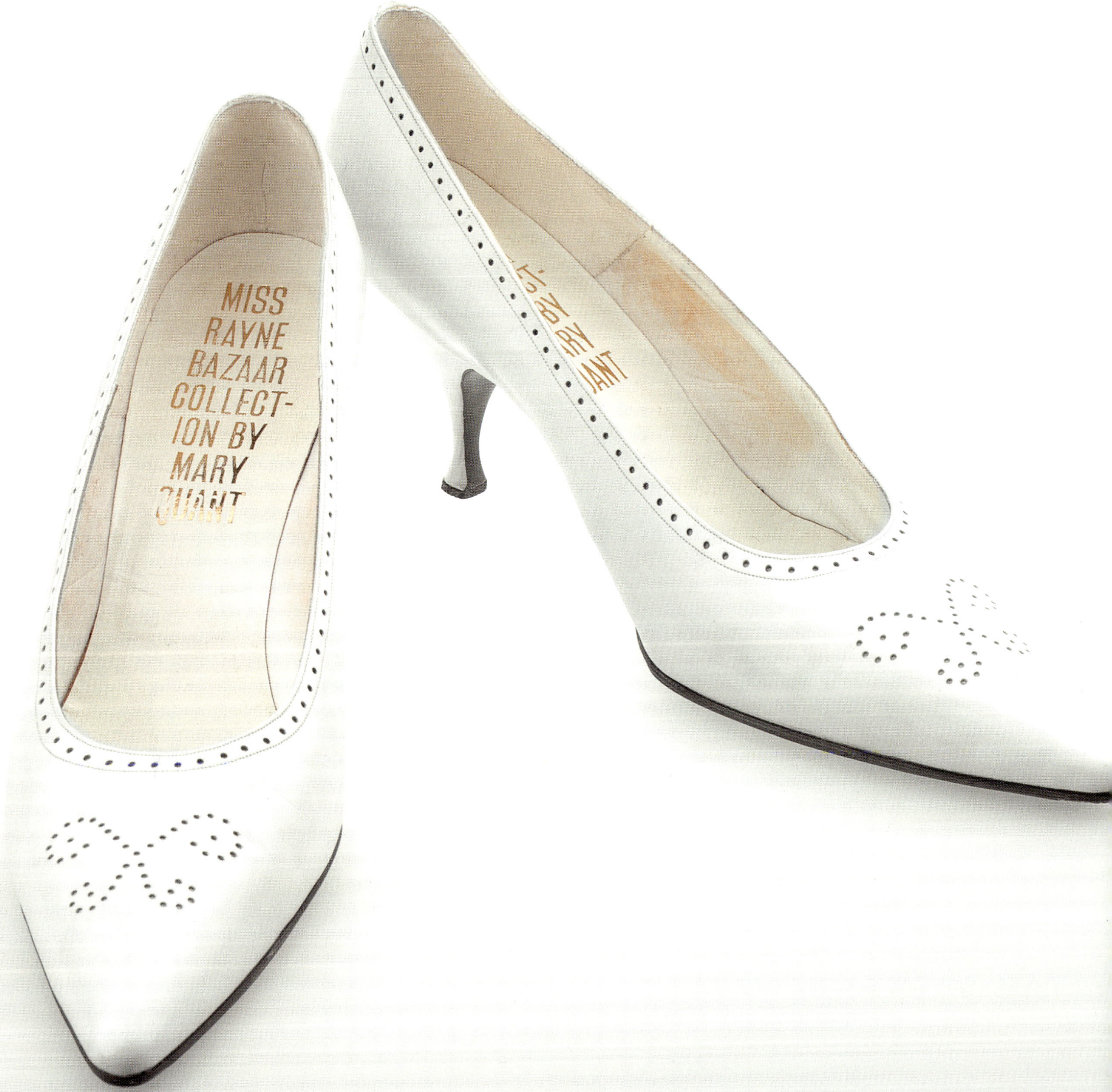
MISS
RAYNE
BAZAAR
COLLECT-
ION BY
MARY
QUANT

Facing page: A pair of white Miss Rayne 'Bazaar Collection' shoes by Mary Quant with very slim Louis heels and punched decoration. Ever-attuned to the changing winds of fashion, Mary Quant was chosen by Edward Rayne as his first designer representing the new young generation of designers in 1960. TRACY DOLPHIN COLLECTION

Below: A pair of maroon velvet Rayne evening shoes with low heels and a simple ribbon and ring strap. c.1969. This design was available in many colours and is a close copy of a popular late 1920s version, one of which is in the collection of the Victoria & Albert Museum. During the '60s, the fashions and music of the 1920s enjoyed a revival due to the influence of the acclaimed BBC dramatisation of John Galsworthy's *Forsyte Saga*, which ran from 1967-1969. MICHAEL PICK COLLECTION

With memories of the successful 1958 press show at La Tour D'Argent in Paris in conjunction with British Airways, from 1970-1987 a Rayne shop was operated on the rue du Faubourg St-Honoré in Paris. Lanvin and Nina Ricci used and promoted Rayne shoes.[9] The Lanvin connection resulted in the Rayne-Andrea Pfister collaboration, building on Edward's success with younger designers following Mary Quant, and including Jean Muir, who rather grandly considered him the 'best British shoemaker of his age. He worked to a quality that matched anything from abroad'. He would no doubt have considered that foreign competition came fairly close to Rayne perfection. In any case, like his father before him, he was later decorated by the French Republic. For service to Anglo-French co-operation in the field of fashion he was appointed a Chevalier de l'Ordre National du Mérite in 1984.

A pair of Rayne Space Age 'disco dazzlers' in brightly burnished metallic silver with wide 'tongues' curling down to a hammered design. c.1970. The design epitomises the disco culture of the period and much of the loud design that was apparent in ultra-fashionable clothes of the period. RAYNE ARCHIVE

Sleek Rayne elegance amid the fashion turmoil of the late 1960s and early 1970s, these court shoes with low tapering heels seem to reflect the history of H. & M. Rayne shoe designs with the assured sunburst effect given by the applied roundels studded with glittering glass brilliants. The model came in bronze, other colours and was re-introduced in later years with varying heel designs. c.1975. MICHAEL PICK COLLECTION

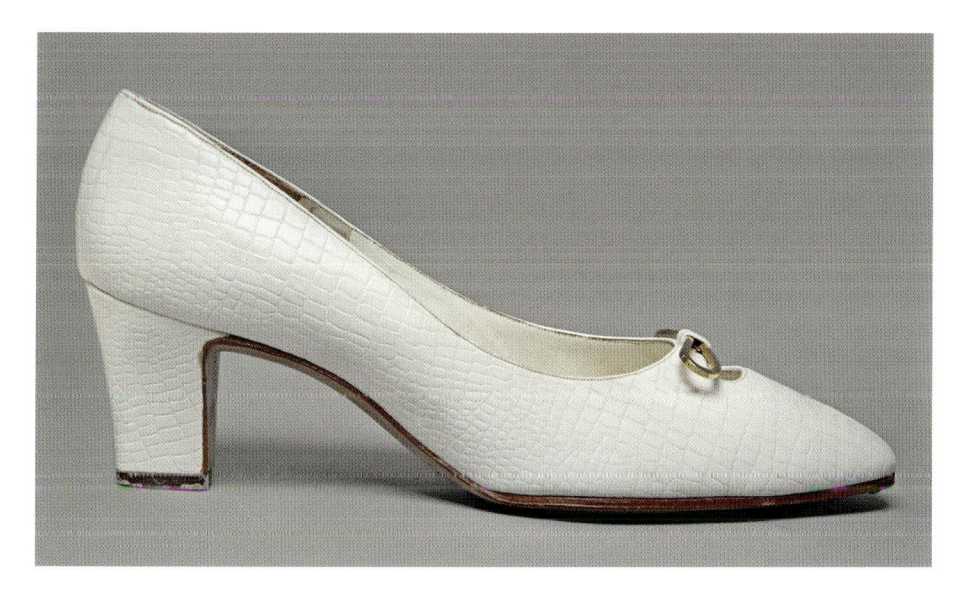

Top left: Another mock reptile summer white Rayne shoe with a small cut-out detail enhanced with gilt trim in the form of a rigid metal bow and less aggressive heels, is a design likely to appeal to older clients, whilst still having the fashionable 'mock-croc' decoration of the uppers. c.1972. RAYNE ARCHIVE

Left: A more sophisticated version of the shiny fashion known as the 'wet look' is found in the pair of Rayne black patent shoes with the silvered chrome-like heels and upswept decoration with metal trim, which was varied on other design of this model. c.1972. RAYNE ARCHIVE

Right: There was a romantic form of dress which expressed itself in velvet and ruffles, something Rayne also catered for, as expressed in the shoes seen on p.123 and in the fabric samples here. JEAN MATTHEW ESTATE

Below: A pair of Rayne yellow fabric-covered light evening sandals with low heels and a ruched fabric gathered through a ring on the vamp forms the other approach to fashion at the time. RAYNE ARCHIVE

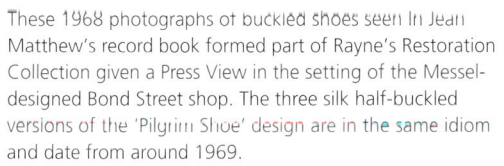

These 1968 photographs of buckled shoes seen in Jean Matthew's record book formed part of Rayne's Restoration Collection given a Press View in the setting of the Messel-designed Bond Street shop. The three silk half-buckled versions of the 'Pilgrim Shoe' design are in the same idiom and date from around 1969.
Record book: Jean Matthew Estate
Shoes: Rayne Archive

Designers

The young fashion designers promoted by Edward Rayne in 1966 were Jean Muir, Gerald McCann and Roger Nelson (facing page). In 1978, Bill Gibb also designed for Rayne as did Clive Shilton for six seasons from 1982 and then Bruce Oldfield in 1986. They all complemented the Rayne style with originality and elegance. In 1971 Edward's beneficial influence was recognised by his election as a Fellow of the Royal Society of Arts.

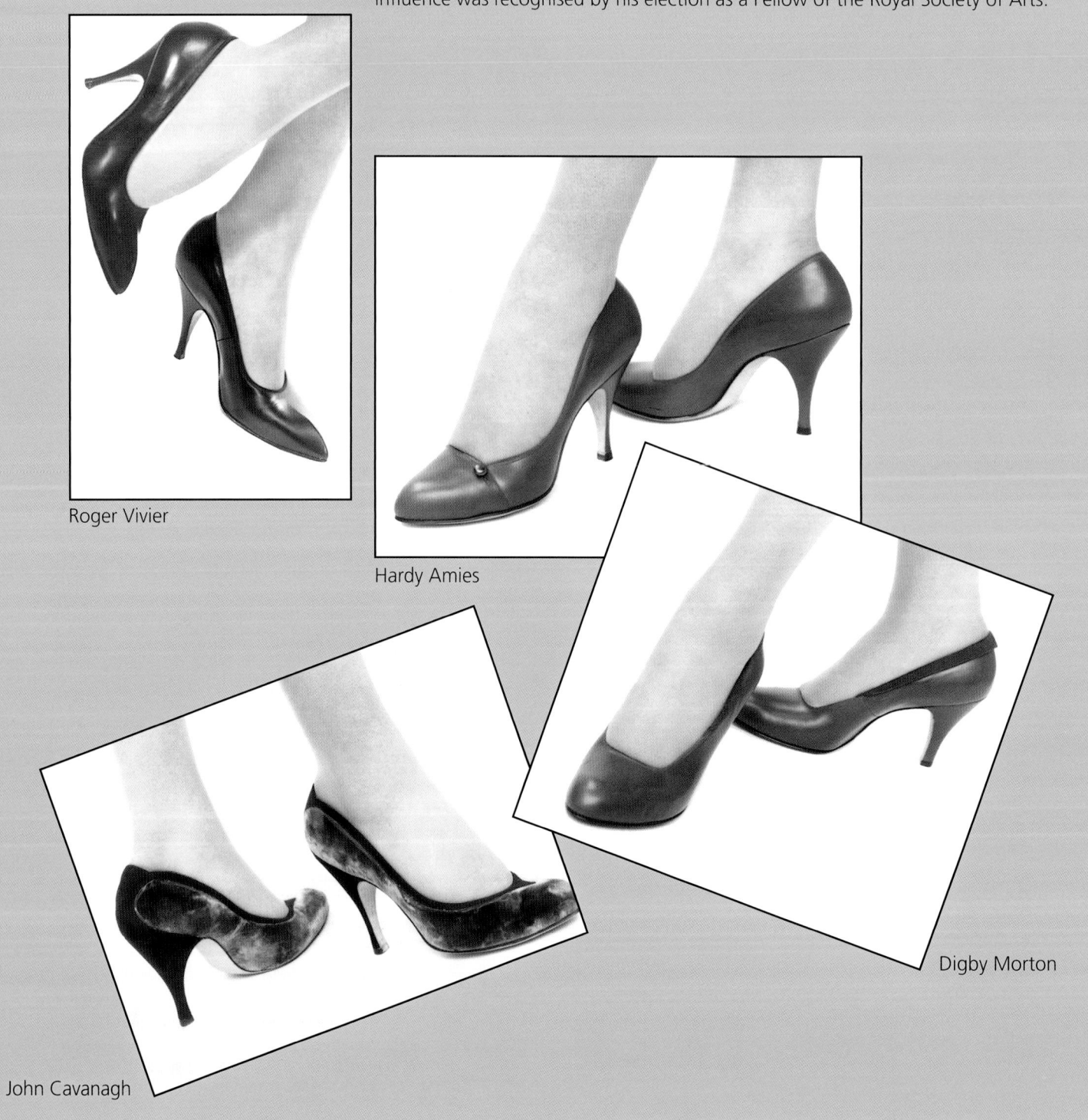

Roger Vivier

Hardy Amies

Digby Morton

John Cavanagh

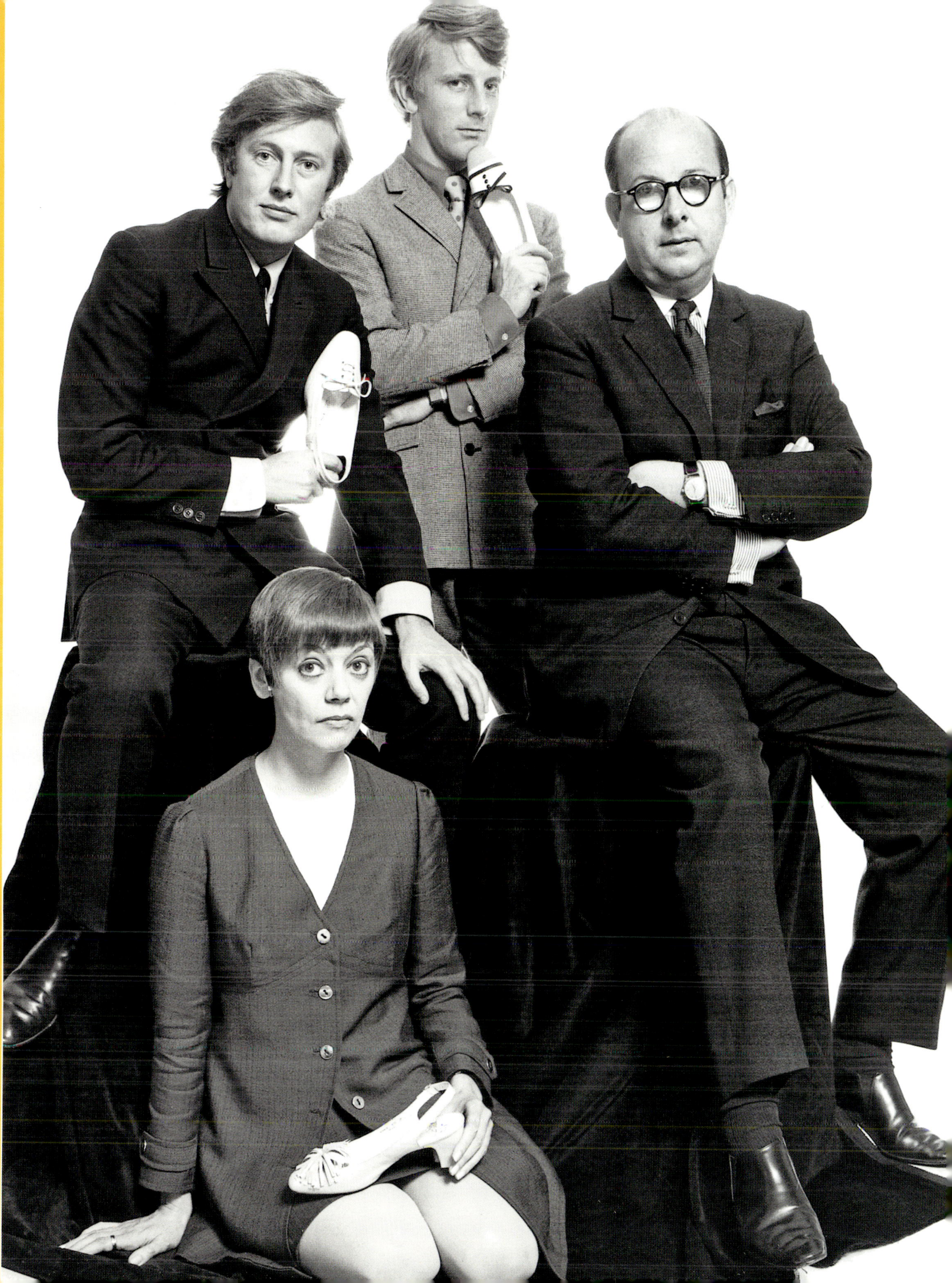

Left and facing page: Sir Norman Hartnell (1901-1979) was generally acclaimed as Britain's leading 20th-century designer, almost from the moment he first opened his business in 1923. His friendship with Joseph and then Edward Rayne resulted in many Hartnell designs for Rayne, not least the 1947 wedding shoes for HRH Princess Elizabeth and her Coronation shoes as Queen Elizabeth II in 1953. He also designed a range of day and evening shoes circa 1946, as well as the 'rose' shoe designed for his 1959 Summer Collection. MICHAEL PICK COLLECTION

Below: These mid-1980s shoes by Bruce Oldfield for Rayne reflect something of the romantic nature of Hartnell's most prestigious commissions. RAYNE ARCHIVE

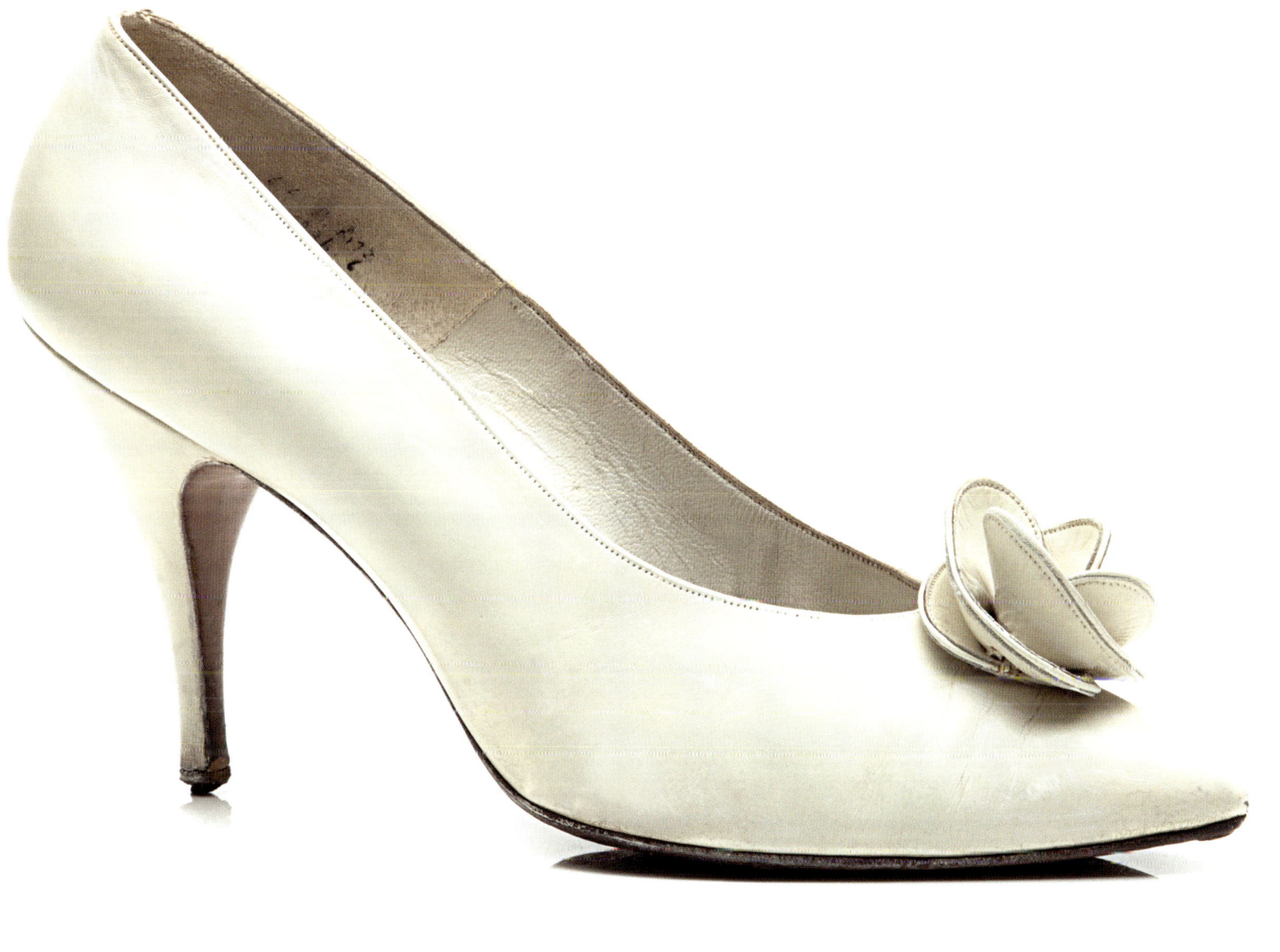

One of the more striking and possibly more uncomfortable Rayne innovations was the use of transparent vinyl uppers, which could prove to be uncomfortably hot in the sun. Allied to the use of Lucite or Perspex for heels, the visual results could be stunning, at their best, as with the pair of satin-bow trimmed sandals with the transparent heels enclosing a leaf and flower-head motif. c.1978. MICHAEL PICK COLLECTION

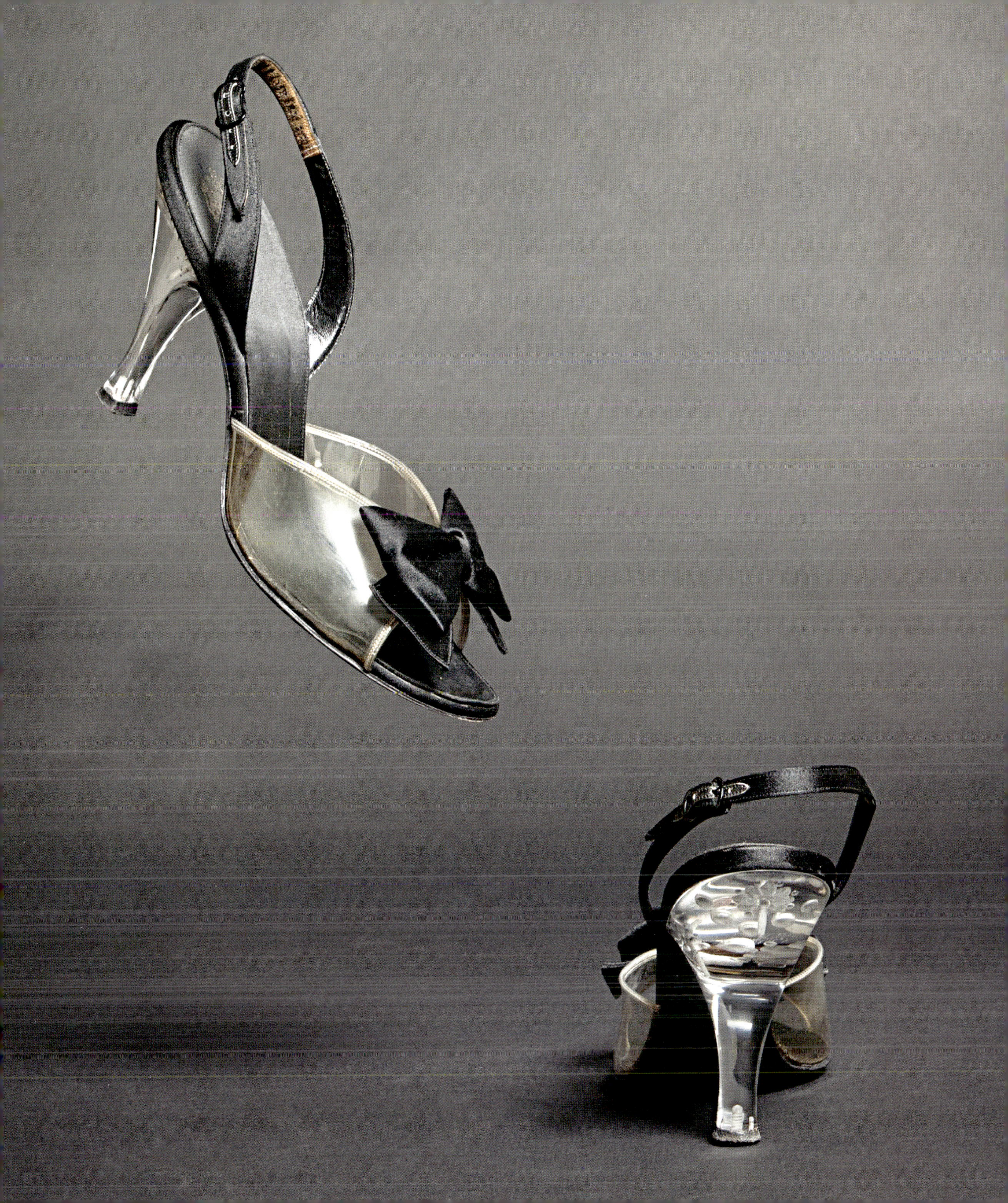

A pair of Rayne classic patent leather brown court shoes with a medium heel and a flat ribbed silk bow. This form of classic Rayne shoe design with a flat bow was first designed for the legendary actress Gertrude Lawrence (1898-1952) in the 1920s; the shape of the bow changed to complement the fashionable shoe designs over the years. A signed portrait photograph by Bertram Park dedicated by Gertrude Lawrence to Jospeh Rayne in 1928 is in the collection of the National Portrait Gallery, London. This design and others like it, became favourites with HM The Queen and can be seen worn in numerous photographs. c.1975. MICHAEL PICK COLLECTION

Capitalising on its British roots, Edward Rayne opened another in-store concession at Harvey Nichols, as with Harrods, Rayne had sold shoes there in the preceding decades and now added the 'Rayne International' label to its output. By 1973 the whole method of retailing was changing fast to adapt to a new generation of consumers, the Debenham Group buying many established local British department stores, all suffering from similar age-related image problems. Rayne was also acquired by the group, together with other British brands, such as Hardy Amies. This not only brought in contributed capital, but benefits for the workforce including pension funds and greater job security. Making and stocking shoes in a wide variety of sizes and shapes is expensive enough, but the outlay continually increased when fashion swung in increasingly wider and unpredictable circles through the 1960s and 1970s when young and older clientele often required different styles.

The everlasting appeal of Rayne satin evening sandals is summed up by this stiletto-heeled pair with bold diamanté-trimmed soft bows dating from the late 1950s and revived in the 1980s. c.1959. MICHAEL PICK COLLECTION

The supply of good quality materials at a reasonable cost was also becoming problematic. When the influential fashion correspondent of *The Times*, Prudence Glynn, met Edward and his factory director in charge of production in September 1976, she was amazed to learn that leather had to be imported from Italy and Germany, because the quality required for Rayne shoes was becoming unavailable in Britain.

Rayne had already begun to import and retail shoes from Italy, as the margins in London were lower and overheads higher. Another problem facing the factory was the decline in available local skilled labour. Shoe making, especially at the luxury end, is a complicated and demanding craft and young workers could find easier work for the same money. Edward was determined to carry on the London factory as long as possible and also tend to the needs of long-term customers determined to buy the best of British craftsmanship, headed by the Royal Family. In 1977, the Silver Jubilee Year, The Queen recognised Edward Rayne's contribution to British business and service to the Royal Family by appointing Edward a Commander of the Royal Victorian Order, within the personal gift of The Queen.[10]

Times and business conditions were increasingly difficult for a company producing a great variety of fashionable shoes of the highest quality. As Edward said in 1980, 'It's an era in which you can't regiment fashion. As women get better and better educated, they are dressing to suit themselves. Appreciating their own taste,' he ended tactfully.[11]

The eighties brought a renewal of power-dressing an updated version of 1940s Adrian or Joan Crawford film style, emphasised by Hollywood films and the world-wide success of the television show *Dynasty* (1981-1989) starring Joan Collins – another Rayne client. The political world was shaken up by Mrs Thatcher, a firm supporter of British fashion and products, including Rayne shoes; but it was the marriage of Lady Diana Spencer to the Prince of Wales that created a new interest in young glamour. The Princess followed what had become a royal tradition and often bought shoes from Rayne, notably to go with some of her most elegant clothes designed by Bruce Oldfield, who designed shoe collections for Rayne in 1986 and 1987.

The business enjoyed good publicity, Edward Rayne was appointed a director of Debenhams from the time of the take-over in 1975 until 1988 and chairman of Harvey Nichols, their flagship store, from 1978 until 1988. In 1978 he took over from Eric Crabtree as chairman of the Fashion Multiples Division and became chairman of Lotus Shoes, a company he had sought to buy in the early 1950s. By 1980 he was in direct control of Harvey Nichols, but in *The Times* (15 January 1980), Prudence Glynn pondered

Rayne's future. The sale of Debenhams by the Burton Group resulted in the sale of H. & M. Rayne to David Graham in 1987, and Edward ceased to have any business interests in what had been his family's firm for a century. As Prudence Glynn put it, 'What an irony for Mr Rayne to be a party to the fate of his own cherished family firm. Not very funny to see your patrimony being bounced about like a squash ball.' His situation brought sympathetic messages from both The Queen and Queen Elizabeth The Queen Mother.

His PR agent Peter Hope Lumley wrote an affectionate 'Personal Tribute' to his client 'Edward Rayne was a bon viveur, loving his food and drink, and resembling nothing so much as a character from *Wind in the Willows* – a benevolent Mr Toad with his huge pebble-lensed spectacles and a rather endearing waddle. But his appearance masked a razor-sharp brain and his work in bringing together the many faceted body of the fashion world was achieved with charm, acute knowledge and love of business, and, above all, a fanatical belief in the potential of the British fashion industry.'

One of the last Rayne designs of the 1980s emulating the 1950s, this colourful bow and ribbon printed blue fabric-covered pair of day shoes conjures up the years of 'power dressing', mixed with the sexiness that is inherent in the best Rayne designs. 1989. TRACY DOLPHIN COLLECTION

Edward's two sons, another Edward junior (who soon resigned) and Nicholas with his wife Lulu, a shoe designer, were still active as the latest Rayne generation working with the new owners. In 1990, H. & M. Rayne was sold again to Richard Kottler; the business itself did not last past 1994. As Jean Matthew wrote, 'by 1987 everything relating to Rayne… was sold… the last Rayne collection with family involvement was for spring 1988' Just as tragically, the unique Oliver Messel interiors of the Rayne Bond Street shop were destroyed over a weekend, just before a preservation order could be applied.

Edward Rayne's successful business career did not end with the loss of the family firm. In 1988 his work in establishing and presiding over the British Fashion Council was recognised by The Queen, who also acknowledged his work for the Royal Family, when he was appointed a Knight Commander of the Royal Victorian Order (KCVO). This might be thought to be the pinnacle of his achievements, but the following year he was instrumental in creating the British Fashion Awards, still a vital part of the British fashion industry's PR machine.

Edward's last years ended as sadly as those of his father Joseph and grandfather Henry. He died at home on 7 February 1992 in a terrible fire, from which his wife luckily escaped. His family records and memorabilia were almost all lost. During his active and productive life he had been the favourite and honoured vendor of shoes to most of the ladies of the British Royal Family and an extraordinary international clientele, including a galaxy of stars of stage and screen. It is a fact that most of the world's most beautiful and notable women of the twentieth century had at some time worn Rayne shoes during his lifetime.

In addition to many awards, Edward Rayne was President of the Royal Warrant Holders Association in 1964 and Honorary Treasurer from 1974 until 1992; a consultant to Marks and Spencer; the instigator of the Burton Group setting up the School of Business Management at the Royal College of Fashion; President of the British Footwear Manufacturers Federation; President of the British Boot and Shoe Institution and of the Clothing and Footwear Institute; a member of the Export Council for Europe and also of both the European Trade Committee and the Franco-British Council. In 1981 he was the first shoemaker to be elected Master of the Worshipful Company of Patternmakers.[12] Henry and Mary Rayne would surely have been proud of their descendant's extraordinary careers during the century following the establishment of their theatrical costume business on the Waterloo Road. With their own drive and initiative perhaps they would have expected nothing less.

Facing page: A pair of highly personal high-heeled tomato-red and silver sling-back high-heeled Rayne shoes, the vamps suggesting an insect, in this case a bee, the signature-mascot of designer Bill Gibb (1943-1989). Edward Rayne had the foresight to include Bill Gibb amongst his 'Young Designers' group and this shoe is a rare specimen of Gibb's designing skills, most usually confined to clothing during his sadly short career. TRACY DOLPHIN COLLECTION

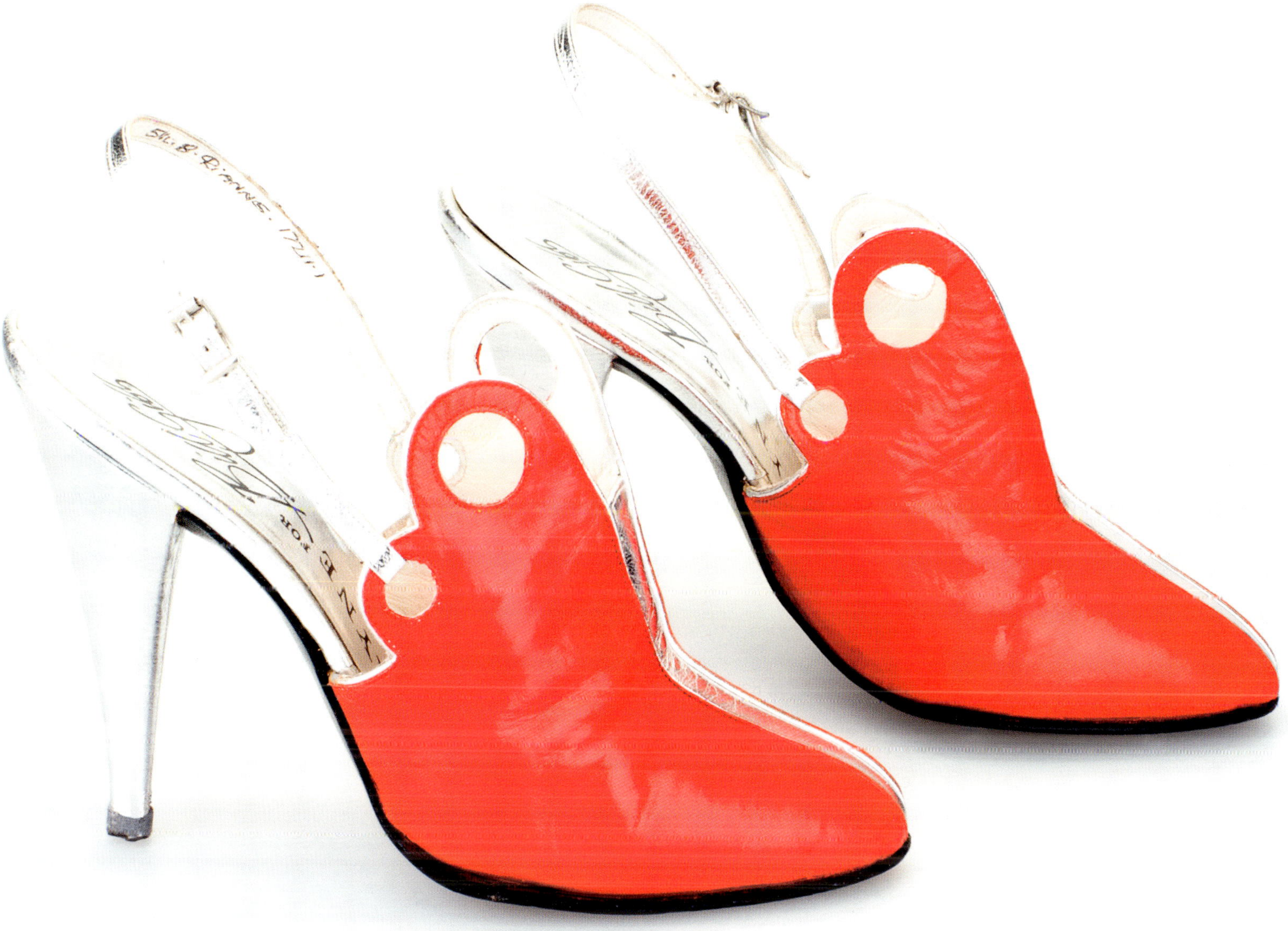

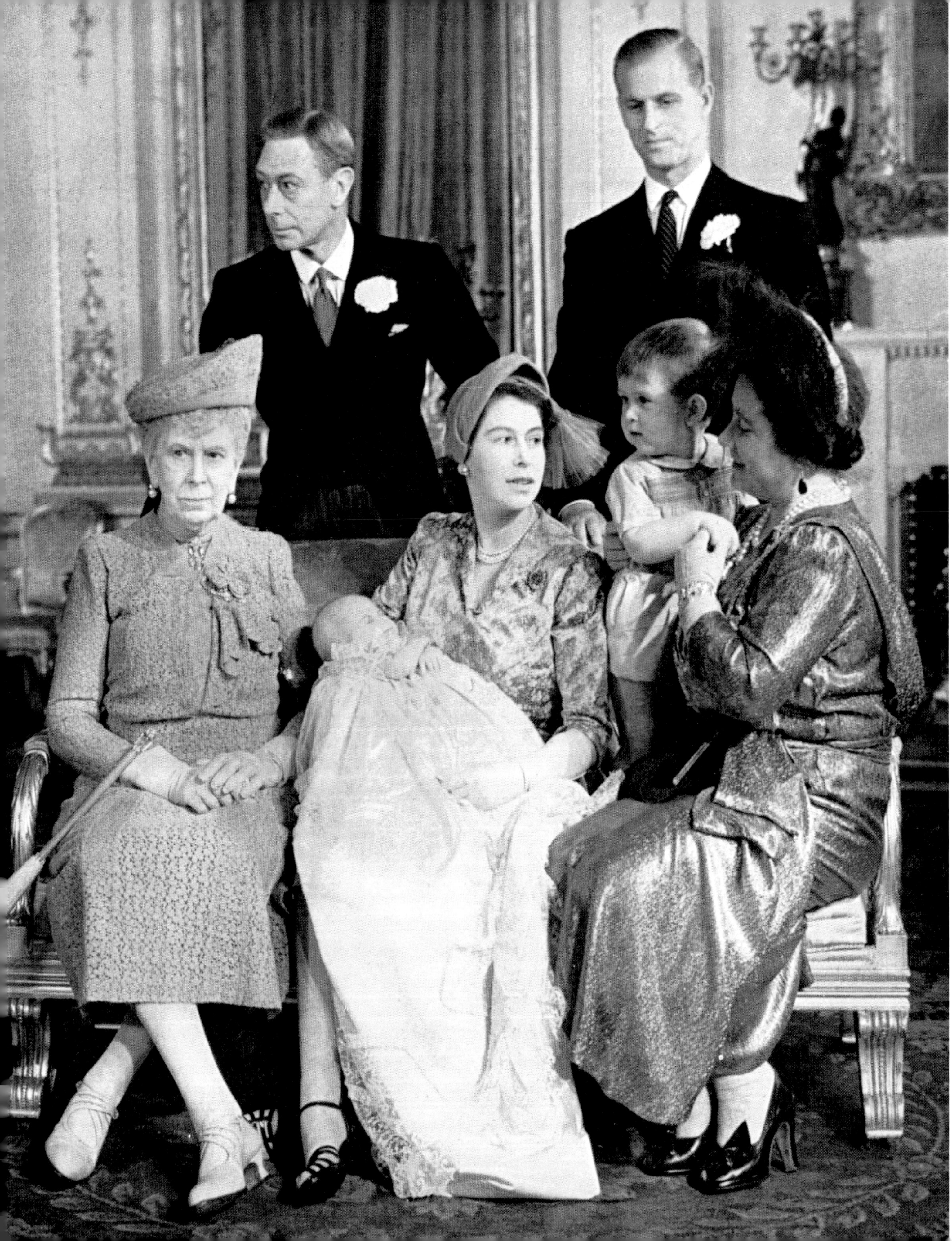

4

SHOEMAKERS TO THE ROYAL FAMILY

Joseph Rayne was granted a Royal Warrant from Her Majesty Queen Mary in the Silver Jubilee Year of 1935. The consort of King George V had been crowned amongst the pomp and circumstance in Westminster Abbey in June 1911 and had formed a focal point of another remarkable living tableaux, the Delhi Durbar of December 1911; in common with all her suppliers, Joseph Rayne was quite aware that there was nothing The Queen needed to be told about clothes or shoes. Once described by an observer as glittering like the Jungfrau with a substantial display of jewels, Queen Mary was noted for her remarkable eye for detail and acute memory. She must have noticed Rayne shoes on those she met and, as an avid theatre-goer, on stage.

From the time of the fashionable exposure of women's ankles around 1910 and the shock of the sight of silk-clad flappers' legs in the 1920s, shoes were of prime importance in a woman's wardrobe. Most obviously, fine shoes for weddings were sought after, as were those for debutantes to wear for their presentation at Court. Mothers and daughters attended any number of receptions, parties and dances, a great source of income to the many trades involved with supplying clothes, hats, gloves and shoes, as well as photographers, caterers, car hire firms and florists, to name the most obvious. Today, investitures, garden parties and Ascot still give a flavour of the peak of this way of life, as do weddings and twenty-first birthday parties in general.

Designing clothes or accessories for the Royal Family involves both a knowledge of the various occasions at which the items will be worn and a sense of theatre. Joseph Rayne had both. The 1920 opening of Rayne's retail shop on New Bond Street placed the business amongst some of the greatest period names in British retailing, many of them devoted to clothing and shoes, notably court dressmakers Handley Seymour, makers of the wedding dress for Lady Elizabeth Bowes-Lyon on her marriage in 1923 to the Duke of York, second son of

Previous page: At the christening ceremony of HRH Princess Anne, now the Princess Royal, on 21 October 1950, HM Queen Mary, HRH Princess Elizabeth and HM The Queen (l-r) all wore shoes by H. & M. Rayne Ltd., each pair of shoes reflecting the wearer's different taste and style of dress. At this date, H. & M. Rayne had the sole Royal Warrant of Queen Mary. The Princess and Queen wore dresses designed by Norman Hartnell. King George VI, HRH Prince Philip, Duke of Edinburgh and HRH Prince Charles, now The Prince of Wales (l-r) are all present. RAYNE ARCHIVE

Facing page: The engagement of HRH Princess Elizabeth and Lt. Philip Mountbatten, later HM Queen Elizabeth II and HRH Prince Philip, Duke of Edinburgh, on 9 July 1947, the Princess wearing shoes by Rayne.

Below: At her marriage in Westminster Abbey on 20 November 1947, the Princess wore Rayne sandals designed by the creator of her wedding dress, Norman Hartnell. He also designed those of the bridesmaids, one of whom was HRH Princess Margaret, together with their Rayne sandals. Hartnell also designed the dress worn by The Queen, later Queen Elizabeth The Queen Mother. RAYNE ARCHIVE

Right: A pencil sketch of the bridesmaids' dress design was made and copied for the Hartnell workrooms and shows his designs for all the sandals. MICHAEL PICK COLLECTION

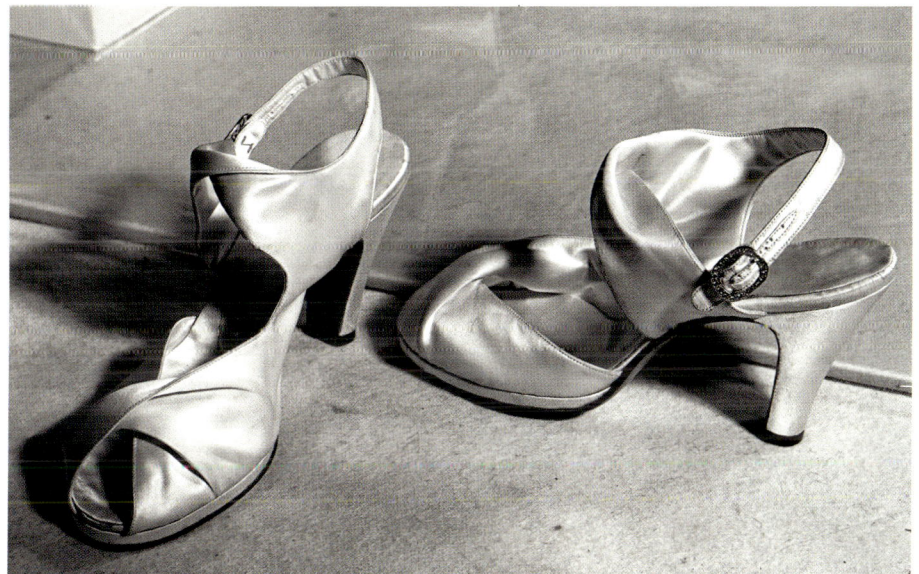

147

The shoes made by Rayne after the design by Norman Hartnell for the marriage of HRH Princess Elizabeth to HRH Prince Philip on 20 November 1947, together with their specially made and lined box. The platform-soled sandals with medium heels are covered with the same off-white satin as the wedding dress and have wide cuffed ankle-straps, no doubt giving some warmth on a chilly autumn day. The ankle straps fasten with diamanté clasps to the side.
BY GRACIOUS PERMISSION OF HM QUEEN ELIZABETH II

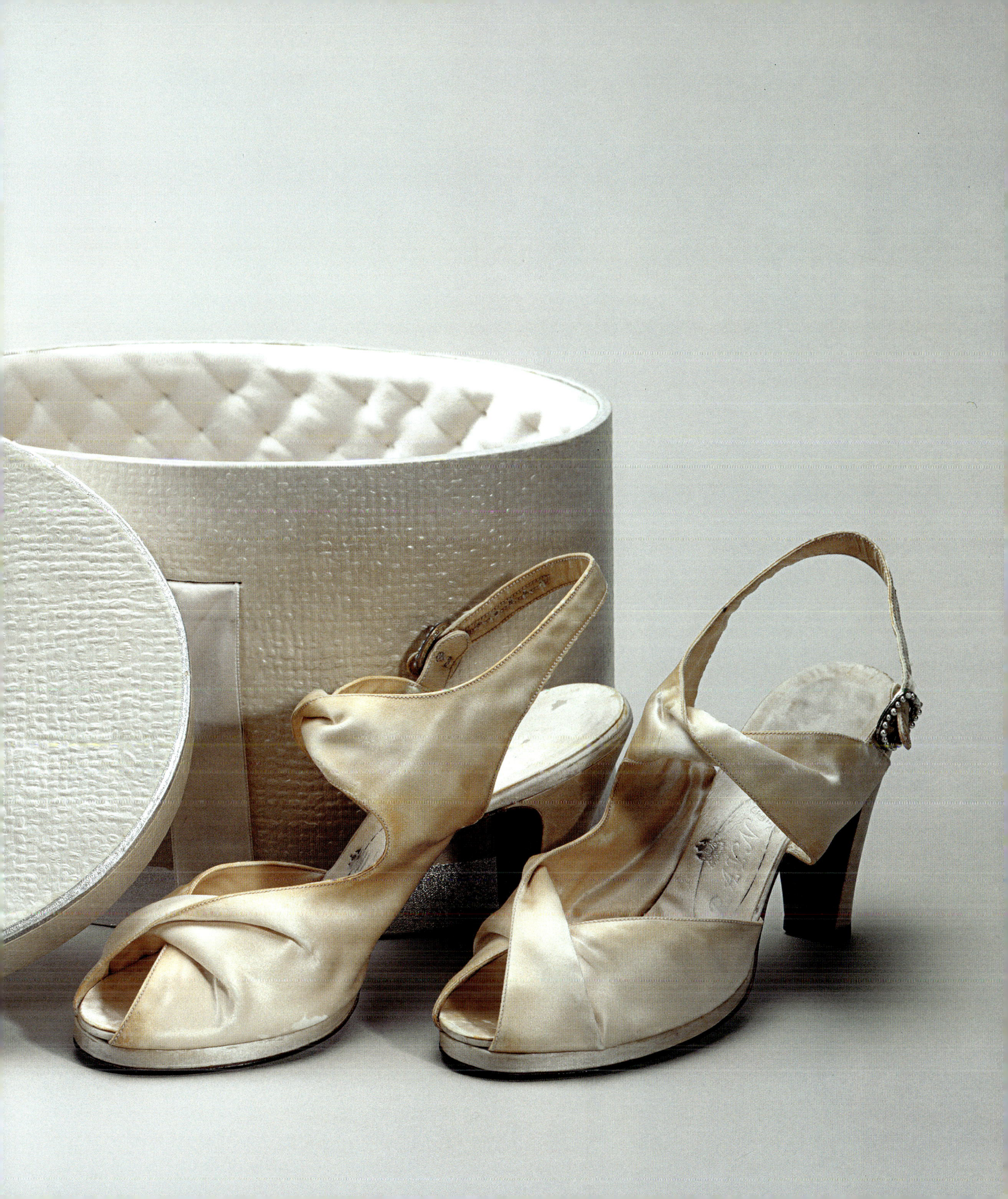

King George V and Queen Mary. The grant of a Royal Warrant to Handley Seymour in addition to that of Reville & Rossiter in nearby Hanover Square by Queen Mary gave the area greater cachet and, no doubt, added to the impression made upon the Queen, who had used Hook, Knowles & Co. Ltd and Peter Yapp – both known as 'boot makers'. By 1936, times had changed and Rayne's Warrant referred to them as 'shoe makers', Yapp still holding a warrant as 'boot makers'.

Until she died in 1953, Queen Mary's shoes varied little from the style prevalent in the early 1900s, reflected in the design of Rayne shoes for Adeline Genée's dancers at that time (now in the V&A). Doeskin in muted shades, low Louis heels and almond toes typified day wear – kid or brocades for evening-wear. Day-shoes came to include buttoned and strapped low pumps; by 1952 it was stated that the Queen ordered ten pairs a year and that the special last on which her shoes were constructed had not been altered for twenty years. Some day-shoes had lizard trim and glacé or patent leather toes with muted brogue detailing, the colour and style complementing Queen Mary's personal style of dressing, which was marginally updated over the decades and even included glittering Norman Hartnell beaded and sequinned sheaths in 1935, the style slightly varying to include some mid-calf dress lengths by 1947. As photographs of the period confirm, Queen Mary's dated style was not unique amongst subjects of her generation: but few had her glamour. George V thought that the Queen's style symbolised continuity through difficult times and epitomised British Imperial splendour, and no-one disagreed.

A record of some shoes and sandals made for the Royal Family by Rayne from 1947-48, includes two wooden-shaped shoe trees for the shoes of HM the Queen (later Queen Elizabeth The Queen Mother) and HM Queen Mary. Left to right: a sandal made for The Queen based on the stock model 'Zarine', with an order sheet; a platform-soled lizard silver piped sandal ordered by The Queen on 3 November 1948; one of several copies of Princess Elizabeth's wedding sandal designed by Hartnell; a thick platform-soled sandal with gilt leather decoration; a pair of thick platform-soled alligator closed sandals with leather ribbon trim; a pair of light platform-soled lattice pierced front sandals; a pair of platform-soled dark suede shoes; a pair of lattice-fronted sandals with high heels. On the shelf behind can be seen a half-finished shoe or sandal. HISTORIC ROYAL PALACES

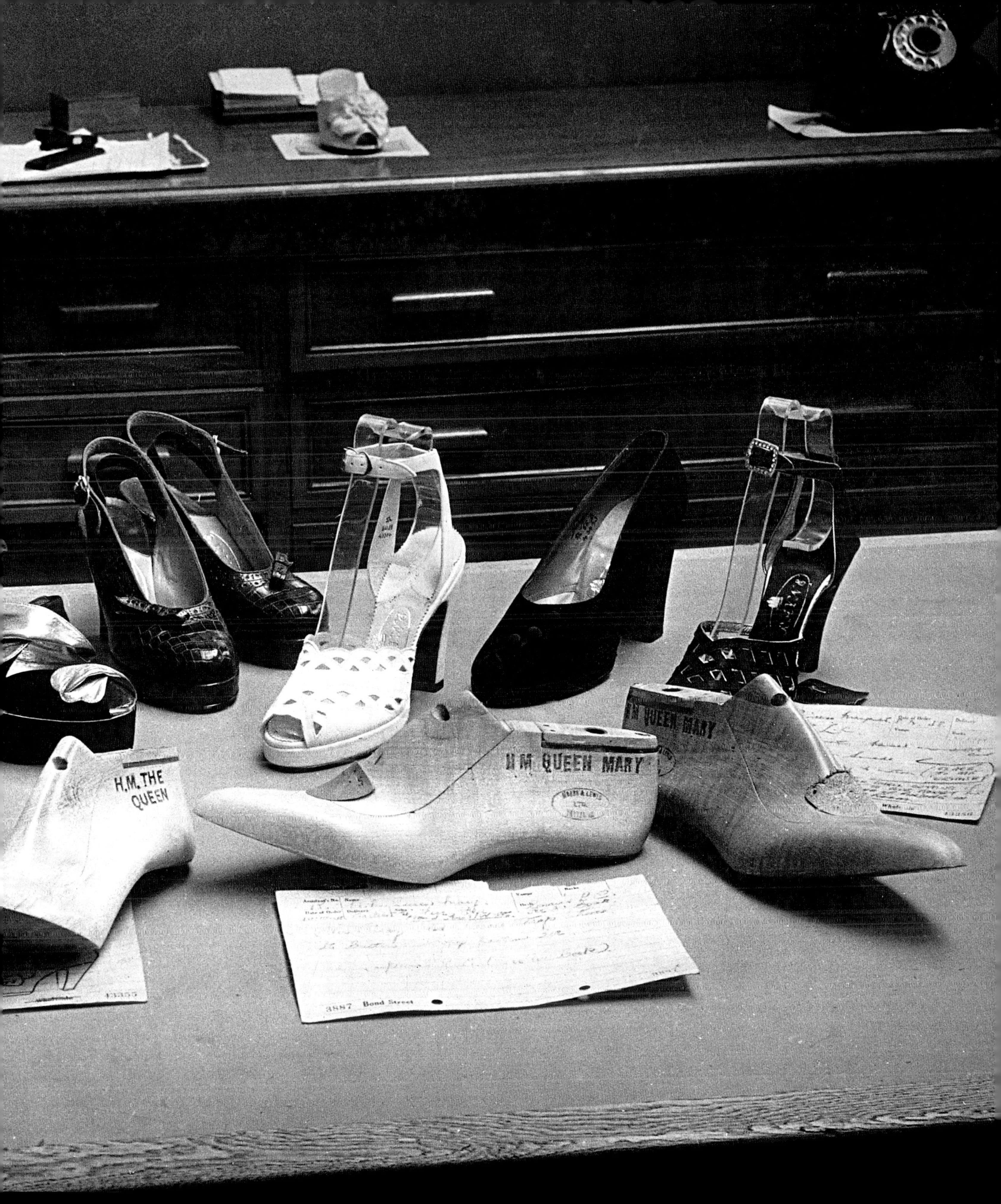
H.M. THE QUEEN
H M QUEEN MARY
H M QUEEN MARY
3887 Bond Street

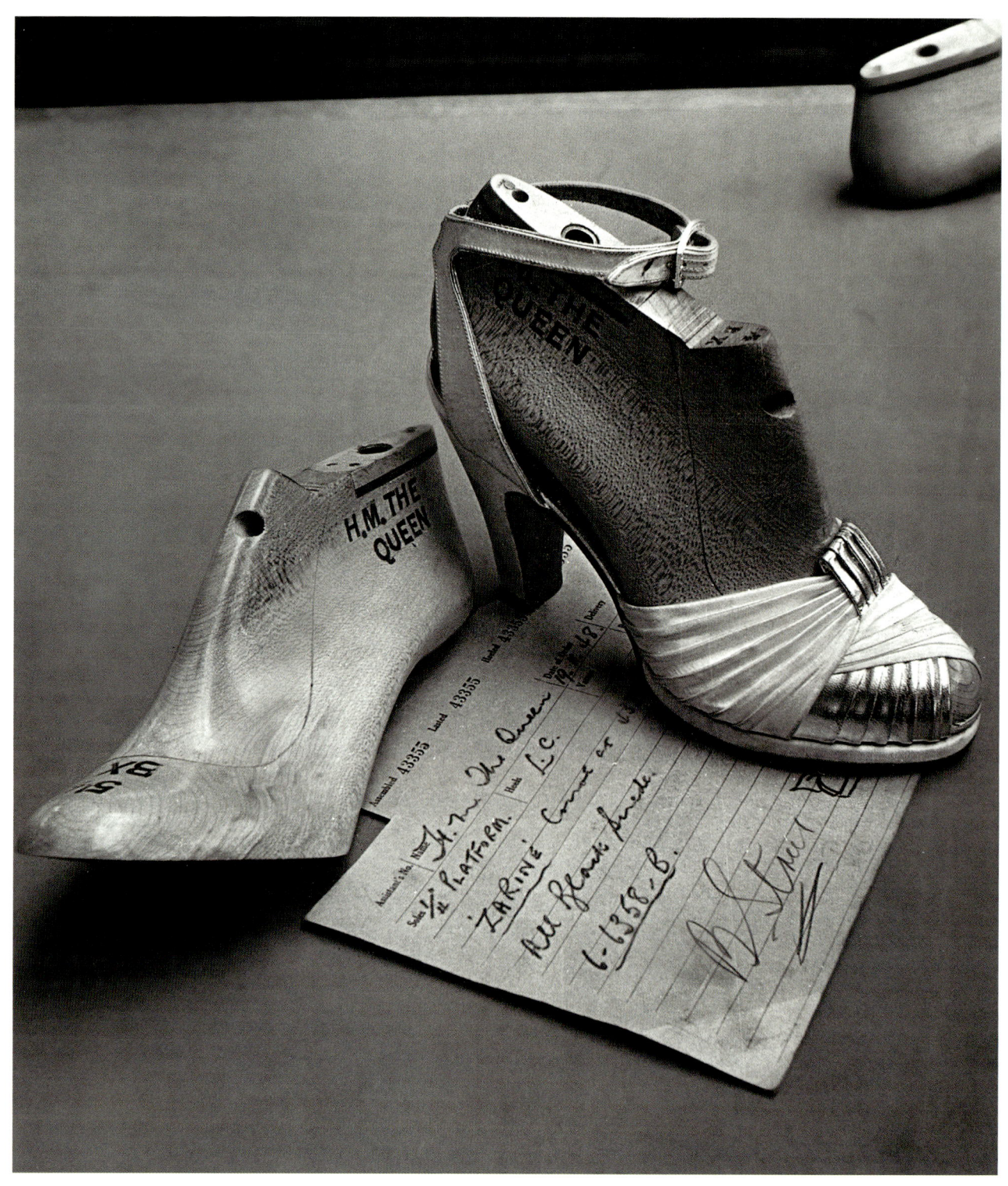

The Rayne stock model 'Zarine' modified to the order attached of 19 November 1948 in 'all black suede' for HM The Queen. The modification of stock models for the royal clients was usual practice, although by the 1970s it was less usual due to the higher labour costs. HISTORIC ROYAL PALACES

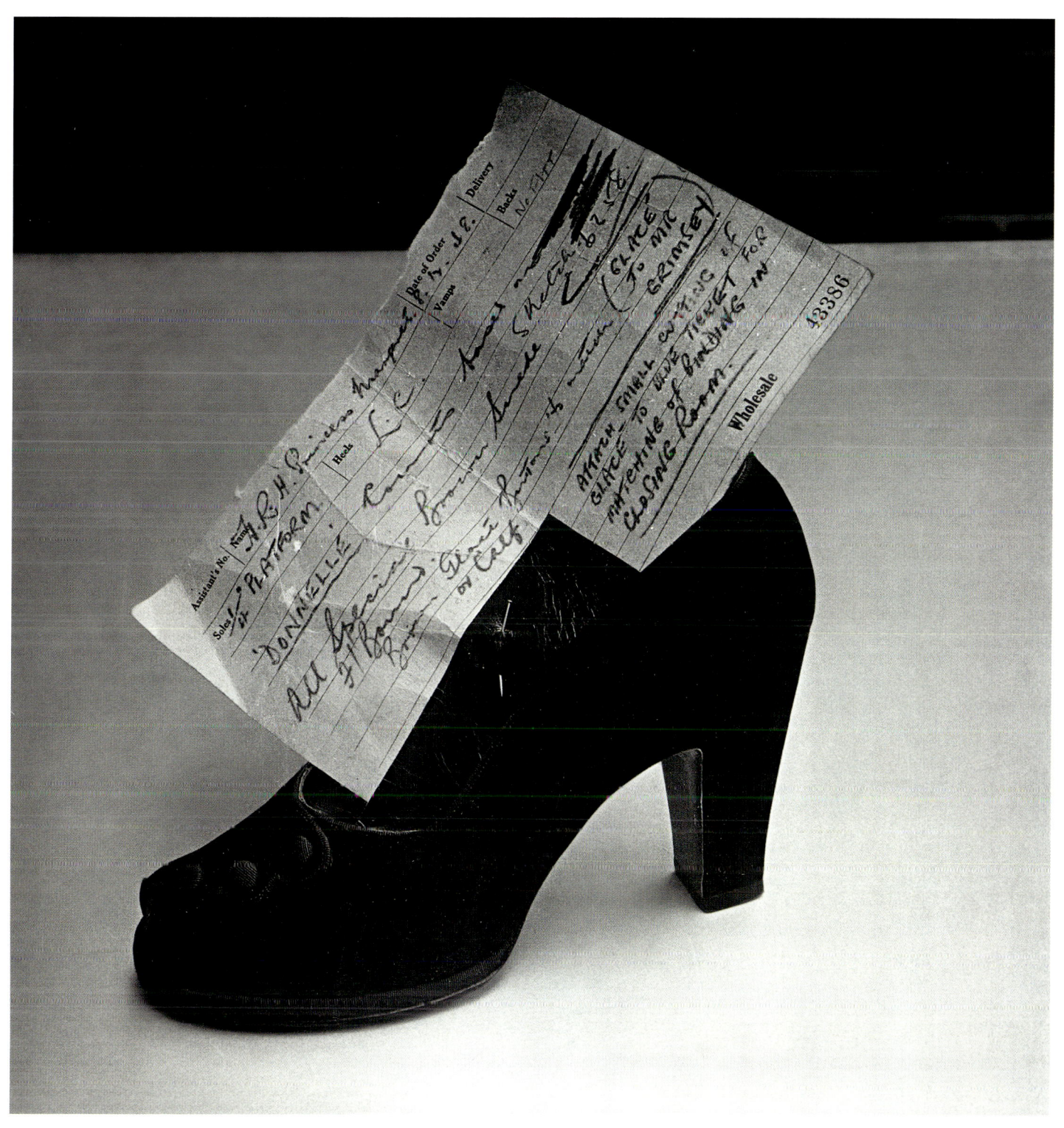

The Rayne stock model 'Donnelle', modified to the order attached of 8 December 1948 in 'special brown suede... with glacé buttons' for HRH Princess Margaret. HISTORIC ROYAL PALACES

A 1948 International Wool Secretariat fashion show attended by HRH Princess Elizabeth wearing Rayne white platform-soled peep-toe sandals with a Norman Hartnell ensemble, the designer sitting on her left. At joint designer fashion shows it became usual for individual designers to sit with the royal guest during the showing of his or her designs. This show was later repeated in Australia. MICHAEL PICK COLLECTION

Versed in so many theatrical designs and productions, Rayne was equal to all the royal commands, and the making of comfortable, durable and elegant shoes was quite usual for the factory. This was of prime importance in the making of all shoes for ladies of the Royal Family with their multifarious engagements in all types of weather. In 1946, Queen Mary saw Rayne's craftsmanship on the screen, when she was present at the Royal Command premiere of Gabriel Pascal's British Technicolor film *Caesar and Cleopatra*, for which Oliver Messel had designed the shoes, all of which were made by Rayne.

As Queen Mary is now such an historic figure from a period no doubt remote for almost all readers, a series of impressions noted by the politician and diarist Sir Henry 'Chips' Channon form usefully succinct vignettes of the effect of the Queen's appearance, notably in her Jubilee Year of 1935, '... in her white and silvery splendour. Never has she looked so serene, so regally majestic, even so attractive. She completely eclipsed the King. Suddenly she became the best-dressed woman in the world.' (6 May, 1935).

The Royal Tour of November 1953-May 1954: The many changes of dress necessary throughout this long tour of Commonwealth countries included corresponding changes of shoes for all climates. Edward Rayne worked closely with the two main designers, Norman Hartnell and Hardy Amies, to create the shoes worn. A few are visible here, left to right: a hospital visit in Auckland during the Tour of New Zealand (23 December-30 January 1954), at Government House, Canberra during the Tour of Australia (3 February 1954-1 April 1954); and in Entebbe, Uganda (28th April 1954-30th April 1954). RAYNE ARCHIVE

Above: The Royal Tour of 1953-1954 following the Coronation of Queen Elizabeth II in 1953 embraced as many of the Commonwealth countries as possible and a few, as in Australia, also saw her in the Coronation Dress at the ceremony of the Opening of Parliament. The long tour necessitated over 100 changes of dress, mainly created by Norman Hartnell and Hardy Amies, with accompanying shoes by Rayne. Few photographs include legs or feet with shoes, but a pair of the many Rayne white ones are seen here. The Queen, as Queen of New Zealand, and Prince Philip were greeted in Auckland by the Governor-General Sir Willoughby Norrie and Lady Norrie, after disembarking from SS *Gothic* on 23 December 1953. RAYNE ARCHIVE

Facing page: A pair of the satin sandals designed by Norman Hartnell and originally made by Rayne for the Royal Wedding of 1947. The low heels have been adapted to the fashionable style of the early 1950s and may well have been suggested to HM The Queen as possible suitable footwear to be worn with the heavy Coronation dress, which was designed by Hartnell on the same lines as the 1947 wedding dress at the command of The Queen. It is not known which sandals were worn on the day, but they were designed by Hartnell in conjunction with Rayne and reported to be of gold brocade. With the additional weight of the Robes of State, the height and secure fastenings of these sandals might well indicate the eventual choice of The Queen. Whatever was worn would have formed virtually the only items of the overall outfit that could have been copied for public consumption. HISTORIC ROYAL PALACES

At the Coronation of King George VI and Queen Elizabeth in 1937, she appeared to Channon, '...ablaze, regal and overbearing...' (12 May, 1937), and later, 'At the Buckingham Garden party...we saw Queen Mary looking like the Jungfrau, white and sparkling in the sun....' (22 June, 1937). No shoes could possibly compete with this, '...Queen Mary glittered with five diamond necklaces around her neck. She was in blue with literally mountains of jewels.' (16 November, 1938). In 1945, 'At the Royal Garden Party Queen Mary was in a cloth-of-gold coat and looked magnificent... Dino Carisbrooke...whispered to me: "My cousin May is rather overdressed." A curious way to describe Queen Mary.' (21 July 1945). It was considered a great honour for Joseph and then Edward Rayne to supply her shoes and as remained the practice with successive royal clients, selections of shoes were sent to them for approval.

Queen Mary's satisfaction with Rayne shoes clearly communicated itself to all the ladies of the British Royal Family, firstly to Queen Elizabeth and her daughters, the Princesses Elizabeth and Margaret; then to the Duchess of Gloucester, Princess Alice, wife of the third son of George V and Queen Mary; and to the Duchess of Kent, Princess Marina, wife of the youngest son.

Queen Elizabeth, Consort of George VI, had a very different style to that of Queen Mary. As the Duchess of York, she had been dressed by Handley Seymour since the 1920s, and first ordered clothes from Norman Hartnell in 1935. Both designers were used until after the Second World War, when Madame Handley Seymour's business closed. Elizabeth loyally ordered her Coronation dress from Handley Seymour; though, bearing her train, the Maids-of-Honour were wearing Hartnell dresses. From 1937 it was Hartnell who provided the majority of her clothes and assisted her with a new style and image, which she maintained until her death in 2002, by which time Hartnell had been dead for almost 23 years.

Jack Jacobus[1] held the Royal Warrant from Queen Elizabeth together with Peter Japp in 1945; by 1955, Rayne and James Allan & Son Ltd of Edinburgh were also Warrant Holders. The Queen wore Jacobus shoes at her Coronation and for the subsequent Royal Visit to France in 1938 and then the Royal Tour of Canada and Visit to North America in 1939 accompanying Hartnell ensembles.

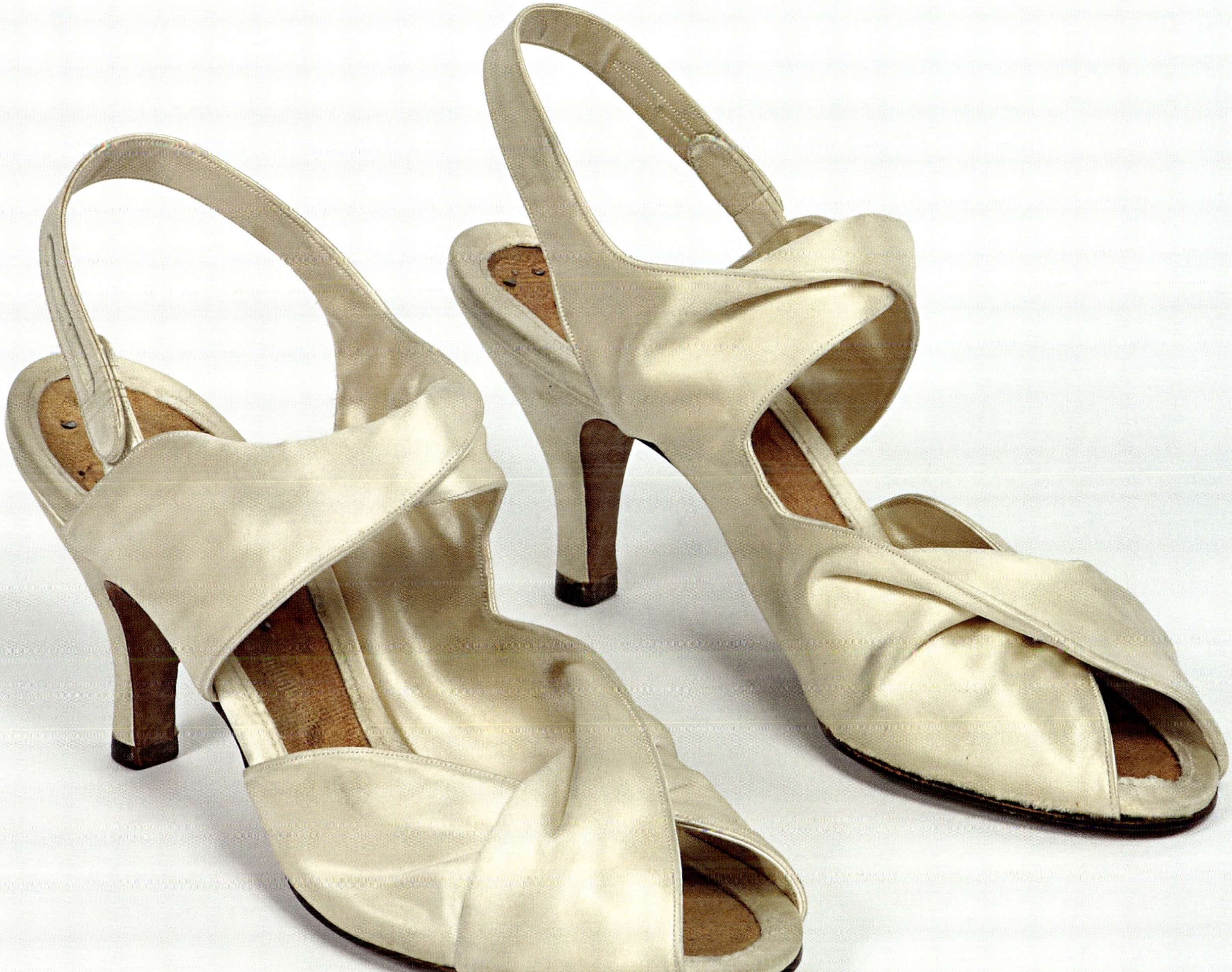

This page: These two shoe designs may have been intended to go with clothes designed by Norman Hartnell and Hardy Amies for HM The Queen's State Visit to the Netherlands in 1958, when the Royal Yacht *Britannia* was used as an impressive symbol of Britain's status and moored in Amsterdam harbour. The slimmer heels of the period are used with slight platform soles to give height and aid the manoeuvring of evening dresses. It is not known if these designs were ever realised.

Top: A design for 'Her Majesty The Queen : Off-white satin closed-back open toe shoe by Rayne with ¼" platform; rhinestone treatment on vamp.' HISTORIC ROYAL PALACES
Below: 'A blue crepe halter back by Rayne with ¼" platform. The whole of the sandal is decorated with mother-of-pearl sequins.' HISTORIC ROYAL PALACES

Facing page: A pair of Rayne pink linen-covered sling-back high-heeled leather-soled sandals with gathered and clasped vamps and open toes made for HM The Queen. The colour closely resembles that of the famous ensemble from Hardy Amies worn by The Queen for her Silver Anniversary Service at St Paul's Cathedral and previously seen in Canada without the hat. c.1976/7. HISTORIC ROYAL PALACES

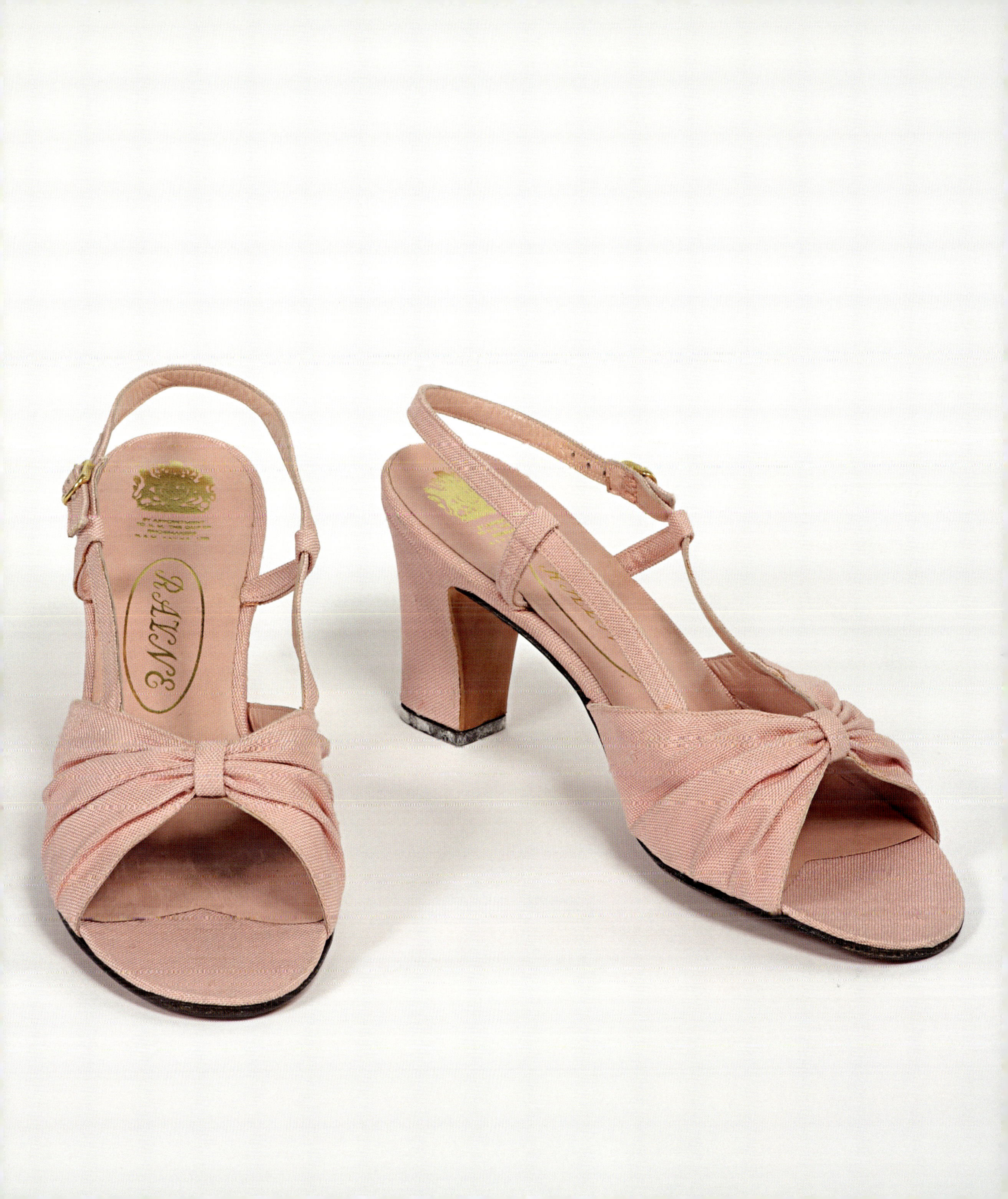
RAYNE

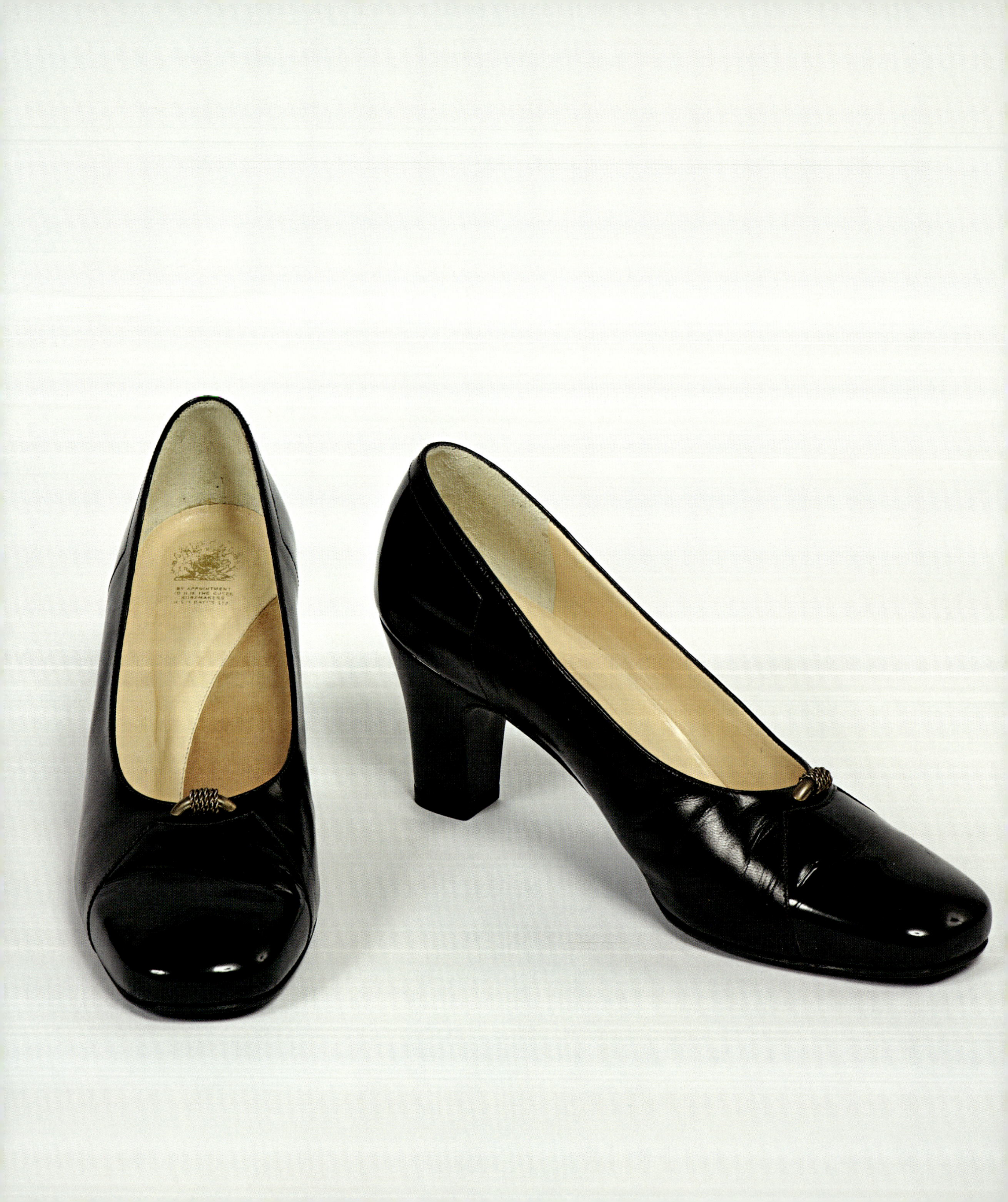
BY APPOINTMENT

Rayne shoes were seen to be worn amid much publicity after the war by both The Queen and her daughters Princesses Elizabeth and Margaret during the Royal Tour of South Africa and Southern Rhodesia, the first of such events since 1939. The Queen had adopted the 1940s style of peep-toe high-heeled sandals with platform soles, often in white suede or calf for daytime, with various colours and often fabrics for the strapped designs for the evening. This began a variant of her own style and the very high heels lent her added height. In 1952 it was stated in an article based on an interview with Edward Rayne, that The Queen ordered 20-30 pairs a year at eight guineas (£8.8shillings) a pair from Mr Rayne personally, when he attended The Queen at Buckingham Palace. '…he would have to bear in mind Her Majesty's liking for neat platform soles – though since the day she stumbled badly in a rutted Sandringham lane she has been less in favour of high heels'. This report may be somewhat exaggerated as high heels were a style followed by The Queen as Queen Mother for almost three more decades, although her famous broken heel during the South African Tour of 1947 may have fuelled this story.[2]

Two years previously, in 1950, young Edward Rayne had learned a lesson he never forgot, when in New York. Grilled by a journalist and plied with Martinis, he managed to avoid discussing his royal clients, but somehow the size of The Queen's foot was divulged. It made the columns of the UK *Daily Worker* and his father, incandescent with rage, summoned their PR agent Peter Hope Lumley and sent him to meet Edward on his return, rather than going himself. Edward had to visit the hawk-like Commander Richard Colville – Press Secretary at Buckingham Palace from 1947-1968 – and explain himself, returning again when the item appeared in an Australian paper. Joseph and Edward were worried that, as a result, The Queen would withhold granting the Royal Warrant. However, they went on to create shoes for a vast number of public and private engagements undertaken by Her Majesty, including visits abroad as The Queen Mother, as well as historic events, such as the Coronation of her daughter Queen Elizabeth II, the marriage of Princess Margaret to Lord Snowdon, and the Investiture of Prince Charles as Prince of Wales. Rayne shoes were highly visible at Royal Ascot and at the appearances of Queen Elizabeth at the gates of Clarence House on her birthday.

Facing page: A pair of Rayne black kid leather court shoes with rounded toes and black patent leather caps, heels and counters and a gilt metal decoration to the front made for HM The Queen. The cream leather insoles have suede arch supports for added comfort and the soles are scored to prevent the wearer from slipping. c.1978. This design and others similar became the one most associated with The Queen's style over the following decades. Historic Royal Palaces

Below: Designs for the shoes to be worn by HM The Queen and Queen Elizabeth The Queen Mother at the marriage of HRH Princess Anne in Westminster Abbey on 14 November 1973. Those for The Queen feature a loosely tied bow and those for The Queen Mother have the preferred slight platform soles and high heels. Rayne Archive

One of a pair of Rayne pink linen-covered platform-soled sling-back leather sandals with small buckles and cut-out to the front resembling a mask. Made for HM Queen Elizabeth The Queen Mother, these epitomise her romantic style and taste for elaborate evening dresses. c.1958. Historic Royal Palaces

One of a pair of Rayne sling-back sandals with high heels and open-toed white nylon mesh vamps trimmed with the same white scalloped leather covering the heels. Small buckles of self-coloured enamelled metal on the straps. Made for and worn by Queen Elizabeth The Queen Mother, these sandals incorporate the nylon mesh found in many of Rayne's most interesting designs of the period. c.1959.   HISTORIC ROYAL PALACES

A pair of Rayne white kid court shoes with decoration of three small strips of leather clasped by gilt rings at the toes and stitching around the uppers. Made with platform soles and the wider leather covered heels fashionable from about 1975, the style was one preferred by HM Queen Elizabeth the Queen Mother for the last decades of her life. c.1985.   HISTORIC ROYAL PALACES

An unusual pair of Rayne children's leather shoes with small flat satin bows made as a sample for the bridesmaids' shoes at the marriage of HRH Princess Margaret and Anthony Armstrong-Jones, later the Earl of Snowdon, on 6 May 1960. HISTORIC ROYAL PALACES

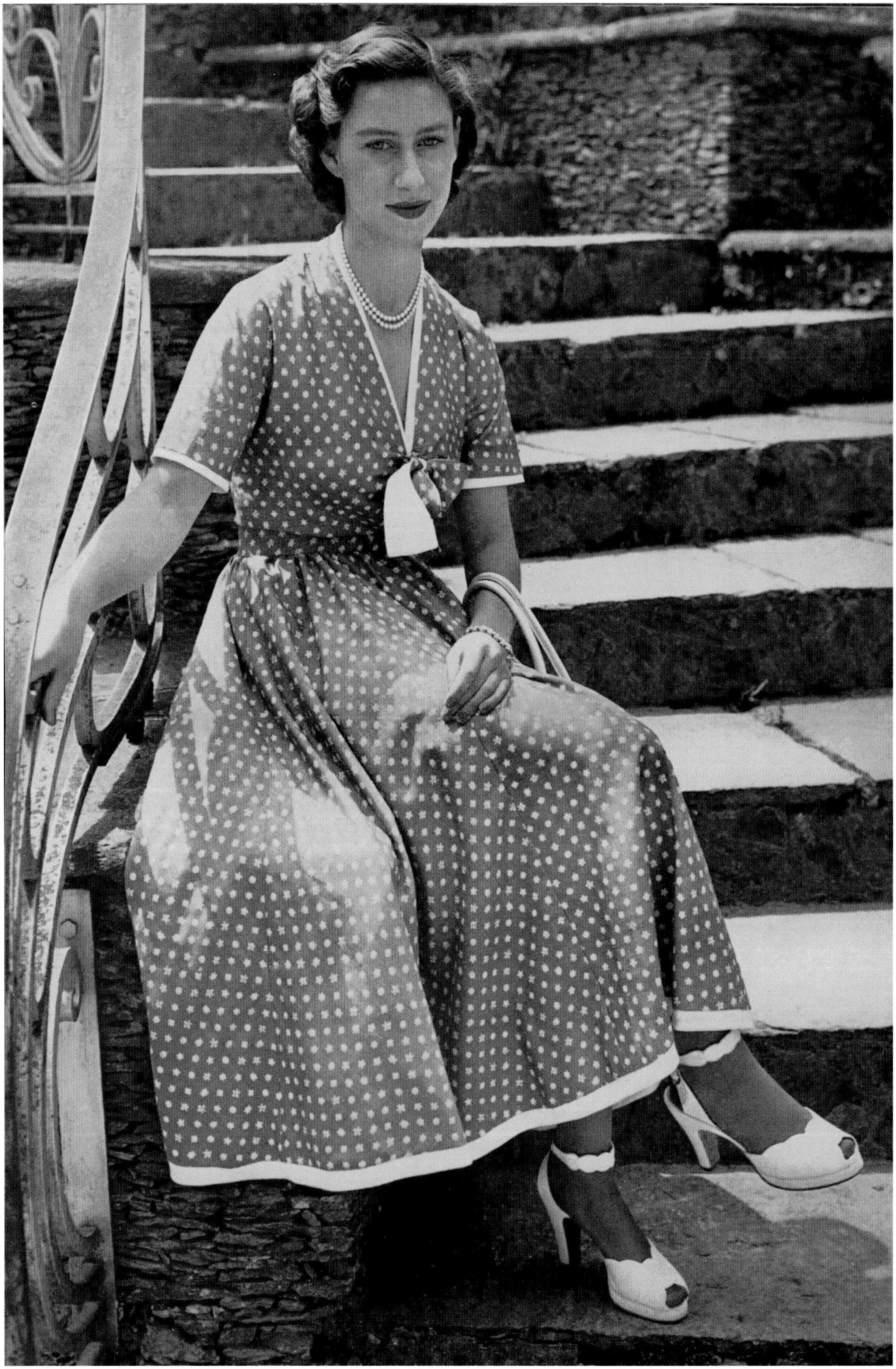

Facing page: HRH Princess Margaret photographed on a visit to Italy in 1949 wearing white Rayne open-toed platform-soled sandals with ankle straps resembling those ordered by her mother, Queen Elizabeth the previous year (see p.150-151). Throughout the late 1940s and '50s, Princess Margaret was treated by the media as a fashion trendsetter and her appearance was eagerly scrutinised world-wide for dress and fashion inspiration. RAYNE ARCHIVE

Below: High-heeled Rayne sandals with platform-soles remained a firm favourite of HRH Princess Margaret throughout her life. This white sling-backed pair has a bold heart motif as decoration at the centre of the straps, which form the vamp. Princess Margaret wore these sandals for the 90th birthday of her mother in 1990 (see p.173). c.1985. HISTORIC ROYAL PALACES

Below and facing page: A pair of Rayne patent pale creamy tan leather sandals with closed vamps above platform soles and with small enamelled decoration. Made for HRH Princess Margaret, these sandals differ little in their design from those of the 1940s, nor do those opposite in tan leather. The slimmer more shapely heels most strongly denote these as being four decades later in date. c.1988. HISTORIC ROYAL PALACES

BY APPOINTMENT TO H.M. THE QUEEN SHOEMAKERS H. & M. RAYNE LTD.
RAYNE

A memorable meeting in New York between Mother Theresa and Diana, Princess of Wales was recorded in June 1997. The Princess was wearing a pair of 'spectator' or two-toned high-heeled court shoes by Rayne. Younger members of the British Royal Family brought their own taste to bear on their individual sense of dress and style. Diana, Princess of Wales became one of the greatest international figures of her age and her extensive patronage of British designers was eagerly sought after. Rayne provided many of her shoes. 1997. RAYNE ARCHIVE

Platform soles remained a favourite, even after their fall from fashion throughout the 1950s and particularly in the late 1960s, when fashion had moved back to the style. Queen Elizabeth had a standing joke with Edward Rayne about her 'football boots', shoes especially designed for her to wear on a muddy pitch for an FA ceremony – these were shoes with specially designed platform soles and thick heels. She even referred to these in a handwritten letter she sent from the Castle of Mey on 18 August 1987, when she commiserated with Edward Rayne on the loss of what she termed his own family's creation.

Edward Rayne collaborated with royal dressmaker Norman Hartnell on many designs for shoes to accompany clothes for Queen Elizabeth and he would go in person with his latest shoe designs for selection and fittings. It was rare for shoes from current designs to be either proposed or selected, though modified versions were sometimes ordered. The benefit of the Rayne factory at Kings Cross lay in its ability to create and make any required design to the highest standards. The factory also repaired or even altered shoes for clients, including royal clients and it was quite usual for anyone ordering a plain white satin shoe to have it dyed to match a fabric sample, something not confined to the Rayne brand.

In collaboration with Hartnell, Rayne made the cream satin sandals with their 'cuffed' ankle straps giving support and some warmth worn by Princess Elizabeth for her wedding in November 1947. He also provided her with a variety of the 1940s fashionable ankle-strapped platform-soled shoes worn in public and also adopted by Princess Margaret, who later had non-slip soles added to those of her very high-heeled shoes – comfort and security first.

Apart from Allan's in Edinburgh, Rayne was the only shoemaker entrusted with making the shoes for Princess Elizabeth and later as Queen. She wore Rayne shoes at her Coronation in 1953. Those worn on the Royal Tour of 1953 to 1954 were in versions of the then fashionable styles, a practice that lasted for as long as Rayne existed, although extremely thin stiletto heels were not seen in public, clearly being too difficult to wear comfortably in most situations, especially on grass or when standing for long periods. Collaboration between Rayne and Hartnell, extended to Hardy Amies as he became more involved with designs for the young Queen and, later, John Cavanagh, a favourite of Princess Marina, Duchess of Kent. Rayne commissioned designs from all three designers for his business during the seasons 1958-1959, and from Digby Morton. Ian Thomas, formerly with Hartnell, became the third dress designer to be favoured by The Queen with a Royal Warrant and he, in turn, collaborated with Rayne on shoes toning with his designs for The Queen.

Edward Rayne was noted for his eye for fashion and style; Rayne-manufactured shoes ably demonstrated this and the input of Jean Matthew and his workforce was also critical to their success, not least for royal shoes. Due to the obvious fact that clothes and accessories worn by The Queen were only identified as they were worn, Edward avidly followed the progress of all royal events, but when asked about his shoes for the Royal Tour in 1954, he sadly complained that he had seen almost nothing of them except a pair of white peep-toe court shoes and a pair of white ankle straps worn in Bermuda and Jamaica – because, as with films, most photography ignored the feet. Nonetheless, everyone knew who had created the shoes and the publicity gained for Rayne and British shoe manufacturing was incalculable.

A pair of black satin platform-soled high reinforced heeled Rayne sandals of sophisticated design, one sling-back strap fastening with a small buckle and a vamp of crossed straps reinforced with nylon mesh side inserts. Enamelled and gilt decoration in the form of a marguerite to the sides. Made for HRH Princess Margaret. c.1989. HISTORIC ROYAL PALACES

Above: The visibility of The Queen in a crowd was heightened by the decision to use brighter colours than usual, Hardy Amies designs being most striking in this respect. Rayne supplied a number of black shoes and sometimes bags, to complement these clothes without in any way fighting the design. This consistent formula began in the late 1960s. This bright yellow ensemble has a spotted turban by Frederick Fox and was worn during the State Visit to Mexico in 1975, and here to view the fireworks display on the Thames during Silver Jubilee Year 1977. HARDY AMIES ARCHIVE

Facing page: The 90th birthday appearance of HM Queen Elizabeth The Queen Mother at the gates of Clarence House on 4 August 1990 with four generations of the Royal Family represented, the eldest all patronising H. & M. Rayne Ltd. and HM The Queen and her mother having awarded the company Royal Warrants in recognition of their long devoted service. Princess Margaret is here wearing the 'heart' sandals seen on page 167. © TRINITY MIRROR/MIRRORPIX/ALAMY

The planning for the Royal Tour naturally included all items in the extensive wardrobe. It covered acres of newsprint around the world. In August 1953, it was reported that both Hartnell and Amies were to supervise the first fittings of clothes at Balmoral and that Rayne was collaborating with them on 'to match the Queen's shoes to her coats, suits and day and evening dresses. As the Queen has often to stand for long hours, they concentrate upon giving her comfort combined with smartness. Although she is rather short, she prefers not to wear ultra-high heels especially in the day time, when her engagements often demand quite a lot of walking or standing. Messrs Rayne therefore often give her platform shoes, as they did for her Coronation shoes in gold-brocaded satin. This adds a little to her height without entailing an uncomfortably high heel.'[3]

Younger members of the Royal Family to wear Rayne shoes included Princess Anne, Princess Michael of Kent and Diana, Princess of Wales – all with their own distinctive styles and all secure in the knowledge that Rayne would never suggest or sell them shoes likely to mirror those of the other members of the Royal Family.

The demise of the Rayne firm brought letters of sympathetic good wishes handwritten by The Queen and Queen Elizabeth The Queen Mother. Both The Queen and Queen Elizabeth wrote of the gratitude to those involved with Rayne over the decades and their loyal service to the Royal Family in general and themselves in particular. The Queen was particularly concerned, as – apart from James Allan & Son in Edinburgh for country shoes – she had only ever used Rayne for her shoes. Amongst the good wishes expressed in several subsequent surviving letters is the expression of hope that Rayne would one day be resurrected, something that has only recently happened with Edward's son Nicholas. As long as Edward Rayne lived, he was still able to assist The Queen and Queen Elizabeth The Queen Mother with the supply of handmade shoes from his own contacts in the shoe trade.

The surviving letters were preserved by Edward Rayne and apart from a signed, framed photograph from Princess Margaret and some Christmas cards are all that remain of a considerable personal archive. The letters with their envelopes slightly blackened by the fire that consumed Edward Rayne and his house are also virtually all that remain of the decades of service and the mementoes of the remarkable company that evolved out of the business begun by Henry and Mary Rayne on the Waterloo Road in Victorian London.

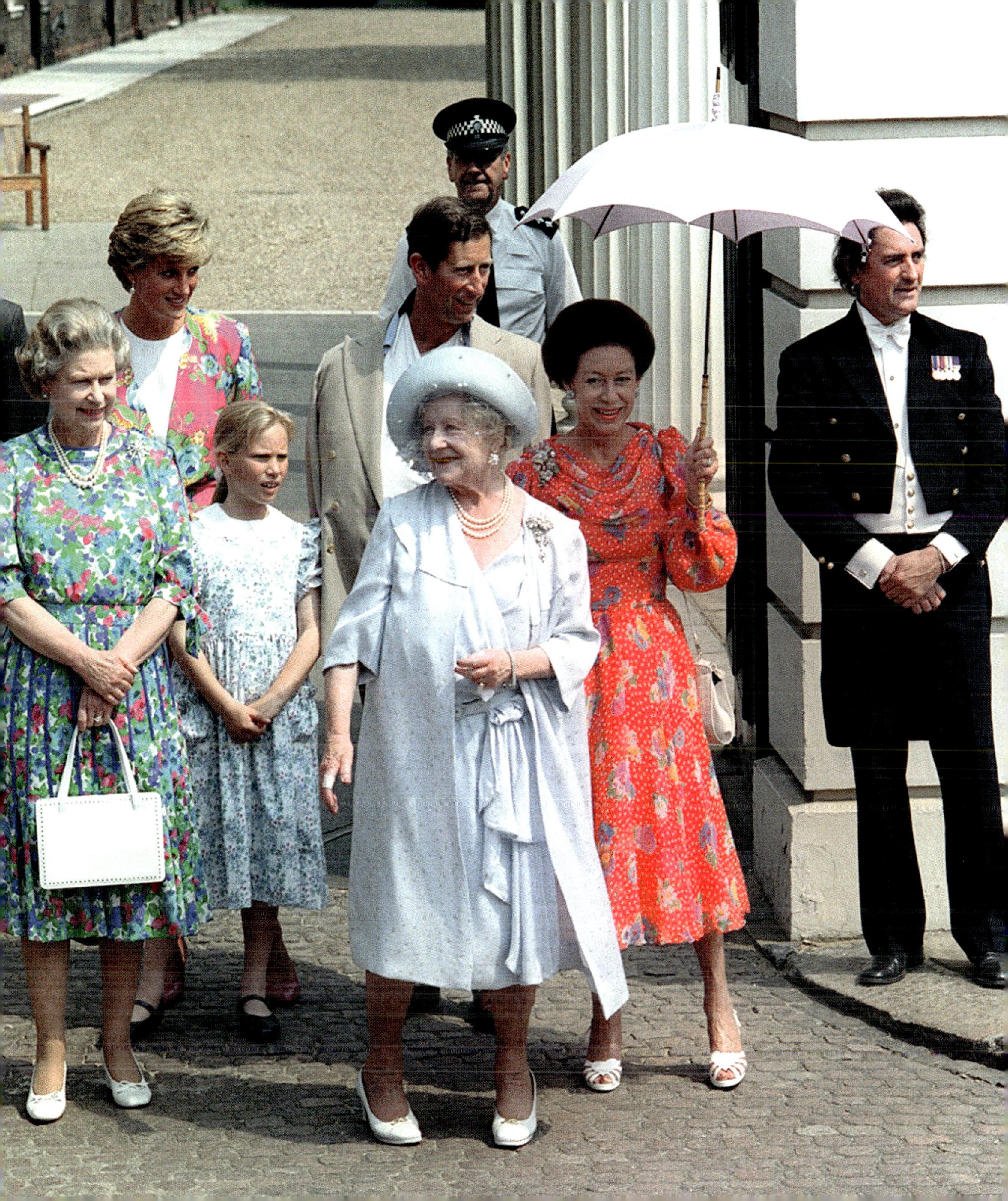

Handbags

Even in the 1930s, H. & M. Rayne Ltd. was advertising bags to match its shoes and this form of merchandising gathered ground in the 1950s. This colourful ensemble of stiletto-heeled shoes and matching evening bag makes a bold statement with the use of a man-made fibre in the floral covering. c.1960. TRACY DOLPHIN COLLECTION

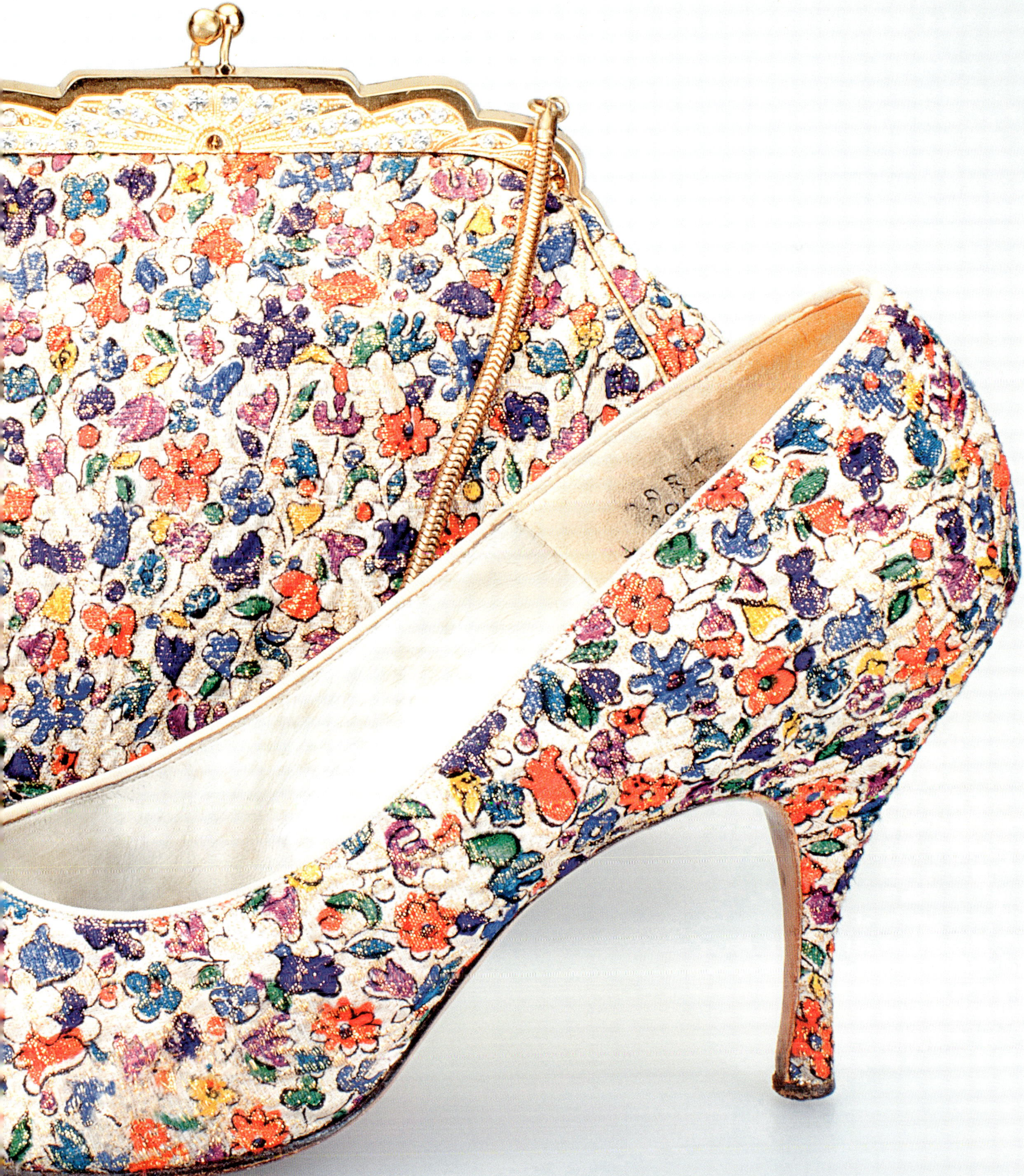

Facing page: The fashion for stiletto shoes reached a peak with the 'needle' heels seen here covered in the same white leather as the trim and small bows on the vamps. The very bold abstract floral design is carried out in a loose-weave man-made textile used on the shoes and matching day bag. c.1962. TRACY DOLPHIN COLLECTION

Right: The Rayne butter yellow leather shoes and bag date from the mid-1950s and typify the similar 'mothers-and-daughters' fashions and styles of the period. Sensible mid-heeled court shoes have flat graduated layers of leather forming the decoration echoed in the pull on the top of the side of the bag, which has a subtle punched line of decoration. c.1955. TRACY DOLPHIN COLLECTION

Below: The strapless sandals and semi-circular bag in a muted Wedgwood blue leather are adorned with sprays of applied porcelain flowers. The sandal is held on by the patent 'Spring'o'Lator' elasticated insole device, which creates a retaining tension between the sole of the foot and the upper of the shoes. Virtually identical shoes were also marketed under the Herbert Levine label in the USA; it seems that they were another example of Rayne and Levine co-operating. c.1958. TRACY DOLPHIN COLLECTION

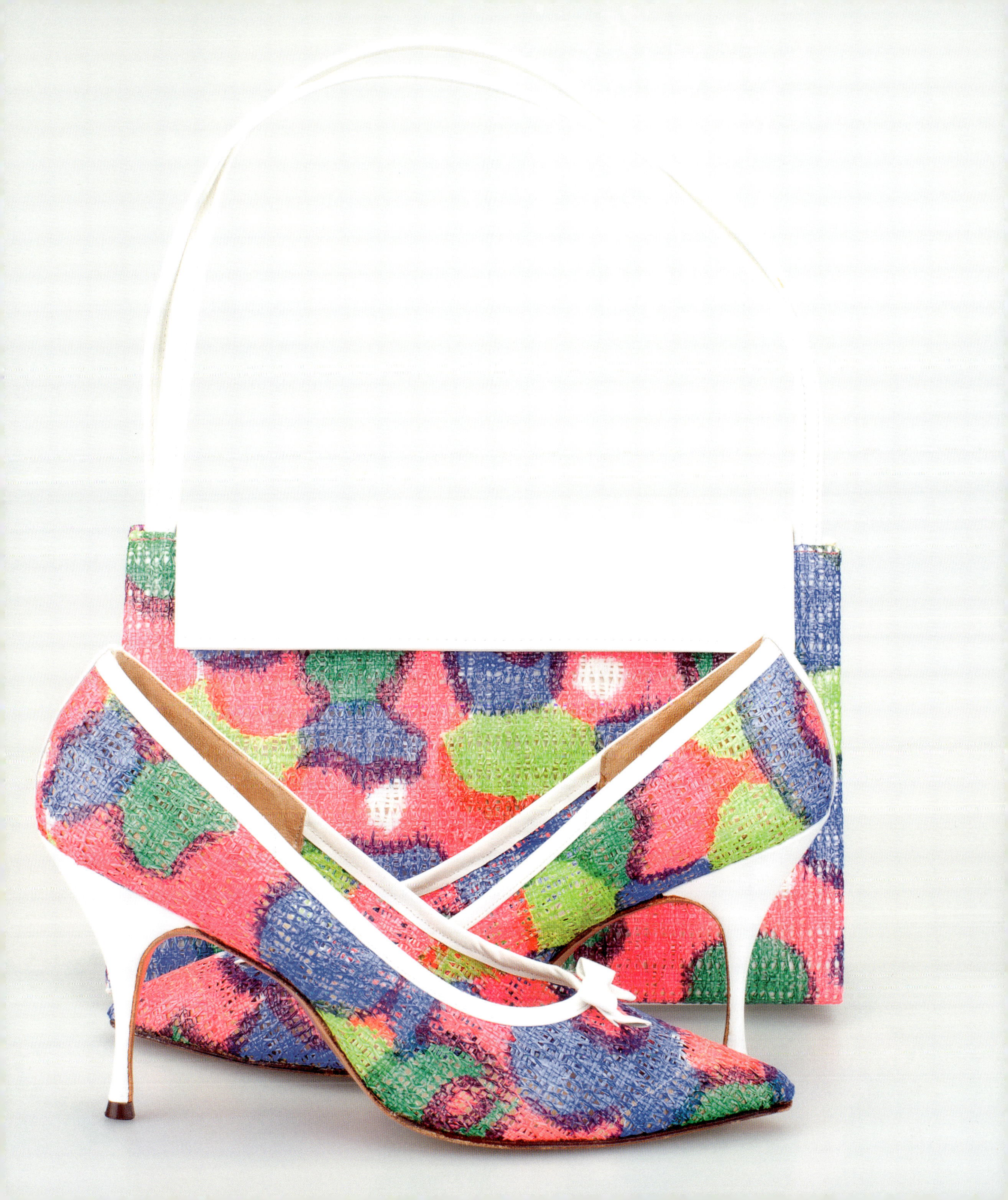

Left: A matching silk covered bag and Rayne version of the diamanté-decorated half-buckled 'Pilgrim' shoe from the 'Romantic' collections. c.1969.
RAYNE ARCHIVE

Below left: A small Rayne scarlet silk-covered and handled evening bag with two opposing diamanté lucky horse-shoes attached by a band of the same silk. c.1968.   RAYNE ARCHIVE

Below: A striking Rayne venture into the 'Wet-Look' of the late 1960s and early '70s. Rayne was an enthusiastic user of 'Corfam', which resembled patent leather, but had softer qualities when handled. This pillar box red bag and the pair of shoes, with their assertive metal decoration, are typical of the fashion at the time for making a bold statement. c.1970.   RAYNE ARCHIVE

Facing page: A pair of Miss Rayne pink leather sling-back sandals with floppy bows and a matching bag with looped handle and loose bow reflect the Swinging London 'Dolly Bird' look of the 1960s. c.1966.   RAYNE ARCHIVE

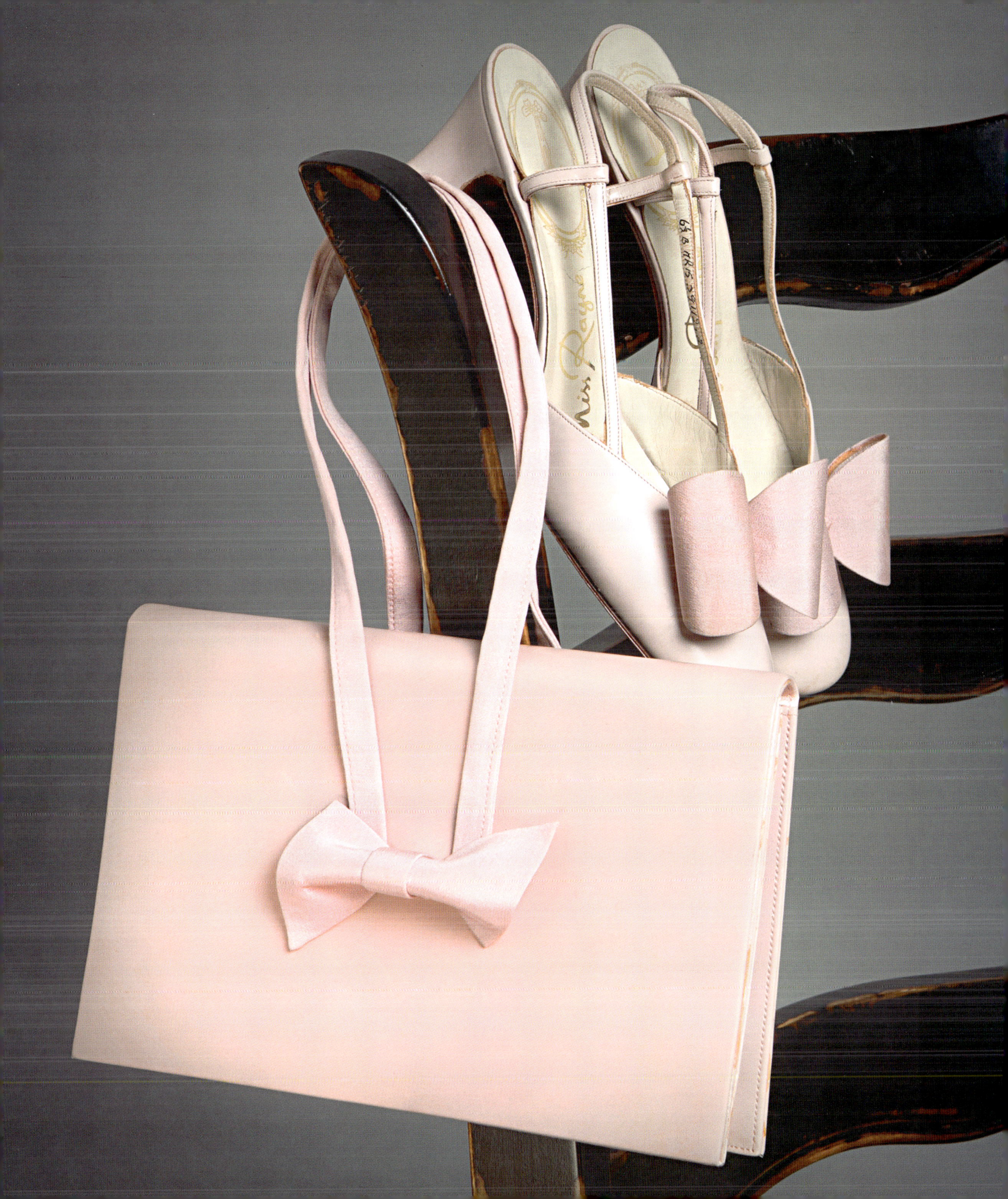

Rayne Today

For over a century H. & M. Rayne Ltd was always at the forefront of innovative shoe design and manufacture. Now into the fourth generation represented by Nick and Lulu Rayne, the French designer Laurence Dacade gives her imaginative twist to successive new collections. Many of the designs are influenced by the great Rayne examples of the past and given subtle new twists, all beautifully executed by Rayne's Italian associates CDivertiamo.

ALL IMAGES PP. 180, 181 AND 189 © RAYNE-CDIVERTIAMO

181

Endnotes

CHAPTER ONE

1. For a detailed history of the area see *Survey of London: Volume 23, Lambeth: South Bank and Vauxhall.* Originally published by London County Council, London, 1951. Waterloo Road pp25-31, York Road pp40-44.

2. The historic activities and numbers of women active as sole or joint traders in Britain has often been underestimated, or deflected by consideration of their appointment to the boards of major manufacturing companies or financial institutions since the nineteenth century. *Women In Business 1700-1850* by Nicola Phillips (The Boydell Press, 2006) considers the diverse and long history of women in business and concludes that their acceptance quite usually depended upon their acceptance and personal standing within local communities, rather than any form of gender discrimination.

3. In the absence of any known memoirs relating to Rayne at this period, *Costumes by Nathan* by Archie Nathan, the managing director of one of London's oldest theatrical costumiers, is full of fascinating details of the business, which undoubtedly resonate with the business of H. & M. Rayne, the costume part of which they bought after the end of the second World War. Nathan also describes the various departments providing every form of garment and accessory, in their case having a specialist arms and armourer at work on the premises for historic or Shakespearean productions.

As a footnote to history, after World War Two, Rayne sold their costume business to Nathans, subsequently Berman and Nathans, in turn bought by Morris Angel Ltd.'s successors.

4. Rayne were not alone in creating cosmetics, by 1907 the outstanding wig-maker William Clarkson was retailing his own 'Lillie Powder For Youth and Beauty – The Greatest Beautifier in the World. Three shades 1/- per box. Absolutely unrivalled for the Complexion.' Equally pertinent as an indicator of the influence to be widespread by those endorsing their products, Clarkson boasted one from Lewis Waller, known for "his good looks ...his virile acting and his vibrant voice" which "rang through the theatre like a bell and stirred like a trumpet". Even at that date, he had many enthusiastic women fans, who formed a club known as the K.O.W. [Keen On Waller] Brigade. This was the continuation of an alternative more self-determining attitude to women's appearance, cosmetics and all matters of their dress.

5. After almost two decades, Henry and Mary Rayne's name was well established beyond theatrical circles and they were a natural source of subscription funding for Brinsworth House, Twickenham as a home for needy music hall artists. Marie Lloyd, who had lent her name to testimonials for Rayne's 'Mona' make-up products was a fellow donor, as was the Scot, Harry Lauder, two of the 600 donors and both legendary names in their own time.

6. Another consideration was that the expansion of Waterloo Station necessitated the demolition of many shops and left Rayne's somewhat isolated; though they did keep a factory and theatrical costumiers store at this address. (see note 1)

7. Although she also patronised other shoemakers, such as Luigi Gamba, an Italian immigrant who by 1912 had a shop specialising in ballet shoes, formerly an Italian hand-made speciality.

CHAPTER TWO

1. The three brothers and Elizabeth had each been left 25% of the business by their father and had their own spheres. The eldest son James (1888-1955) had been born in Dalston, just three years after Henry and Mary Rayne founded their business. Witness to the rise in the family fortunes, his aptitude and interests clearly lay in the fascinating theatrical contacts nurtured by his parents and Uncle 'Himmy'. Later, he ran the costume side of H. & M. Rayne at 15 Rupert Street. He married in 1913 and had two daughters and fought in the First World War being invalided out in 1917.

The second son Joseph Edward (1892-1951) was in charge of the shoe factory and the third, Charles (1893-1950) followed his Uncle 'Himmy' as manager of the second Rayne shop opened in 1932 at 152 Regent Street on a long lease that was still in place and cost-effective six decades later. Charles left due to ill health in 1938; however, he was left to manage the whole Rayne business during the war as his poor health exempted him from military service. Of the four daughters, the eldest, Elizabeth born 1886 married in 1908, divorced and was free to be manageress of the New Bond Street shop, later making a difficult second marriage. Jessica and Susan married and were not actively involved with H. & M. Rayne.

2. Her brother Claude settled in London and worked for Standard Oil, latterly in Italy.

3. *Kentucky New Era*, 22 April, 1911.

4. During the war, he had proved useful to the literary editor, critic, poet and roisterer Henry Savage, the pugnacious husband of his sister Elizabeth. Savage was the son of the local pub owner in Raynes Park, fought in the Boer War and, seeking escape from his personal problems in the ranks during First World War, found himself worse off. In his memoirs, *The Receding Shore* (published in 1933 and infuriatingly free of dates) he recalls, 'My wife had had enough of me and we separated'. This was around 1914, but his Rayne family connections would prove invaluable in early 1917.

Savage was about to be charged with disobeying orders and desertion in the face of the enemy and was put to digging trenches pending further action, 'One morning a car arrived for me, "They're at Flexicourt," said Cully, the Major's bat-man and chauffeur, grinning. "You ain't 'arf for it. The bloke wants to see you first." The "bloke" was my brother-in-law. He, too, was not at all delighted on seeing the lost sheep again. "It'll be a nice job getting you out of this," he said, "You ought to be boiled." "Send me to a Road Construction Company," I suggested. "I'm sick of the Staff." "If it can be wangled," he reflected, "But you'll have no privileges. You'll have to navvy on the roads." So it came about, at the informal court martial which followed, that I lost my stripes and was ordered to a Construction Company.'

5. There are no known surviving photographs of Henry and Mary Rayne, their family nor of their houses and business. The only vignette of the lives of the three Rayne brothers comes from the memoirs of their brother-in-law Henry Savage, bohemian husband of Elizabeth Rayne. He mingled with various music hall stars, mixed with racing and boxing types and gives a human insight into the life of young Edwardian men with some money, that has its equivalent today. 'Dissolute' was the word he applied to this life of young and not so young men; it was a world that ceased to resonate with the post-war sober attitudes and life of Joseph Edward. Savage wrote, 'Felix [Bertrand] ... three of my brothers-in-law [all the Rayne siblings], a young airman and myself had won money at Sandown Park and celebrated with a dinner at a Wimbledon restaurant. A lively dinner it was... the breakages bill being heavy... a party of Yeomanry resplendent in new uniforms, having entered the restaurant [Felix] ordered several dishes of mashed potatoes and started pelting them ... they took it in good part ...we left for ... the local theatre, where we engaged a box. Before long a wrestling match was taking place in the box... when Little Tich, the star of the evening, came on stage so many indignant people rose up in protest that I though it advisable to slip out...The next we heard were expostulations and bumpings as the Box E party were being thrown down the back stairs. I was congratulating myself on having seen the last of them for the night, but fate having directed my foot-steps to an adjacent hostelry, there they were drinking and there we stayed until the landlord refused to serve us any more. Deciding, then, for home we chartered a decrepit four-wheeler ... at a curve in some tramway lines [Felix] suddenly seized the reins, the horse stumbled and over went the cab on one side. It was a miracle that no-one was injured...We went in all directions, a comic position being that of one of the inside passengers, who stood bolt upright in the overturned cab with his head through the window.' pp93-94.

6. By the 1930s there were other Bond Street shops selling imported American shoes, not least Dolcis, then selling some expensive and unusual shoes.

7. This was the store that was famously transformed some twenty years later into the Rayne shop designed by Oliver Messel.

8. Both Fountain House and the factory survived the War intact, although the Waterloo Road building was destroyed with much of the surviving Victorian area .

9. Oliver Messel designed the costumes.

CHAPTER THREE

1. Norman Hartnell, Silver and Gold, Evans Brothers, London, 1955, p.85.

2. Interview by Cynthia Judah, 'She Plans Shoes For The Queen', *Picture Post*, 18 September 1954, pp 40-41.

3. *Shoe & Leather*, 6 September 1973.

4. Various shots show Jean Matthew at a workbench fitting rhinestones into the uppers and heels of shoes.There is a close-up of a woman's feet wearing some fabulous evening shoes with gem-studded platforms. More feet are wearing some gem-studded high heeled mules called 'Scanty'. See:

5. By this point Delman had been bought by the General Shoe Corporation. As GENESCO, this diversified over the next decades forming lucrative licensing agreements with the major European designers, including, for example, Hardy Amies Menswear.

6. *Wedgwood Review*, November 1958.

7. Mary Quant, *Quant by Quant*, Cassel, London, 1965, p106.

8. Kenneth Partridge was one of the young innovative designers of the Swinging Sixties, his Jaeger windows attracted great publicity and amongst his clients were two of The Beatles and Norman Parkinson. Partridge was one of the first television decorating specialists to take on a problem room for a member of the public and give it inspired re-decoration with flair. Made by the BBC, *In Your Place* had two series, the first in black and white and the second amongst the first transmissions in colour: "That was exciting," as Mr Partridge remembers (March 2015).

9. Although French manufacturers such as Charles Jourdan were popular worldwide and many well-made fashion shoes were made at less cost in Italy than in the Rayne factory.

10. It rounded off his friendship with Norman Hartnell, termed by Prudence Glynn in *The Times* in 1977 'our first fashion Knight', when he was also appointed a Knight of the Royal Victorian Order, as was another friend Hardy Amies. Although Edward and Hardy did not have the same long friendship founded in the war and the sense of pre-war humour that resulted in Edward and Norman appending their own nicknames on greetings cards to one another in the usual pre-war snobbish terms as 'The Cobbler' and 'The Little Woman Round The Corner'. Having made their own success, they could afford to joke. A more frosty Hardy would not have appreciated this, hence Hartnell's nickname for him: 'Hardly Amiable'. In 1986 the younger range of Rayne shoes was named 'Cobbler' having bought the firm 'Chelsea Cobbler'.

11. Press clipping from unidentified newspaper

12. Obituary, *The Times* February 10 1992.

CHAPTER FOUR

1. The centre of the front to The Queen's Theatre on Shaftesbury Avenue included the new boot and shoe makers shop of Jack Jacobus at numbers 39–46. He was one of the two owners of the eight-year lease on the whole block, an indication of how well established his business was. It sold elegant and inventive shoes of very high quality into the 1950s. Jack Jacobus was awarded a Royal Warrant by Queen Elizabeth, Consort of King George VI, having supplied her with shoes since the 1920s. She wore Jacobus shoes with her Coronation dress by Handley-Seymour in 1937.
2. *Housewife* magazine, 1952, p99.
3. *Townsville Daily Bulletin*, Australia, Wednesday 19 August, 1953.

The Rayne Factory

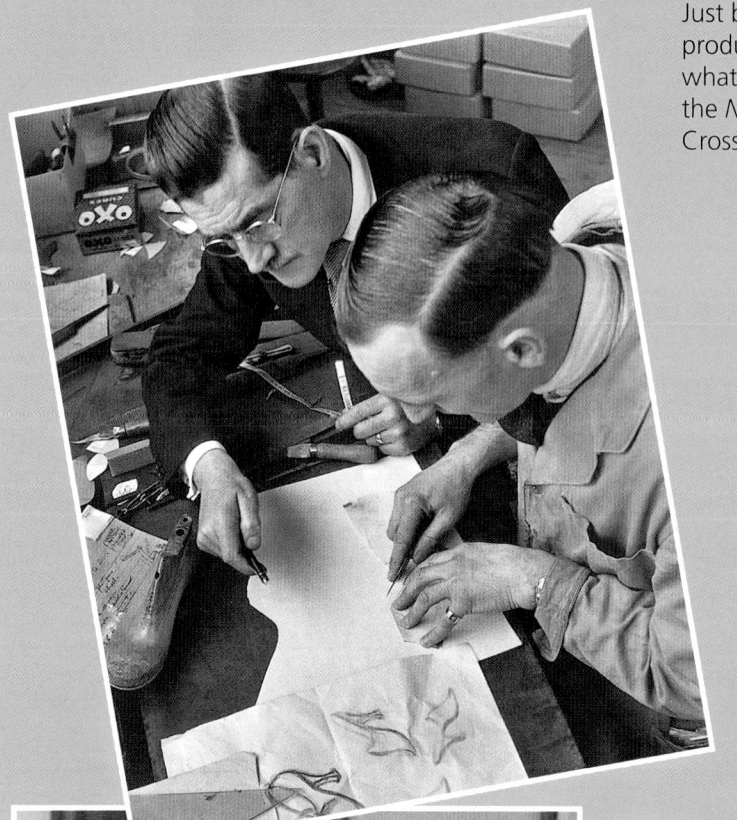

Just before the outbreak of the Second World War, Rayne shoe production was moved from the Waterloo Road premises into what had originally been built as the auxiliary printing plant for the *News of the World* newspaper in Tileyard Road, Kings Cross, London. There it remained until it was closed in 1990.

Clockwise from top left: Mr Tredwen Snr discusses the production of a new design with Norman Cook, 1956; Jean Matthew examining leather with a factory expert, 1956; In the office showroom – Edward Rayne, Jean Matthew and factory manager Norman Cook examining new shoes c.1956.
JEAN MATTHEW ESTATE

Facing page: The factory building had modern facilities lacking in the former premises. Machinists in the closing room stitching the uppers together, 1956.
JEAN MATTHEW ESTATE

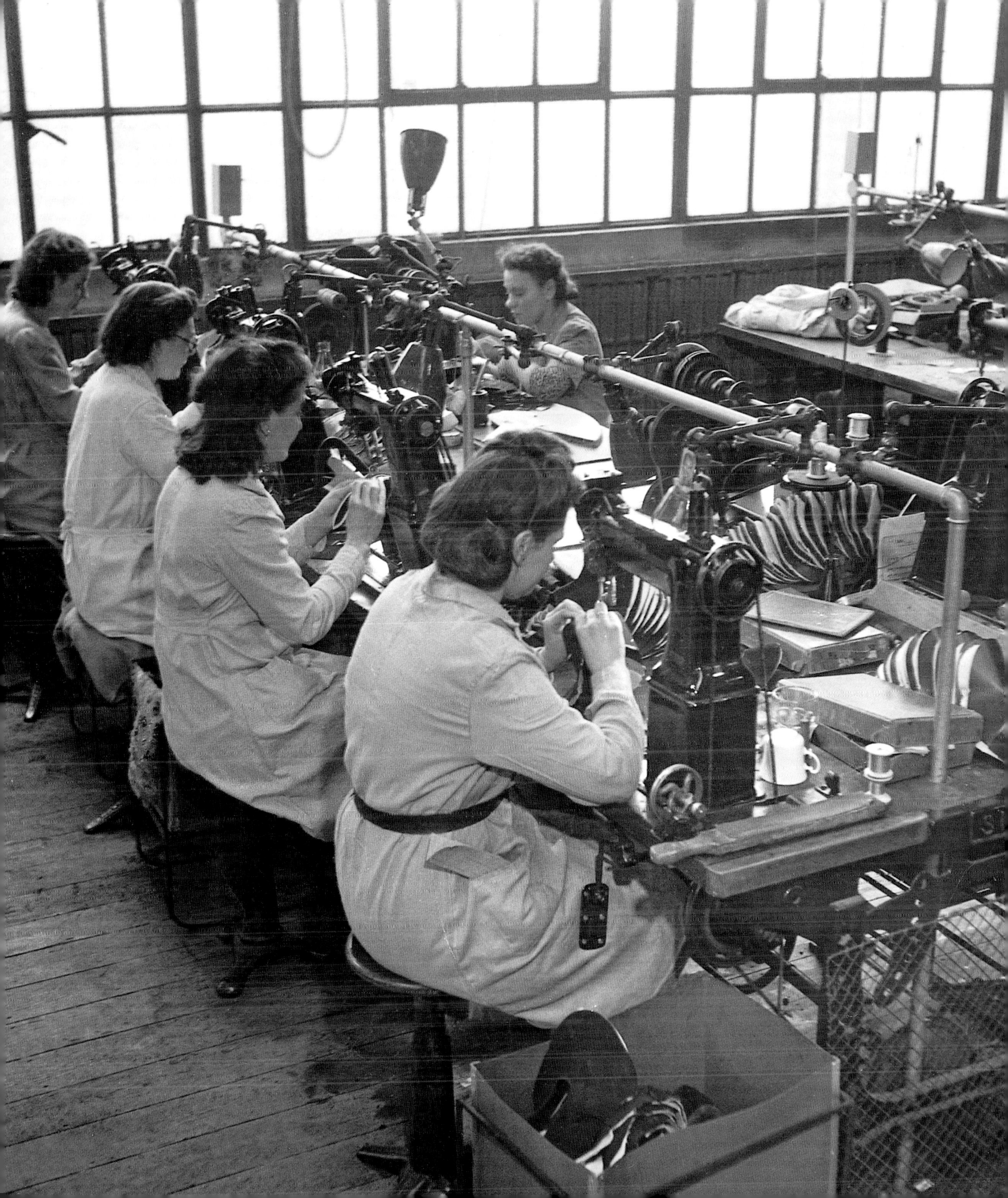

Bibliography

BOOKS

Amies, Hardy, *Still Here*. London: Weidenfeld & Nicolson, 1984.

Baedeker's Guide to London. Leipzig, 1890.

Balmain, Pierre, *My Years and Seasons*. London: Cassell, 1964.

Barnes, Alison, *Royal Sisters Volume Three*. London: Pitkin, 1951.

Beaton, Cecil, *The Glass of Fashion*. London: Weidenfeld & Nicolson, 1954.

Beaumont, Cyril W., *Supplement to Complete Book of Ballets*. London: C.W. Beaumont, 1942.

Bell, Quentin, *On Human Finery*. London: Allison & Busby, 1992.

Birt, Catherine, *Royal Sisters Volume One*. London: Pitkin, 1949.

Bossan, Marie-Josephe, *The Art of the Shoe*, Parkstone Press, 2004.

Bradford, Sarah, *Elizabeth: A Biography of Her Majesty The Queen*. London: William Heinemann Ltd, 1996.

Brahms, Caryl, *Footnotes to the Ballet*. London: Lovat Dickson Ltd., 1936.

Brendon, Piers & Whitehead, Phillip, *The Windsors: A Dynasty Revealed*. London: Hodder & Stoughton, 1994.

Breward, Christopher; Conekin, Becky & Cox, Caroline (eds.), *The Englishness of English Dress*. Oxford: Berg, 2002.

Breward, Christopher; Ehrman, Edwina; and Evans, Caroline, *The London Look: Fashion from Street to Catwalk*. New Haven, CT: Yale University Press / Museum of London, 2004.

Buckton, Henry (ed.), *By Royal Command*. London: Peter Owen, 1997.

Carter, Ernestine, *20th Century Fashion: A Scrapbook, 1900 to Today*. London: E. Methuen, 1975.

Carter, Ernestine, *The Changing World of Fashion*. London: Weidenfeld & Nicolson, 1977.

Chase, Edna Woolman & Chase, Ilka, *Always In Vogue*. London: Gollancz, 1954.

Clark, Brigadier S.F., *The Royal Tour: Parts One to Four*. London: Pitkin, 1953-1954.

Cousins, Angela, *Kids From Over The Water, An Edwardian working-class childhood in south-east London*. Cirencester: Mereo, 2013.

Deans, Marjorie, *Meeting at the Sphinx*. London: Macdonald, Nd [1946].

De Courcy, Anne, *1939: The Last Season*. London: Phoenix, 2003.

De Guitaut, Caroline, *The Royal Tour: A Souvenir Album*. London: Royal Collection Publications, 2009.

De la Haye, Amy (ed.), *The Cutting Edge: 50 Years of British Fashion, 1947-1997*. London: V&A, 1996.

De Valois, Ninette, *Invitation to the Ballet*. London: John Lane, 1953.

Derrick, Robin & Muir, Robin (eds.), *Unseen Vogue: The Secret History of Fashion Photography*. London: Little, Brown & Company, 2002.

Dior, Christian, *Dior By Dior*. Translated by Antonia Fraser. London: Weidenfeld & Nicolson, 1957.

Doe, Tamsin, *Patrick Cox ; Wit, Irony & Footwear*. London: Thames & Hudson, 1998.

Eastoe, Jane, *Elizabeth: Reigning In Style*. London: Pavilion Books, 2012.

Ferragamo, Salvatore, *Shoemaker of Dreams: The Autobiography of Salvatore Ferragamo*. London: George G. Harrap Ltd, 1957.

Field, Leslie, *The Queen's Jewels: The Personal Collection of Elizabeth II*, Weidenfeld & Nicolson, London. 1987.

Fogg, Marnie, *Boutique: A '60s Cultural Phenomenon*. London: Mitchell Beazley, 2003.

Garland, Madge, *Fashion: A Picture Guide To Its Creators and Creations*. Harmonsworth: Penguin, 1962.

——, *The Indecisive Decade*. London: Macdonald, 1968.

Giroud, Françoise & Van Dorrsen, Sacha, *Dior: Christian Dior 1905-1957*. London: Thames & Hudson, 1987.

Glynn, Prudence, *In Fashion: Dress In the Twentieth Century*. London: George Allen & Unwin, 1978.

——, 'Tread softly for you tread on £29', *The Times*, Thursday 30 September, 1976.

Halstead, Ivor, *Bond Street*. London: Barcliff Advertising & Publishing, 1952.

Hartnell, Norman, *Silver and Gold*. London: Evans Brothers, 1955.

Haskell, Arnold, *Balletomania: the story of an obsession*. London: Victor Gollancz, 1934.

—— (ed.), *Ballet to Poland*. London: Adam and Charles Black, 1940.

——, *Ballet Panorama: an illustrated chronicle of three centuries*. London: B.T. Batsford, 1943.

——, *Balletomane at Large: an autobiography*. London: Heinemann, 1972.

Heald, Tim, *A Peerage for Trade: a History of the Royal Warrant*. London: RWHA / Sinclair-Stevenson. 2001.

Henry, O., *101 Stories*, London: The Folio Society, 2002.

Keenan, Bridget, *The Women We Wanted to Look Like*, London: Macmillan, 1977.

Lambert, Eleanor, *The World of Fashion: People, Places, Resources*. New York & London: Bowker, 1976.

Lewis-Crown, Peter, *House of Lachasse: The Story of a Very English Gentleman*. London: Delancey Press, 2009.

Lyall, Gavin, *The Pictorial Story of The Royal Tour of India and Pakistan And The State Visits to Nepal and Iran*. London: Pitkin Pictorials, 1961.

MacCarthy, Fiona, *Last Curtsey: The End of the Debutantes*. London: Faber & Faber, 2006.

Marschner, Joanna & Behlen, Beatrice, *Hats and Handbags: Accessories from the Royal Wardrobe*. Historic Royal Palaces, 2003.

Marshall, Francis, *London West*. London and New York: The Studio Ltd, 1944.

Massingberd, Hugh, *Her Majesty Queen Elizabeth The Queen Mother Woman of the Century*. London: Macmillan, 1999.

Mayhew, Henry, *London Characters and Crooks*. London: The Folio Society, 1996.

McDowell, Colin, *A Hundred Years of Royal Style*, London: Muller Blond & White, 1985.

——, *The Literary Companion to Fashion*. London: Sinclair-Stevenson, 1995.

——, *Forties Fashion and the New Look*, Introduction by Hardy Amies. London: Bloomsbury, 1997.

——, *Shoes: Fashion and Fantasy*. London: Thames and Hudson, 1989.

Menkes, Suzy, *The Royal Jewels*. London: Grafton, 1985.

Molloy, John T., *New Women's Dress For Success*. New York: Grand Central Publishing, NYC. 1996.

Muir, Robin, *Norman Parkinson: Portraits In Fashion*. Bath: Palazzo Editions, 2010.

Mulvagh, Jane, *The Vogue History of 20th-Century Fashion*. London: Bloomsbury Books, 1988.

Nathan, Archie, *Costumes by Nathan*. London: Newnes, 1960.

Page, Betty, *On Fair Vanity*. London: Convoy Publications Ltd, 1954.

Palmer, Alexandra, *Dior: A New look. A New Enterprise*. London: V&A Publishing, 2009.

Parkinson, Norman, *Would You Let Your Daughter*. London: Weidenfeld & Nicolson, 1985.

Pedersen, Stephanie, *Shoes – What Every woman Should Know*. London: David & Charles, 2005.

Pick, Michael, *Royal Design, Loyal Style*. The London Collections, 1977.

——, *Be Dazzled!* New York: Pointed Leaf Press, 2007.

——, *Hardy Amies*. Woodbridge: Antique Collectors' Club, 2012.

Pimlott, Ben, *The Queen: Elizabeth II and the Monarchy*. London: HarperCollins, 2001.

Pope-Hennessey, James, *Queen Mary 1867-1953*. London: George Allen & Unwin, 1959.
Pratt, Lucy & Woolley, Linda, *Shoes*. London: V&A Publications, 2008.
Pringle, Colombe, *Roger Vivier*. Paris: Assouline, 2005.
Pringle, Margaret, *Dance Little Ladies: The Days of the Debutante*. London: Orbis, 1977.
Quant, Mary, *Quant by Quant*. London: Cassell, 1966.
Reddish, Claude, *A Chronicle of Memories*. 1950
Rexford, Nancy E., *Women's Shoes in America 1795-1930*. Kent, OH: Kent State University Press, 2000.
Rhodes James, Robert (ed.), *"Chips" – The Diaries of Sir Henry Channon*. London: Weidenfeld & Nicolson, 1967.
Riello, Giorgio & McNeil, Peter, *Shoes: A History from Sandals to Sneakers*. London: Bloomsbury Academic, 2006.
Robb & Edwards, Anne, *The Queen's Clothes*. London: Express / Elm Tree Books, 1977.
Robinson, Julian, *Fashion In the Forties*. London: Academy Editions, 1976.
Ross, Josephine, *Society in "Vogue": The International Set between the Wars*. London: Condé Nast Books, 1992.
Savage, Henry, *The Receding Shore*. London: Grayson & Grayson, 1933.
Saville, Margaret, *Royal Sisters Volume Two*. London: Pitkin, 1950.
——, *Royal Sisters Volume Five*. London: Pitkin, 1953.
Scott, Elizabeth, *Royal Sisters Volume Four*. London: Pitkin, 1952.
Seebohm, Caroline, *The Man Who Was Vogue*. London: Weidenfeld & Nicolson, 1982.
Steele, Valerie, *Shoes – A Lexicon of Style*. New York: Rizzoli, 1999.
Strong, Roy, *Cecil Beaton : The Royal Portraits*. London: Thames & Hudson, 1998.
Swann, June, *Shoes*. London: Batsford, 1982.
Talbot, Godfrey, *The Royal Family*. Surrey: Country Life Books. 1980.
——, *Queen Elizabeth The Queen Mother*. Surrey: Country Life Books. 1978
Thaarup, Aage, *Heads and Tales*. London: Cassell, 1956.
Thomas, Wynford Vaughan, *Royal Tour: 1953-1954*. London: Hutchinson, 1954.
Trasko, Mary, *Heavenly Soles: Extraordinary Twentieth-Century Shoes*. New York: Abbeville Press, 2007.

Trewin, J.C. , *The Gay Twenties: A Decade of the Theatre*. London: Macdonald, 1958.
Trewin, J.C., *The Turbulent Thirties: A Further Decade of the Theatre*. London: Macdonald, 1960.
Vickers, Hugo, *Cecil Beaton: The Authorised Biography*. London: Weidenfeld & Nicolson, 1985.
Walford, Jonathan, *The Seductive Shoe: Four Centuries of Fashion Footwear*. London: Thames & Hudson, 2007.
——, *Shoes A-Z: Designers, Brands, Manufacturers and Retailers*. London: Thames & Hudson, 2010.
Watt, Judith, *The Penguin Book of Twentieth Century Fashion Writing*. London: Viking, 1999.
Wilcox, Claire & Mendes, Valerie, *Modern Fashion In Detail*. London: V&A Museum, 1991.
Withers, Audrey, *LifeSpan*. London: Peter Owen, 1994.
Wulff, Louis, *Her Majesty Queen Mary*. London: Sampson, Low, Marston & Co.Ltd., 1949.
Young, Sheila, *The Queen's Jewellery*. London: Ebury Press, 1969.
Yoxall, H.W., *A Fashion of Life*. London: William Heinemann Ltd., 1966.

ARTICLES
Avenue Magazine, 'Hardy Amies' by Michael Pick, April 1999.
Boot and Leather News, 'Portrait of a Designer', 6 September, 1973.
British Airways *High Life* magazine, 'The worlds prettiest shoe shop'. March 1986.
Daily Graphic, 'The Royal Tour of Canada', by Anne Packard, London, 1951.
Daily Mail, 'Blow to the well-heeled as royal shoemaker goes bust', 1 February 1994.
Footwear News, 'Britain's Rayne, 69, Dies in Fire at Home', by James Fallon, 17 February 1992.
——, 'The Great Design Houses (Shoe Designers Gucci, Rayne, Delman, Bally and I. Miller)' by Bonnie Baber et al., 17 April 1995.
——, 'The Great Fashion Merchants' by Laurien MacDonald, 17 April 1995.
——, '1940-49—Stylish Sacrifices' by Maryann LoRusso, 26 April 1999.
——, 'Walk of Fame—Celebrities ...' by Maryann LoRusso, 26 April 1999.
Guardian, Edward Rayne obituary, 8 February 1992.
——, Edward Rayne profile by Colin McDowell, 10 February 1992.
Independent, Edward Rayne obituary, 11 February 1992.

——, Eric Crabtree obituary, 19 September 1995
Natal Daily News, 'Shoes should not have to be broken in says Queen's shoemaker', Monday 7 July 1958.
Picture Post, 'Top Shoe Man', 25 March 1953.
——, 'She Plans Shoes Fit For A Queen', 18 September 1954.
Ritz Magazine, 'Raynes Talk to Jonathan Scott' c.1981.
Sunday Times Magazine, 'The Face of British Fashion' by Rebecca Tyrrel, 16 October 1989.
Times, The, 'The British Look', 10 December 1951.
Times, The, Edward Rayne obituary, 10 February 1992

MAGAZINES & JOURNALS
Dundee Courier, The, 1930-1950.
Elegante Welt magazine, Issue 3. Düsseldorf: Arno Buchholz, March 1954.
Era, The, (weekly paper), 1885-1920.
Harpers & Queen, 1970-2003.
Harper's Bazaar, 1935 -2003.
House & Garden.
Queen, The, 1930-1970.
Survey of London, vol 23, 1951.
Tatler, The, 1 Aug 1951 et seq.
Vogue Magazine, 1920-1992.
Women's Wear Daily, 1935-1985.

OTHER SOURCES
Bunbury, Turtle, 'The Irish family who Founded Rayne Shoes'. www.turtlebunbury.com, February 2014.
Hope Lumley, Peter, 'Sir Edward Rayne A Personal Tribute'. Privately printed eulogy, 1992.
London Fashion Exhibition, 'Edward Rayne CVO Profile by Angus Stewart', March 1980.
Matthew, Jean, *unpublished notes on Rayne history*. c.1987.
National Archives, The, First World War Records of Joseph Rayne.
Rayne, Edward, 'Fashion In Footwear - The Perpetual Challenge' Lecture at Museum of London to Friends of Fashion, 12 January 1983.
Rayne, Edward, Unfinished draft for an autobiography. 1988.
Rayne, Nicholas, Various correspondence with family members.Rayne Ltd, H.&M., *A Selected List of Costumes for Fancy Dress Balls, Skating Carnivals, Amateur Theatricals, Pageants, etc*. London: H. & M. Rayne Ltd., c.1920.
Rayne, H& M, Booklet on Old Bond Street Oliver Messel designed new shop. London, 1959
Rayne H. & M., Booklet for new seasons shoes, c 1964.

Acknowledgements

The author and publishers wish to thank HM The Queen for her gracious permission to publish the colour image sent to the author of Her Majesty's wedding shoes and the use of information in letters to Sir Edward Rayne to Her Majesty and Her late Majesty Queen Elizabeth The Queen Mother.

The author and publishers are grateful to Lady Sarah Chatto and Viscount Linley for permission to use imagery of the shoes of Her late Royal Highness Princess Margaret, Countess of Snowdon.
The author is indebted to Nicholas Rayne for his enthusiastic and invaluable support, also for the loan of commissioned imagery and documents from the Rayne Archive.

The author and publishers thank CDivertiamo srl, Nicholas Rayne's associates in Italy, for their co-operation.

We are particularly grateful to Tracy Dolphin for her permission to use items form her Rayne collection.

Many people and institutions have generously given information and assistance to the author and any omissions from the list below are completely inadvertent: Angels The Costumiers: Richard Green, Angela Santos; Edmund Bird, Heritage Advisor to the GLA; Condé Nast Publications: Brett Croft, Ms Belen Cuesta, Ms Stephanie Halfmann, Harriet Wilson; Mrs Caroline Creer, Head of Secretariat, Private Secretary's Office, Buckingham Palace; Miss Peggy Cummins (Mrs Derek Dunnett); Deutsche Kinemathek - Museum für Film und Fernsehen, Berlin: Barbara Schröter, Andrea Ziegenbruch; Fashion Institute of Design & Merchandising L.A.: Kevin Jones, Christina Johnson; Ms Shirley Goddard; Miss Julie Harris; Miss Anna Harvey, Vice President & Senior Editor, Brand Development Condé Nast International Ltd.; Mrs Jean Ireland; Timothy Jones, English Heritage; Michael Lake; Ms Melissa Leventon; The late Mrs Jean Matthew; Thomas Messel; Museum of London: Ms Beatrice Behlen, Ms Sarah Williams; Austin and Howard Mutti-Mewse; National Gallery of Victoria International, Melbourne, Australia: Ms Paola Di Trocchio, Jennie Moloney; Norman Parkinson Archive: Alex Anthony; Bruce Oldfield; Richard Paice; Kenneth Partridge; Edward Rayne; Nick and Lulu Rayne; Royal Albert Memorial Museum and Art Gallery, Exeter: Ms Shelley Tobin; Royal Archives: Miss Pamela Clark, Ms Alison Derrett; Royal Warrant Holders Association: Ms Pippa Dutton; David Russell; Northampton Museum and Art Gallery: Ms Rebecca Shawcross; Eiji Takahatake; Ms Francesca Thomas; Topsham Museum: Ms Rachel Nichols; Ms Liz Tregenza; Hugo Vickers; Victoria & Albert Museum: Ms Sarah Belanger, Keith Lodwick, Ms Helen Persson, Ms Jane Pritchard; Mrs Rita Waite; Ms Dinah Warnock; Ms Heather White; Edward Young, Deputy Private Secretary to HM The Queen.

With grateful thanks to the photographers:
Brendan Hall of Colour White (www.colourwhite.com); Henry Jaremko- Silvercanvas Photography (www.silvercanvas.com); Emilie Bailey (www.emiliebailey.com).

The author thanks ACC Publishing:
James Smith, Susannah Hecht, Lynn Taylor, Stephen Mackinlay, Tom Conway and Jane Emeny.

Author's Biography

MICHAEL PICK is a London-based fine arts and design consultant. He was a director of Stair & Company Ltd (London and New York) and Partridge Fine Arts plc. A Fellow of the Royal Society of Arts, he is the author of seven books on design and the decorative arts, on which he has lectured and written extensively in the UK, overseas, and on board RMS *Queen Mary 2*. He has contributed to numerous publications, including *The Times*, *Daily Telegraph*, *Independent*, *Apollo*, *The Connoisseur*, *Antiques*, *The Antique Collector*, *Tatler*, *Harpers & Queen*, and *Vogue*. In the late 1970s and 1980s he worked freelance with fashion PR Percy Savage and has also broadcast on television in the UK and abroad.

A founder Committee Member of the Twentieth Century Society (then The Thirties Society), the officially recognised British post-1900s architectural preservation group, his commissions have included the complete renovation of the Norman Hartnell Mayfair building with its art-moderne interiors. He is the author of *Be Dazzled!* on the Life of Norman Hartnell, and of *Hardy Amies*. He was Guest Curator of the Fashion and Textile Museum's exhibition 'Hartnell to Amies' and subsequently at Tullie House, Carlisle. He was appointed Guest Curator at the Fashion and Textile Museum for the 2015 exhibition 'Rayne: Shoes for Stars'.

Index

Page numbers in **bold** refer to illustrations

2001: A Space Odyssey (1968) **14**; 14
Addinsell, Richard 67
Adelphi theatre 32
Aeolian Hall, London 46
Albert Hall, The 46
Albert, Prince (*see also*: King George VI) 50
Alia 22
Alice, Princess (Duchess of Gloucester) 156
Allan & Son Ltd, James 156, 170, 172
Amies, Hardy **14**, **132**, **172**; 11, 13, 14, 65, 90, 93, 94, 138, 155, 156, 158, 170, 172
Andress, Ursula 6
Anne, Princess (Princess Royal) **144**; 161, 172
Apollo theatre 34
Arnaud, Yvonne 33
Ascot **46**; 50, 146, 161
Astaire, Adele 33
Auguste 22

Bacon, Mai 33
Balfour, Betty 33
Ballet Russes 34
Bannerman, Margaret 33
Bardot, Brigitte **112**; 46
Baroda, Maharani of 121
Bata shoes 78
Battersby, Martin **10**, **15**; 11, 122
Beatles, The 6
Beeton, Cecil 67, 68
Bennett, Arnold 33
Bergdorf Goodman 56, 57, 94
Best, Edna 33
Blanche, Ada 24
Blaney, Norah 33
Bobby department store, Bournemouth 82
Bogarde, Dirk 113
Bowes-Lyon, Lady Elizabeth (*see also*: Elizabeth, Queen) 50, 65
Braithwaite, Lilian 33
Brayton, Lily 33
Bridgewater, Guy 46
Britannia, HMY 158
British Boot and Shoe Institution 142
British Fashion Awards 142
British Fashion Council 7, 116, 142
British Footwear Manufacturers Federation 142
British Technicolor 68
Britten & Bannister Ltd (Britt Bann shoes) 74
Bron, Eleanor 6
Brough, Fanny **32**; 32
Browne, Irene 33
Burton Group 141, 142
Butlers Bootmakers 113

Caesar and Cleopatra (1945) 67, 68, 110, 113, 155
Camberwell Palace theatre 22
Canterbury Music Hall 20, 22
Cantilever Shoe Company 93
Carisbrooke, Dino 156
Carno, Fred 18
Casino Royale (1967) 6
Cavalcade (1931) 60
Cavanagh, John **132**; 94, 170
Cdivertiamo 180
Channon, Sir Henry "Chips" 155-6
Chaplin, Charlie 20
Charing Cross Road shop **26**, **32**; 23, 30, 32, 33, 34
Charles, Prince (Prince of Wales) **144**, **173**; 140, 161
Charlot, André 54
Chase, Edna Woolman 58
Chester, Betty 33
Chevalier, Maurice 18
Christie, Julie 6
City of Melbourne Ball (1954) 94
Clark, Mary *see*: Rayne, Mary
Cleopatra (1963) 112
Clothing and Footwear Institute 142
Cochran, C.B. 54, 60, 110
Collier, Constance 33
Collins, Joan 140
Collins, José 33
Colman, Prentice & Varley PR agency 111
Colville, Cmdr Richard 161
Compson, Betty 33
Compton, Fay 33
Cooke, Norman **184**; 93
Cooper, Gladys 18, 33
Cooper, Lady Diana 11
Corfam **178**; 121
Cort, Morna (Morna Leigh) 90
Courtneidge, Cicely 33
Coward, Noel 60
Crabtree, Eric 140
Crawford, Joan 6
Crawford, Mimi 33
Croft, Annie 33
Crown Neolite soles 116
Cummins, Peggy **6**; 6

Dacade, Laurence 180
Daily Worker 161
Daly's department store, Glasgow 90
Daly's theatre 32, 34
Dangerous Moonlight (1941) 67
Darling (1965) 6
Daveney, Keturah 18, 33
Davies, Bette 61
Davies, Marion 61
Debenham Group 138, 140-1
Delman shoes **57**, **58/59**; 7, 13, 56, 60, 65, 67, 78, 94, 100, 113, 121

Delman, Herman 56, 60
Delysia, Alice 33
Denney, Anthony **79**
Diaghilev, Sergei 34, 36
Diana, Princess of Wales **170**, **173**; 7, 14, 140, 172
Dickson, Dorothy 33
Dietrich, Marlene 14, 61, 110, 111
Dior, Christian 7, 78, 82, 94, 100
Docker, Lady Norah 94
Doctor at Sea (1955) 113
Dolcis 93, 100
Dully Sisters 33
Dorchester Hotel 110, 111
Drury Lane Theatre 60
Dupont 121
Dynasty (1981-89) 140

Edelman leather (Teddy and Arthur Edelman) 121
Edward, Prince (Duke of Windsor) 93
Edwardes, George 32
Elizabeth Princess (Queen Elizabeth II) **144**, **146**, **150**, **154**, **155**, **156**, **158-61**, **172-3**; 13, 14, 61, 74, 82, 90, 94, 116, 134, 138, 140, 141, 142, 147, 150, 156, 158, 161, 170, 172
 – Coronation (1953) 90, 94, 134, 156, 161, 170, 172
 – Royal Tour (1953-54) **155**, **156**; 90, 94, 155, 156, 170-2
 – Wedding (1947) **147**, **148/9**, **150/1**, **157**; 82, 90, 134, 147-8, 150, 156, 170
Elizabeth, Queen (Lady Elizabeth Bowes-Lyon; Queen Elizabeth The Queen Mother) **144**, **150**, **152**, **161-4**, **173**; 13, 40, 50, 73, 74, 82, 89, 90, 122, 141, 146, 148, 150, 156, 161, 167, 172
Elsom, Isobel 33
Elson, Anita 33
Emma Conns' Royal Victoria Hall and Coffee Tavern 20
Empire Theatre of Varieties 34
Era, The 24
Ervine, St John 54
Escape (1948) 6
Esther Costello (1957) 6
European Trade Committee 142
Evans, Edith **54**; 33
Evins, David 121
Export Council for Europe 142

Ferragamo, Salvatore 13, 60, 78
Festival of Britain (1951) 78
Fleetwood, Ken **14**
Fokine, Michel 36
Forbes-Robertson, Sir Johnston **21**
Forsyte Saga (1967-9) 127

Fox, Frederick **172**
Franco-British Council 142
Franke, Mrs Arthur **42**

Gaiety Girls, The 29, 32
Gaiety theatre 32
Galsworthy, John 127
Gatti's, Villers Street 22
Gatti's Palace of Varieties (*aka*: Gatti's-in-the-Road) 20, 36
Gay, Maisie 33
Genée, Adeline 34, 150
General Shoe Corporation of America 94
George V, King 50, 55, 60, 146, 150
George VI, King (Duke of York) **144**; 73, 147, 156
Georges department store, Melbourne 94
Gibb, Bill **143**; 132
Glamour magazine 93
Globe Theatre 54
Glynn, Mary 33
Glynn, Prudence 141
Gothic, SS 156
Graham, David 141
Granger, Stewart 68
Granville theatre 22
Gray, Sally 67
Griffin & Spalding's store, Nottingham 90

Hale, Binnie 33
Hamilton Bridge Club 74
Hamlet **20-21**
Handley Seymour, Madame 50, 146, 150, 156
Hard Day's Night, A (1964) 6
Harper's Bazaar 121
Harris, Julie **6**; 6
Harrison, Rex 6
Harrods 138
Hartnell, Norman **14**, **40**, **41**, **134**, **135**, **144**, **147**, **148/9**, **154**, **157**; 13, 14, 50, 65, 82, 90, 94, 122, 133, 144, 150, 155, 156, 158, 170, 172
Harvey, Anna 7
Harvey Nichols 7, 54, 138, 140
Helen! (1932) 110
Hellstern 78
Help! (1965) 6
Henri Bendell store 113
Henry, O. 60
Herbert Levine (*see also*: Levine, Beth & Herb) 100, 176
Hicks Theatre (*later*: The Globe) 34
Hobson, Valerie 61
Holiday Camp (1947) 6
Hook, Knowles & Co. Ltd. 150

Hope Lumley, Peter 90, 93, 111, 141, 161
Horrockses 90
Humpty Dumpty (1903-04) 33

Imperial Russian Dancers 36
INCSOC (Incorporated Society of London Fashion Designers) 82, 111, 113, 122
Ingram, Richard 74
International Wool Secretariat **154**
Irving, Henry 24

Jacobus, Jack 73, 156
Jaipur, Maharani of 121
Janis, Elsie 33
Japp, Peter 156
Jays Ltd 32
Jazz Singer, The (1927) 36
Jeffries, Ellis 33
Jellinek, Peter 93
John Pant Ltd 113
Joseph shoes 61
June 33

Kendal, Marie 20
Kendall, Kay 6
Kenmare, Lady 11
Kerr, Deborah 6
Knoblauch, Edward 33
Korda, Alexander 61
Kottler, Richard 142
Kubrick, Stanley 14
Kyashi, Lydia 36

Langtry, Lillie 13, 29
Lanvin 128
Lauder, Harry 20, 32
Launer 110
Lawrence, Gertrude 33, 61, 138
Laye, Evelyn 33, 110
Leather, Hide and Wool Exchange, The 29
Leigh, Morna *see*: Cort, Morna
Leigh, Vivien **61**; 14, 61, 67, 68, 110
Leno, Dan 20, 23, 24, 33
Lesley, Rice & Co. Ltd 65
Levey, Ethel 33
Levine, Beth & Herb (*see also*: Herbert Levine) 100, 121
Leybourne, George 20
Lillie, Beatrice 33
Little Michus, The (1905) 34
Little Tich 20
Live and Let Die (1973) 6
Liverpool Symphony Orchestra 46
Lloyd, Arthur 20
Lloyd, Marie 20, 24
London Films 61
London Pavilion theatre 34

Lord, Kitty **16**, **19**; 18
Lotus Shoes 140
Lucite **136-7**; 121
Lyric theatre 34

Macdonald, Grant 54
Margaret, Princess **150**, **152**, **165-9**, **171**, **173**; 74, 82, 90, 147, 156, 161, 170, 172
Marina, Princess (Duchess of Kent) 156, 170
Marks and Spencer 142
Marsh, Mae 33
Marshall & Snelgrove stores **90**; 54
Mary, Queen **144**, **150**; 13, 50, 56, 60, 65, 73, 146, 150, 156
Matthew, Jean **39**, **93**, **184**; 40, 93, 100, 110, 121, 131, 142, 171
McCann, Gerald **133**; 132
Mcintosh, Elsie 94
Melba, Dame Nellie 46
Messel, Oliver **108-11**; 7, 8, 14, 68, 109-11, 113, 131, 142, 155
Michael of Kent, Princess 172
Milestones (1915) 33
Millar, Gertie 32
Miller, I. 94
Millerkin shoes 94
Miss Rayne collection **10**, **15**, **87**, **92**, **126**, **179**; 11, 74, 94, 110, 121
Mistinguett 100
Molyneux 90
Mona powder **23**, **24**, **25**; 24, 46
Monkman, Phyllis 33
Morris Angel Ltd 32
Morton, Digby **132**; 65, 82, 170
Muir, Jean **133**; 7, 14, 128, 132

Nathan 22, 74
National Shoe Fair, Chicago (1958) 107
Nelson, Roger **133**; 132
New Look **76**, **78**; 78, 82
New Victoria Palace Theatre (*later*: Old Vic) 20
New York Herald Tribune 113
Nijinsky 34
Nina Ricci 128
Norie, Lady **156**
Norie, Sir Willoughby **156**

Oberon, Merle 61
Old Vic (*see also*: New Victoria Palace Theatre) 34
Oldfield, Bruce **134**; 7, 14, 132, 140
Oscars 6

Paquin 32
Paragon theatre 22
Park, Bertram 138
Partridge, Kenneth 122

Pascal, Gabriel 67, 155
Patti, Adelina 24
Pavlova, Anna **34**, **34**, **37**; 33, 34-36
Pelz, Otto Jnr 60
Perugia, André 13, 78, 94, 100, 102
Peverelli, Baron de 46
Pfister, Andrea 128
Philip, Prince (Philip Mountbatten; Duke of Edinburgh) **144**, **146**, **156**; 94, 148
Pierre Hotel, New York 11
Pinewood studios 67
Plaza Hotel, New York 107
Prince of Wales theatre 32

Quant, Mary **126**; 7, 116, 121, 128
Quayle, Anna 6
Queen Elizabeth, RMS 6, 90
Queen magazine 122
Queen's Theatre 34

Randall Shoes 121
Randall, H.E. 93
Rayne Casuals collection 74, 94, 191
Rayne-Delman 94, 113, 121
Rayne family (*see also*: Meta Reddish; James Ryan):
– Charles 55, 56, 60
– Sir (Henry) Edward **9**, **11**, **12**, **15**, **108**, **184**; 6, 7, 11-14, 40, 55, 65, 67, 68, 74, 76-143, 161, 170, 171, 172
– Edward Jr. 142
– Elizabeth 60
– Eveleen 20
– Henry (Edward Henry Ryan) 16-37, 45
– Himalaya ('Himmy') 32
– James 55, 60, 74
– Joan 55, 60
– Joseph Edward 42-75, 134, 146, 161
– Lulu 7, 8, 142, 180
– Mary (née Clark) 16-37, 45
– Morna 6
– Nicholas 7, 8, 14, 142, 172, 180
Reddish, Claude 45-6
Reddish, Meta (Mrs Joseph Edward Rayne) **42**; 45-6, 55, 60
Rene 113
Retford, Ella 33
Reville & Rossiter 150
Rivett **75**
Robert's Wife (1938) 54
Rollerball (1975) 7
Royal Cambridge Theatre of Varieties 22
Royal College of Art, fashion dept 93
Royal College of Fashion 142
Royal Russian Opera Ballet 36
Royal Society of Arts 132

Royal Warrants 7, 13, 56, 74, 93, 142, 144, 146, 150, 156, 161, 170, 172
Russell, Peter 65
Ryan, James 18, 20

Saks Fifth Avenue 56
Schopp department store, Stuttgart 90
Seymour, Jane 6
Shaftesbury Avenue 29, 34
Sharaff, Irene 113
Shaw, George Bernard 32, 67, 68
Sheppard, Eugenia 113, 121
Shilton, Clive 132
Simmons 22
Simon and Laura (1955) 6
Simpson, Wallis (*later*: Duchess of Windsor) 61
Sketch, The 24
Spring Chicken, The (1905) 32
Stiebel, Victor 65
Strathmore, Earl and Countess of 50
Stutz, Geraldine 93, 113
Sunday Times magazine 122
Swan & Edgars department store 92

Taylor, Elizabeth 14, 68, 110, 111, 113
Terry, Ellen 24
Thaarup, Aage 90
Thatcher, Heather 33
Thatcher, Margaret 140
Theatre Royal 33
Theresa, Mother 170
Thomas, Ian 170
Thorndike, Sybil 33
Times, The 140
Toms, Carl 122
Tredwen Snr, Mr **184**
Tresmand, Ivy 33

Vance, Harry 20
Vivier, Roger **132**; 7, 56, 94, 100, 121
Vogue **46**, **56**, **57**, **79**, **105**; 45, 50, 52, 54, 55, 56, 60, 61, 65, 82, 100

Walbrook, Anton 67
Washington Star 78
Watts, Martha 13
Wedgwood Collection **107**; 107
Wilde, Oscar 32
Wilhelm, Mr (William Charles Pitcher) 32
Worshipful Company of Patternmakers 142
Worth 6
Wright, Haidee 33

Yapp 150

Ziegfeld, Florence 34

Overleaf: A jaunty colourful advertisement for Rayne 'Casuals' – a complete range of shoes suitable for holiday or casual wear – as indicated by the address of the Rayne shop at 152 Regent Street, traditionally catering more for the younger, county or suburban customers, who wanted smart durability rather than the lace, fabric or exotic leathers found at the Bond Street address. 'Casuals' were also widely sold across the British Isles in the many department store outlets featuring Rayne shoes. 1955. RAYNE ARCHIVE

RAYNE

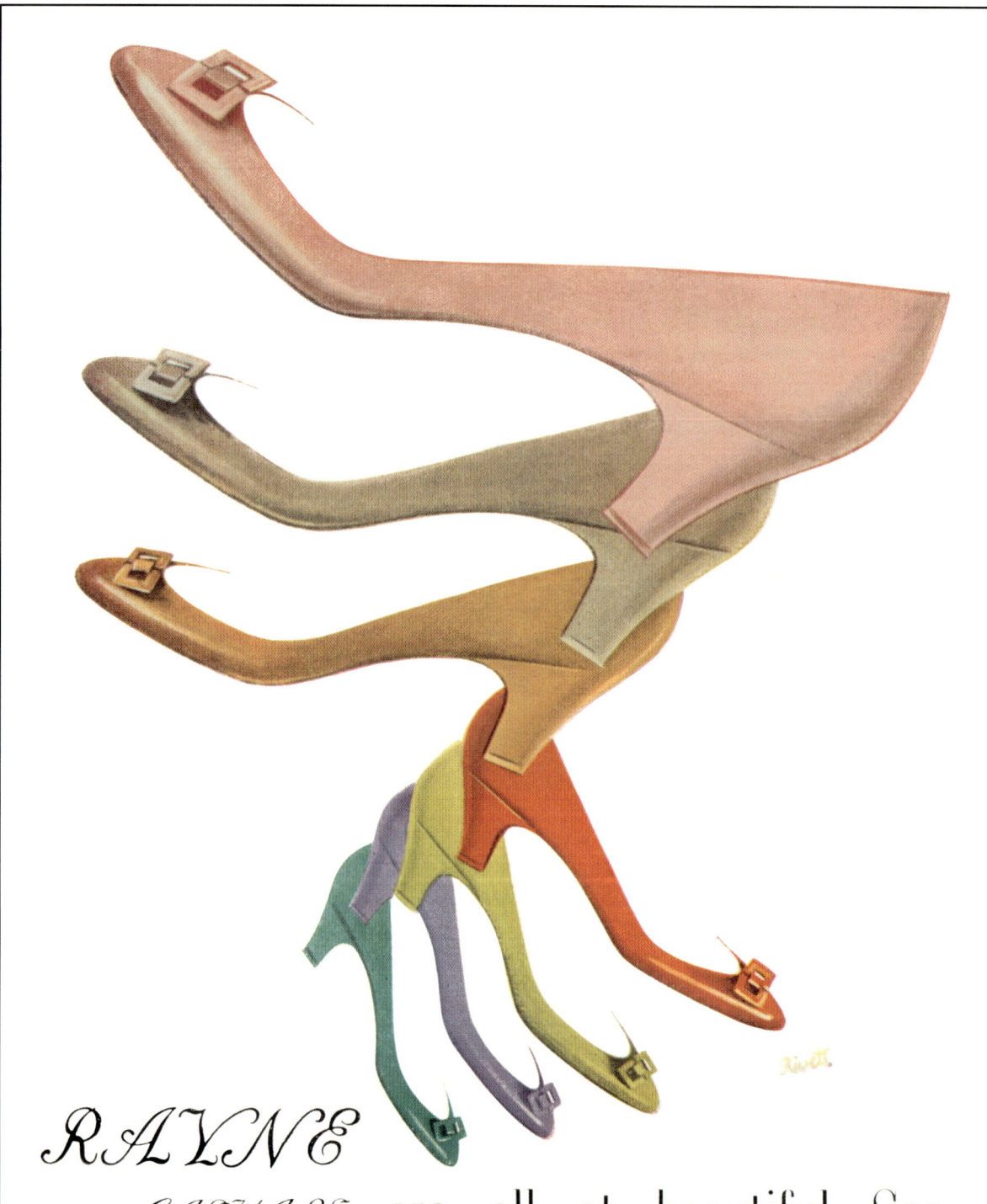

CASUALS are all at beautiful Sea
—all the colours of a Sunny Shore

Florana Calf by **Bolton Leathers** Ltd.   *Rayne Casuals at H. & M. Rayne, Ltd., 152 Regent St., W.1*

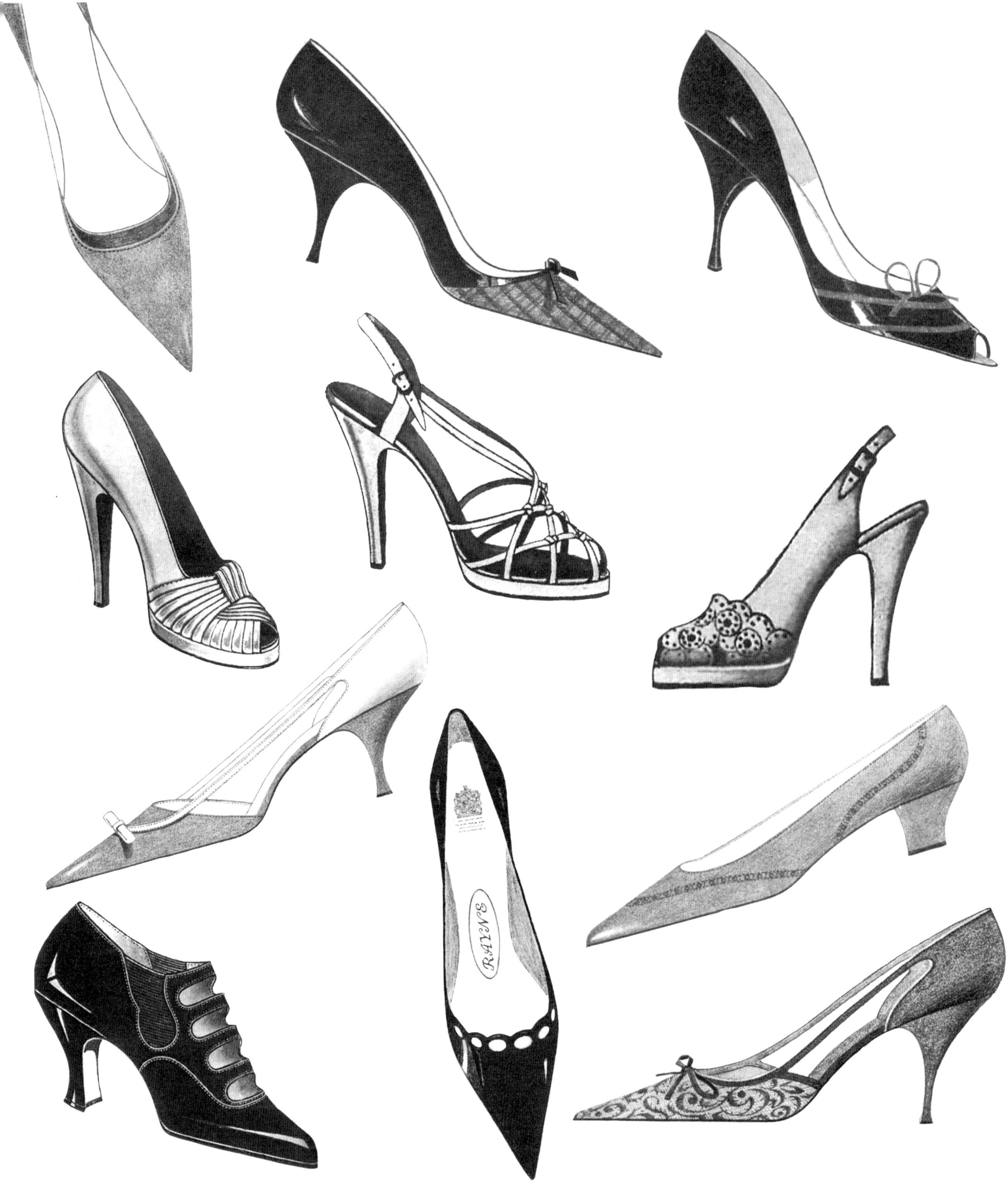
RAYNE